WEIGHT WATCHERS®
Healthy Life-Style
C·O·O·K·B·O·O·K

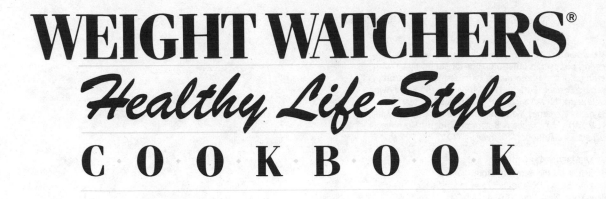

WEIGHT WATCHERS®
Healthy Life-Style
C O O K B O O K

Over 250 Recipes Based on the
Personal Choice® Program

Set design and photography by Gus Francisco

NAL Books

WEIGHT WATCHERS is a registered trademark of
Weight Watchers International, Inc.

We would like to thank the following for kindly lending us serving pieces and other props or for supplying us·with settings for the photo insert: Laura Ashley, New York, N.Y.; Richard Bennett Pottery, Housatonic, Mass.; Brandywine Restaurant, New York, N.Y.; Paul Chaleff Pottery, Pine Plains, N.Y.; James Madden, Bayshore, N.Y.; Judy Milne, New York, N.Y.; Queens Botanical Gardens, Flushing, N.Y.; Barbara Zitz Antiques, Rhinebeck, N.Y.

NEW AMERICAN LIBRARY
Published by the Penguin Group
Penguin Books USA Inc., 375 Hudson Street,
New York, New York 10014, U.S.A.
Penguin Books Ltd, 27 Wrights Lane,
London W8 5TZ, England
Penguin Books Australia Ltd, Ringwood,
Victoria, Australia
Penguin Books Canada Ltd, 2801 John Street,
Markham, Ontario, Canada L3R 1B4
Penguin Books (N.Z.) Ltd, 182–190 Wairau Road,
Auckland 10, New Zealand

Penguin Books Ltd, Registered Offices:
Harmondsworth, Middlesex, England

First published by New American Library,
a division of Penguin Books USA Inc.

First Printing, January, 1991
10 9 8 7 6 5 4 3 2 1

 REGISTERED TRADEMARK—MARCA REGISTRADA

LIBRARY OF CONGRESS CATALOGING-IN-PUBLICATION DATA
Weight Watchers healthy life-style cookbook / photography by Gus
    Francisco.
        p.   cm.
    ISBN 0-453-01023-7 ; $19.90
    1. Reduced-sodium diet—Recipes.
2. Reduced-cholesterol diet—Recipes.   I. Weight Watchers International.
RM237.8.W45   1991
641.5'63 — dc20   90-13817
                                                               CIP

Printed in the United States of America
Set in ITC Goudy Sans Book
Designed by Julian Hamer
Food stylist: Nina Procaccini
Prop stylist: Laurie Beck
Illustrations by Dolores R. Santoliquido
Introductions by Anne Hosanky
Nutrition analysis by Hill Nutrition Associates, Inc.

Acknowledgments

A dish doesn't prepare itself, neither does a cookbook. Both require proficient and caring hands. Weight Watchers International is fortunate to have those dedicated hands on board. We pay well-deserved tribute to our Publications Management Department, with a special bow to General Manager Eileen Pregosin for her vigilant and perceptive guidance.

In the busy test kitchen at Weight Watchers International, an inspired corps of chefs worked for nearly a year developing and testing more than 250 recipes, as well as creating the food styling for the mouth-watering photographs you'll find in these pages. Our admiring thanks to chefs Nina Procaccini, Susan Astre, Christy Foley-McHale, and Judi Rettmer, as well as test kitchen assistant Jacqueline Hines.

Recipes have to be translated, not only into savory dishes but also into easy-to-follow language. We are grateful for the unflagging efforts of our editorial staff—Patricia Barnett, Isabel Fleisher, Elizabeth Resnick-Healy, Melonie Rothman, and April Rozea—who researched, edited, and proofread this manuscript through countless revisions, abetted by the secretarial expertise of Nancy Biordi.

Last, but far from least (like dessert!)—our appreciation to Barbara Warmflash, General Manager, Products and Licensing, who deftly managed the myriad other details involved in steering this cookbook from our kitchen to yours.

—Weight Watchers International

Contents

Introduction

With today's busy life-styles, having the best foods with the least fuss is every cook's dream. That's why the more than 250 recipes in this book are all geared to getting you in and out of the kitchen quickly—while still providing some of the most delectable, nutritious dishes you've ever tasted. And our recipes, which are based on the Weight Watchers food plan, help make it a pleasure to control your weight.

Every recipe can be prepared within an hour—many in just half that time. More than 50 recipes take advantage of the jet speed of the microwave oven, and every recipe is headed by a note telling you the approximate total time needed for preparation.

But speed is never obtained at the expense of good nutrition. A savvy life-style for the nineties is one that focuses on healthful eating and an awareness of proper nutrition. Our recipes are based on the most up-to-date nutritional information available and we share that data with you. Each recipe contains analyses for calories, protein, fat, carbohydrate, calcium, sodium, cholesterol, and dietary fiber. In addition, many recipes are highlighted by a symbol indicating that we've controlled the sodium, fat, and/or cholesterol levels. A special section provides information on the thinking underlying the current nutritional guidelines.

To help you with your weight-control efforts, each recipe provides Selection Information, explaining how the dish fits into the Weight Watchers food plan. To make it even easier, there are 14 recipe-keyed one-day menu planners that do a lot of your thinking for you. And there is a handy additional index that enables you to find in a flash the recipes that will meet your particular needs.

You'll also find a wealth of helpful cooking tips, such as how to enhance flavors without adding sodium, fat, or cholesterol, as well as a convenient spice chart that gives a quick view of which seasonings "marry" well with different foods. And if you're shy about admitting that you don't understand various cooking directions, you'll be delighted to see that we've included a glossary of cooking terms.

The recipes (which are mostly for two servings) take you through the day from breakfasts and brunches to suppers and snacks. There are taste-ful recipes for appetizers, soups, and dips; poultry, meat, fish, and shellfish; legumes; egg substitutes and cheese; side dishes; desserts and beverages.

Every recipe has been prepared and tested in the test kitchen of Weight Watchers International. That's your best guarantee of high quality, for Weight Watchers is staffed by the most qualified nutritionists, home economists, and chefs, all of whom understand *your* life-style needs.

The Weight Watchers organization has been an acknowledged leader in the weight-control field for more than 27 years. In that time, Weight Watchers has grown from a handful of people to millions of enrollments. People of all ages, from children to senior citizens, attend weekly meetings virtually around the globe. In addition, the popular expanding line of convenience foods, best-selling cookbooks and engagement calendars, and exercise audio cassettes are all dedicated to the continuing concept of a healthy life-style. You can be confident that this cookbook provides not only an express trip through the kitchen but a delicious route to nutritious eating.

Recipes That Fit Your Life-Style

Does a delicious, nutritious dish, prepared in just about the time it takes you to read this chapter, seem too good to be true? If so, this is the cookbook for you—all of these recipes can be prepared within an hour and many in even less time.

To get the most from our recipes, read the guidelines on the following pages. They'll help you create appetizing dishes faster and more effortlessly than you ever dreamed possible.

First, however, let's take a look at the most important ingredient in our recipes: *good nutrition*.

What Is "Good Nutrition"?

Never cut corners on nutrition. The key to healthy eating—and to a safe and healthy weight loss—is to eat a *variety of nutritious foods in moderation*.

A healthful menu plan should provide your body with basic nutrients while staying within caloric limits. The reason variety is so important is that no single food can supply all the essential nutrients in the amounts needed. Cutting out one type of food isn't the answer to weight loss, since it's the *amount* of protein, fat, and carbohydrate that determines its caloric content. The more you vary your choices, the less likely you are to develop either a deficiency or an excess of any nutrient. Variety also helps avoid the pitfall of boredom, which can lead to detours from the Food Plan.

To stay healthy your body needs approximately 40 different nutrients, including protein, fat, carbohydrate, fiber, vitamins, minerals, and water. These nutrients have a lot of work to do in your body.

Protein builds and maintains body tissue and is an excellent source of iron and B vitamins. The best sources of protein are poultry, lean meats, fish, eggs, milk, cheese, legumes, and peanut butter.

Carbohydrate is the body's primary energy source and also provides fiber and B vitamins. Fruits, vegetables, cereals, breads, legumes, and whole grains are excellent sources of carbohydrate.

Dietary fiber—so prominent in the news these days—is found in two forms: soluble and insoluble. *Insoluble fiber* helps maintain regularity and is found in bran products, whole grains, legumes, fruits, and vegetables. *Soluble fiber* may help to lower blood cholesterol levels and to control levels of blood sugar. Some good sources of this type of fiber are oats, barley, beans, and fruits, especially apples.

Vitamins and *minerals* are also essential for proper body functioning and each has its own role to play. For instance, vitamin B_1 helps cells convert carbohydrates into energy, vitamin C helps strengthen body tissues, and vitamin A is important for good vision.

Iron, so vital for the formation of red blood cells, is one of the most difficult minerals to get in adequate supply, especially for women. Some good sources are lean meats, poultry, shellfish, liver, legumes, and whole or enriched grains.

Calcium builds and maintains strong bones and teeth. Without adequate calcium your body has to take what it needs from your bones, which may cause them to become weak and brittle and to fracture more easily. The most well-known sources of calcium are, of course, milk and other dairy products. In addition, calcium is found in canned sardines and salmon (with bones), tofu, cooked soybeans, and oranges and in such vegetables as cooked collards, turnips, mustard greens, broccoli, and spinach.

The Trio to Be Wary Of

Sodium—Cholesterol—Fat—The red flag goes up in any nutrition-conscious mind at those words. However, these "villains" have their useful sides, too.

Sodium

Sodium is an important regulator of the fluid balance in your body. By attracting water into the blood vessels, sodium helps maintain normal blood volume and pressure—making small amounts of sodium a necessity. However, too much may contribute to high blood pressure which can, in turn, lead to heart and kidney diseases and strokes. Sodium may also be a problem in weight loss, since it can mask the actual loss and even send the scale up because of water retention (caused by sodium's effect on the body's water balance).

Sodium occurs naturally in certain foods, and overzealous cooks may add additional amounts in the form of table salt. In addition, sodium is often added in the processing of prepared foods such as canned vegetables, meats, and poultry; prepared salad dressings; cured, smoked, canned, and dried fish; cheese and processed cheese products, foods, and spreads; baking soda and baking powder; and food preservatives such as monosodium glutamate (MSG).

The guideline to remember is that your daily intake of sodium *should not exceed 3 grams (3000 milligrams)*. (Did you know that just ¼ teaspoon of salt contains a whopping 533 milligrams of sodium?)

Here are some ways to avoid excess sodium:

• Ignore the salt shaker when cooking pasta, vegetables, rice, soups, and cereals. (Let each person add her/his own salt at the table.)

• Use reduced-sodium versions of soy sauce and broth in your favorite recipes or season with herbs and spices.

• When cooking canned legumes, drain and rinse with cold water before using, to remove some of the excess sodium.

• Do a balancing act: reduce or eliminate the amount of salt called for in a recipe containing a high-sodium item (for example, pickles, celery, olives, sauerkraut, and canned or frozen vegetables with added salt).

• Take advantage of the popular new reduced-sodium products currently on the market, such as reduced-sodium tomato sauce and cheese. (Some of our recipes call for reduced-fat cheese, which is often lower in sodium as well.)

Cholesterol

"LDL" . . . "HDL" . . . Those initials are on everyone's cholesterol-counting lips these days. But what do these terms really mean? Put quite simply, LDLs are low-density lipoproteins, while HDLs are high-density lipoproteins. Both types carry cholesterol and fats in the bloodstream.

The "bad" cholesterol is LDL, which apparently promotes the deposit of cholesterol on artery walls, increasing the risk of heart disease. On the other hand, the "good" cholesterol, HDL, is believed to carry cholesterol away from the arteries.

There are two types of cholesterol: *blood* (serum) and *dietary*. Blood cholesterol, a fat-like substance manufactured by the body, is found in every living cell and is essential for normal functioning. Dietary cholesterol is found in foods of animal origin (meats and dairy products).

Research has shown that a diet rich in saturated fat and cholesterol tends to raise blood cholesterol levels, increasing the risk of heart disease. *Therefore, we recommend that you limit your cholesterol intake to an average of 300 milligrams per day* (based on your weekly intake). This can be done by reducing your consumption of butter, hard cheeses, heavy cream, red meats, eggs, and organ meats. You should also limit foods made with coconut, palm, and palm kernel oils.

Plant foods, on the other hand, are free of dietary cholesterol. So be sure to include healthful amounts of complex carbohydrates and high-fiber foods such as whole grain breads and cereals, legumes, and fresh fruits and vegetables.

Don't make the mistake of thinking that eliminating a particular food or eating just one type will solve the cholesterol problem. Your best remedy is to get into the habit of making nutritious low-fat menu choices.

Fat

The plus side of fat is that it's a major source of energy. It also cushions body organs, acts as an insulator, enables the body to carry fat-soluble vitamins, and provides essential fatty acids. It's easy to see that small amounts of fat are a necessary part of our daily diet. The other side of the coin is that too much fat (especially the saturated variety) has been linked to heart disease and some types of cancer.

There are three types of fat in foods: *saturated fat,* found primarily in animal foods such as meats, butter, and cream, as well as in coconut, palm, and palm kernel oils; *polyunsaturated fat,* present in most liquid vegetable oils, including corn, soy, safflower, sesame, cottonseed, soybean, and sunflower; and *monounsaturated fat,* found in olives and olive oil, avocados, and peanut and canola (rapeseed) oils.

The three types play very different roles in the cholesterol scene. Saturated fat is the villain that tends to raise blood cholesterol by increasing the LDL levels. Polyunsaturated fat is both helpful and nonhelpful. It apparently reduces the total blood cholesterol level by lowering LDLs, but seems to lower HDLs as well. The fat that gets the highest rating is monounsaturated, which seems to lower LDLs while leaving HDLs unaffected.

Regardless of whether the fat is saturated or not, it's still high in calories. Each gram contains 9 calories, more than double the calories in equivalent amounts of carbohydrates or protein.

Since a low-fat diet helps with weight control, give yourself a boost by following these fat-reducing suggestions:

- Steam or microwave vegetables without added fat, rather than sautéing them in butter, margarine, or oil.
- When preparing homemade broths, soups, and stews, refrigerate them before serving so that the fat can congeal and be easily removed.
- Use lean cuts of meat and remove any visible fat before eating.
- Use a rack when baking, roasting, or broiling beef, lamb, or pork, so that the fat will drip off. When boiling these meats, discard any fat that cooks out.
- Remove the skin from poultry (it's a source of saturated fat) before pan-broiling, sautéing, stir-frying, or stewing. When baking, broiling, or boiling poultry, remove the skin before serving.

Become knowledgeable about nutrition by making it a habit to read product labels. They provide nutrition information that will help you succeed on the Food Plan. Some products, for instance, are permissible on the Weight Watchers food plan only if they meet certain nutritional guidelines.

In addition, some of the recipes in this book call for items of specific caloric content and the label will clue you as to whether it's the appropriate product.

How to Read the Recipes

- On each recipe the approximate preparation time is given. This does *not* include marinating, freezing, cooling, or chilling time, since these tasks can be taking place while your attention is on other things. (For example, a dish can marinate in the refrigerator overnight, while a dessert can cool during the time you're enjoying the meal.)

- Following each recipe is Selection Information (e.g., Each serving provides: 1 Milk; 2 Proteins; 30 Optional Calories), explaining how one serving fits into the Weight Watchers food plan. You'll find this information helpful when preparing your menus, since it helps you keep track of your Selections. *If you make any changes in the recipe be sure to adjust the Selection Information accordingly.*

- In step with the current emphasis on nutritional awareness, each recipe also includes a per serving nutritional analysis for calories, protein, fat, carbohydrate, calcium, sodium, cholesterol, and dietary fiber. These amounts are based on the most up-to-date data available. *Be aware that these figures will be altered by any changes you make in a recipe, whether or not it affects the Selection Information.* The nutritional analysis for recipes containing cooked items (such as rice, pasta, or vegetables) assumes that no extra salt or fat is added during cooking.

- Many recipes have a symbol indicating that they are reduced in sodium, fat, and/or cholesterol. For optimum healthfulness, we've often used such foods as egg substitutes, reduced-fat cheeses, and low-sodium broths.

 on a recipe that contains 2 or more Proteins indicates that each serving has 50 milligrams or less of cholesterol. All other recipes with this symbol contain 25 milligrams or less of cholesterol per serving.

 indicates that 30% or less of the calories come from fat.

 on a recipe that contains 2 or more Proteins indicates that each serving has 400 milligrams or less of sodium. All other recipes with this symbol contain 200 milligrams or less of sodium per serving.

Cooking Cues

Organize Before Starting

Before beginning to prepare a recipe, read it through so that you know exactly what you'll have to do before you begin. To save you time, we've kept ingredients to a minimum. Make sure you have everything you need within easy reach, including utensils. Proper organization saves time, too.

Have the Proper Cookware

Use nonstick cookware so that you can cook with little or no fat. If you don't own this type of cookware, spray an ordinary pan with nonstick cooking spray.

Make Use of Cooked Meats

To help speed up cooking time, many of the recipes call for cooked meat or poultry—a savory (and economical) way to use up leftovers. If you don't have any on hand, purchase precooked meats, such as barbecued chicken, roast beef, or ham, from your supermarket's take-out department.

Thaw in a Time-Saving Way

When thawed ingredients are called for, the most time-wise way is to let them thaw overnight (in the refrigerator, not out on the counter!) or let your microwave oven do a speedy thawing job.

Start with Pre-Preparation Amounts

The weights of fresh fruits and vegetables given in the recipes are the weights *before* any peeling, cutting, or other procedure. For example, if a recipe calls for one pound of apples, cored, pared, and diced, start with one pound; then proceed according to recipe directions.

Weigh and Measure Properly

Never gauge amounts by guesswork. Take time to weigh and measure carefully. It's important for the success of the recipe, as well as for accurate portion sizes.

- Foods should be weighed on a food scale.
- Liquids should be measured in a standard glass or clear plastic measuring cup. For amounts of less than ¼ cup, use standard measuring spoons.
- Dry ingredients should be measured in metal or plastic measuring cups that come in ¼-, ⅓-, ½-, and 1-cup sizes. Be sure to level the amount with a knife or spatula. To measure less than ¼ cup, use standard measuring spoons and level the contents the same way.
- "Dash" means approximately ¹⁄₁₆ of a teaspoon (½ of a ⅛-teaspoon measure or ¼ of a ¼-teaspoon measure).

- Weights in recipes are given in pounds and fractions of a pound. Following are the ounce equivalents:

1 pound = 16 ounces	½ pound = 8 ounces
¾ pound = 12 ounces	¼ pound = 4 ounces

Serving Sizes

When preparing a recipe for more than one serving, mix ingredients well and divide evenly so that each portion will contain equal amounts.

Multiplying or Dividing Recipes

Recipes can be doubled, tripled, etc.—or halved—but seasonings *cannot* be automatically multiplied or divided. Begin by using less than the multiplied or divided recipe would call for, then, if necessary, increase the amount according to your taste.

Marinating

It's best to marinate foods in glass or stainless-steel containers, rather than aluminum, since marinades usually contain acidic ingredients which may react adversely with the aluminum.

Tip: Marinating items in a securely fastened leakproof plastic bag eliminates having to wash a container.

Refrigerating/Freezing

- If a cooked food is to be chilled or frozen, first allow it to cool slightly. Placing a very hot food in the refrigerator or freezer may affect the efficiency of the appliance, as well as warming the other foods in it.
- The best way to refrigerate or freeze a large quantity of food is to divide it into smaller portions after cooking. They'll cool faster, reducing the chance of spoilage.
- All refrigerator items should be securely covered. To prevent freezer burn, make sure that all foods that are going to be frozen are covered or wrapped properly.

Oven Suggestions

- Remember that ovens—like cooks—aren't identical, so always check for doneness as directed.

- Keep tabs on the accuracy of your oven thermostat by checking it from time to time. Any discrepancy may affect the quality of your cooking. To determine whether the thermostat is registering correctly, place an oven thermometer on a rack centered in the oven. Set the oven temperature, wait 10 to 15 minutes, then check the thermometer. If the actual oven temperature doesn't match the temperature setting, adjust the setting higher or lower as needed to compensate for the difference until the oven can be repaired.

- To prevent heat loss, close the oven door promptly after putting food in and don't open the door unnecessarily.

- When baking, place the pan in the middle of the center oven rack so that air can circulate freely, enabling the food to bake evenly. It's best to use one oven rack at a time. If using two, position them so that they divide the oven into thirds. Stagger the pans so that they're not directly above each other.

- When broiling, the standard distance from the source of heat is four inches. This guideline should be followed unless the recipe specifies otherwise.

Tip: When using only some of the cups in a muffin pan, prevent the pan from warping or burning by partially filling the empty cups with water. When you're ready to remove the muffins from the pan, carefully drain off the boiling hot water.

Microwave Ovens

"Microwaving": this is a popular word in our current kitchen vocabulary. Not only does a microwave oven provide an express route through cooking and thawing, it does so while the kitchen stays comfortably cool. These ovens have also transformed the brown-bag scene by making it possible to bring a microwavable meal to your office (provided that it has a microwave oven) and prepare a hot lunch in minutes.

Because of this ease and popularity, we've included more than 50 microwave recipes in this cookbook. They were tested in 650- to 700-watt microwave ovens with variable power levels. These levels control the percentage of power introduced into the oven cavity and automatically cycle power on and off. Lower power levels cook more slowly; higher levels cook faster. The power levels may also vary depending on the brand of oven.

Our recipes use the following power levels:

HIGH (100%)
MEDIUM-HIGH (60–70%)
MEDIUM (50%)
LOW (10–20%)

If the levels in your microwave oven are different from these, you may need to adjust the recipe. If you own a lower-wattage oven, increase the cooking time, check it, and cook longer, if necessary. For higher-wattage ovens, decrease the cooking time slightly.

When cooking in your microwave oven, be sure to use cookware that is specifically recommended for use in the microwave oven, such as microwavable casseroles with matching covers. When food is arranged on a microwavable plate or in custard cups, an inverted microwavable pie plate or saucer can serve as a cover.

Becoming Familiar with Some Ingredients

BACON—Bacon is occasionally used because of its special taste and unbeatable aroma. Whenever possible a recipe variation has been included that does not include bacon.

BROTH—Canned ready-to-serve low-sodium broth is used in many of the recipes. This convenient product adds flavor to a dish while keeping the sodium level under control.

BUTTER—When the recipe calls for butter or whipped butter, use the lightly salted kind unless sweet butter is specified. Although most of our recipes use lower-saturated fat alternatives (such as nonstick cooking spray, margarine, vegetable oil, or olive oil), at times a small amount of butter is included because it can go a long way toward enhancing the flavor of a recipe.

CHEESE—The cheese used in our recipes is very often the *reduced-fat* variety, since other kinds can add a substantial amount of fat to your diet. This variety is often lower in sodium as well.

EGGS—Because of the danger of salmonella, certain precautions should be taken with eggs:

- Never buy cracked or dirty eggs. If you find any cracked ones in the carton, discard them immediately.
- Only purchase eggs stored in a refrigerator case.
- Refrigerate eggs as soon as possible. Store them in their carton so they won't absorb odors from the refrigerator. Don't wash them before storing or using.
- Don't eat raw eggs or foods made with raw eggs.
- Cook eggs until both the whites and the yolks are firm, not runny; "over well" is safer than "sunny-side up."
- Avoid foods that are rich in eggs that are only lightly cooked, such as soft custards and meringues.
- Don't leave eggs—either raw or hard-cooked—out of the refrigerator for longer than two hours.
- Use fresh eggs within five weeks and hard-cooked ones within one week.

- Leftover uncooked egg whites and yolks should be refrigerated immediately and discarded after four days.
- Any areas of the kitchen that come in contact with raw eggs should be washed with hot soapy water.
- Serve eggs and egg-rich foods promptly after cooking.

Tip: When using eggs, break each one individually into a cup or bowl before combining with each other or with additional ingredients. This avoids wasting other items if an egg is spoiled or a piece of shell falls into it.

EGG SUBSTITUTES are made mostly of egg white (the high-protein portion of the egg). They are cholesterol-free (some brands are also fat-free) and are usually available in the supermarket freezer section.

Keep frozen egg substitutes frozen until needed. Thaw the container in the refrigerator or speed thawing by putting the container under cold running water.

FRUITS and FRUIT JUICES (canned and frozen) should not contain added sugar (sugar substitutes are permitted). Canned fruit may be packed in its own juice or in another fruit juice, blend of juices, or water.

GELATIN—When dissolving unflavored gelatin over direct heat, keep the heat low and stir constantly since gelatin burns very easily.

LIQUEURS—If a specified liqueur is unavailable, you may substitute one of your favorites.

OILS—Vegetable oils have certain characteristics that make them appropriate for specific recipes. However, one can often be substituted for another. In recipes where no particular type is specified, you have the option of using safflower, sunflower, soybean, corn, cottonseed, or any combination of these. However, olive, walnut, and peanut oils have distinctive flavors so use when specified. When Chinese sesame oil is indicated, use the *dark* (rather than the light) kind. The light is relatively flavorless and may be used as a substitute for any other vegetable oil, whereas the dark variety, which is made from toasted sesame seeds, has a rich amber color and characteristic sesame flavor.

Nut and seed oils (such as walnut, hazelnut, peanut, almond, and sesame) should be stored in the refrigerator after they've been opened, so they won't become rancid or develop odors. Since these oils are usually more expensive, buy in small quantities and store them properly. (Other oils may be stored in the cupboard.)

SHELLFISH—*Clams* and *mussels* should be purchased live and have shells that are tightly closed. Give any slightly open shells a hard tap. They should snap shut. If they don't, discard them. Remember that shells open during cooking. (To avoid last-minute dashes to the store, buy more shellfish than the recipe requires. Any leftovers can be used as part of a meal the next day.)

VEGETABLES called for in the recipes mean *fresh* ones, unless otherwise indicated. You may substitute canned or frozen varieties, but the cooking times should be adjusted accordingly. Canned or thawed frozen vegetables would take less time; those frozen solid may take slightly longer. Be aware that canned vegetables may also increase the sodium content of the recipe.

CHILI PEPPERS contain volatile oils that can make your skin and eyes burn. When working with these hot peppers, wear rubber gloves and be careful not to touch your face or eyes. Before continuing with the recipe preparation, thoroughly wash your hands and the knife and cutting board to remove all traces of the peppers.

LETTUCE called for in the recipes assumes either iceberg or romaine. Four lettuce leaves provide one Vegetable Selection. If you use any other type of lettuce (such as Boston or Bibb), 8 lettuce leaves provide one Vegetable Selection.

WHIPPED TOPPING—This lower-calorie alternative to whipped cream is used in a few dessert recipes. As a way to cut back on saturated fat, when the topping is just a garnish, the recipe has a variation that does not include it.

NOTE: To take you on a culinary adventure, some of the recipes include exotic ingredients such as sun-dried tomatoes, shiitake mushrooms, and balsamic and raspberry vinegars. Once found only in the finest restaurants, today these elegant treats are as accessible as your neighborhood supermarket. We invite you to broaden your experiences by trying them. However, in case your tastes run to the less daring, familiar alternatives are provided in the recipes.

Seasonings

What nutritional allies herbs and spices are! They increase tastiness without compromising health since they can easily be substituted for flavorings too high in fat, sodium, or cholesterol.

We recommend using fresh herbs in many of our recipes. When appropriate, the amount of dried herb that may be substituted is also indicated. If the recipe doesn't have a dried alternative, use fresh herbs.

When substituting fresh spices for ground spices, use approximately 8 times the amount (for example, 1 teaspoon minced pared gingerroot instead of 1/8 teaspoon ground ginger).

Some Well-Seasoned Suggestions

- Dried herbs are stronger in flavor than fresh. Therefore, use less.
- For cold spreads, dips, and dressings, add herbs several hours ahead of time to allow the flavors to blend.
- When using fresh herbs, to release the most flavor cut the leaves very fine.
- Fresh herbs can easily be stored in the freezer. Simply rinse the herb in cold water and freeze in a resealable plastic freezer bag. The frozen herb can be added during cooking (thawing isn't necessary).

"Marrying" Seasonings to Compatible Foods

BEEF	Black or green peppercorns, chili powder, dill, garlic, paprika, powdered mustard, rosemary, sage
EGGS	Basil, chervil, chili powder, chives, curry powder, paprika, red or black pepper, tarragon
FISH	Basil, bay leaf, cilantro (Chinese parsley), dill, fennel, garlic, pepper, rosemary, saffron, tarragon
LAMB	Curry, garlic, ginger, mint, mustard, rosemary, saffron, sage
PORK	Cloves, coriander, garlic, ginger, lemon, rosemary
POULTRY	Dill, garlic, ginger, oregano, paprika, powdered mustard, sage, tarragon
VEAL	Garlic, ginger, marjoram, mustard, oregano, thyme
VEGETABLES	Allspice, basil, chervil, chives, cilantro (Chinese parsley), dill, garlic, marjoram, mint, nutmeg, parsley, red pepper, rosemary

Easy Garnishing

Savvy chefs know that nutritious food should be a feast for the eyes as well as the palate. We like to present attractive dishes, especially when entertaining—but not at the cost of hours of preparation. Fortunately, the simplest dishes can be dressed up in glamorous style with the aid of some very easy garnishing techniques.

DIPS can be made colorful by sprinkling them with chopped scallions (green onions) or grated carrots.

FISH dishes take on appetizing attractiveness when accompanied by lemon or lime wedges dipped in finely chopped parsley or paprika. Or try an easy citrus twist: cut into a slice of lemon or lime from the edge to the center, then twist in opposite directions.

FRUIT SALADS and **COOKED VEGETABLES** appear more savory when sprinkled with grated lemon, orange, or lime peel, while strips of orange peel or mint leaves add a cool appeal to fruit salads.

LETTUCE leaves ''blush'' attractively when colored by paprika.

SALADS take on a new look when garnished with carrot curls or dressed up with tomato wedges or slices that have been dipped in finely chopped parsley.

SOUPS gain visual appeal when chopped scallion (green onion), grated carrot, or the ever-popular popcorn is added (popcorn should be counted toward your Bread Selections). A bowl of steaming broth can be deliciously garnished with chopped fresh herbs such as parsley, tarragon, dill, rosemary, basil, or chives.

VEGETABLES and **SOUPS** look more elegant when sprinkled with small amounts of grated Parmesan cheese (count it toward your Optional Calories).

USING FRESH HERBS in your recipe? Garnish with a matching sprig.

FOR AN IMAGINATIVE "SERVING BOWL" for a dip or an egg or tuna salad, use a hollowed-out bell pepper (green, red, or yellow) or a small cabbage.
   P.S. When garnishing isn't called for, you can still brighten the appearance of foods by arranging them creatively on a pretty dish.

Tips for Toting

''Brown-bagging'' has become a way of life because it's convenient, necessary, and economical. Many of our recipes lend themselves to a portable life-style.
   Here are helpful hints to keep in mind when packing meals or snacks.

Cold Foods

- Pack chilled foods in an insulated bag or lunch box.
- Use well-chilled ingredients when making sandwiches.

- Make a week's worth of sandwiches in advance and freeze them for freshness. Then just take one with you in the morning; it will be thawed by the time you're ready for lunch. Peanut butter, meat, and poultry fillings freeze well. (Do *not* freeze raw vegetables, such as lettuce or tomato, since this may affect their texture. And never freeze mayonnaise fillings.)
- When possible, keep the brown-bag meal refrigerated until time to eat. Foods such as meats, poultry, fish, and eggs may spoil if kept at room temperature longer than two hours.

Hot Foods

- When toting hot foods, keep them above 140°F (hot to the touch).
- Hot foods should be packed in an insulated vacuum container. To help keep foods hot longer, preheat the container by filling with hot water and allowing it to stand for several minutes. Then pour out the water and fill the container with hot foods.

Appetizers, Soups, and Dips

Dip into an array of dishes that get your meal off to a nutritious start. Guests will applaud your cholesterol-reduced Tofu-Tahini Dip, and no one need know it only takes a cool (no cooking) five minutes to prepare. And something Popeye never knew is that his favorite vegetable could show up at a party as Spinach Pinwheel Hors d'Oeuvres. Soups don't have to be limited to dinner; for a change-of-pace luncheon add our novel Buttermilk-Walnut Soup. Not home at lunchtime? Simply ladle soup into an insulated vacuum container for a filling pick-me-up.

P.S. Our dips make snappy snacks, too!

Spicy Deviled Eggs ⬦ⓢ

4 hard-cooked eggs
2 tablespoons plus 2 teaspoons
  reduced-calorie mayonnaise
2 tablespoons *each* finely
  chopped red bell pepper, green
  bell pepper, and celery
2 teaspoons minced scallion
  (green onion)
½ teaspoon seeded and minced
  jalapeño pepper
Dash *each* chili powder, hot
  sauce, and Worcestershire
  sauce
Garnish: diced red bell pepper

*Deviled eggs make an attractive hors
d'oeuvre or a totable lunch.*

1. Cut eggs in half lengthwise; remove egg yolks to small mixing bowl, reserving whites.

2. Add remaining ingredients except garnish to egg yolks and, using a fork, mash until combined. Spoon an equal amount of yolk mixture into each egg white half. Cover and refrigerate until ready to serve.

3. To serve, garnish with diced red bell pepper.

APPROXIMATE TOTAL TIME: 15 MINUTES

MAKES 4 SERVINGS

Each serving provides: 1 Fat; 1 Protein; ¼ Vegetable
Per serving: 107 calories; 6 g protein; 8 g fat; 2 g carbohydrate; 28 mg calcium; 123 mg sodium; 216 mg cholesterol; 0.2 g dietary fiber

Ham 'n' Cheese Biscuits ▽ⓒ

½ ounce *each* reduced-fat Cheddar cheese, shredded, and diced turkey-ham

2 teaspoons reduced-calorie mayonnaise

1 teaspoon *each* sweet pickle relish and country Dijon-style mustard

4 ready-to-bake refrigerated buttermilk flaky biscuits (1 ounce each)*

1. Preheat oven to 400°F. In small mixing bowl combine all ingredients except biscuits, stirring until thoroughly combined; set aside.

2. Carefully separate each biscuit into 2 thin layers, then partially separate each layer, forming a pocket. Spoon an equal amount of ham mixture into each pocket; crimp edges of each biscuit to enclose filling.

3. Arrange biscuits on nonstick baking sheet and bake until biscuits are lightly browned, 8 to 10 minutes. Serve immediately.

* Keep biscuits refrigerated until ready to use. Separate dough into layers as soon as biscuits are removed from refrigerator; they will be difficult to work with if allowed to come to room temperature.

APPROXIMATE TOTAL TIME: 20 MINUTES

MAKES 4 SERVINGS, 2 BISCUITS EACH

Each serving provides: ¼ Fat; 1 Bread; 25 Optional Calories
Per serving: 111 calories; 3 g protein; 5 g fat; 13 g carbohydrate; 32 mg calcium; 421 mg sodium; 3 mg cholesterol; dietary fiber data not available

Scallion-Cheese Filled Tomatoes ▽_C ▽_S

6 cherry tomatoes
¼ cup finely chopped scallions (green onions)
1 ounce chèvre (French goat cheese)

1. Cut a thin slice from stem end of each tomato. Scoop out and discard pulp, reserving shells; set aside.

2. In small bowl combine remaining ingredients, mixing well. Fill each reserved tomato shell with an equal amount of scallion-cheese mixture.

3. Preheat broiler. Set tomato shells on nonstick baking sheet and broil until cheese is bubbly, about 1 minute. Serve warm.

APPROXIMATE TOTAL TIME: 10 MINUTES

MAKES 2 SERVINGS, 3 TOMATOES EACH

Each serving provides: ½ Protein; ½ Vegetable; 10 Optional Calories
Per serving: 60 calories; 3 g protein; 4 g fat; 3 g carbohydrate; 31 mg calcium; 90 mg sodium; 13 mg cholesterol; 1 g dietary fiber

Spinach Pinwheel Hors d'Oeuvres ⩒c ⩒f

1 tablespoon plus 2 teaspoons
  olive *or* vegetable oil
½ cup finely chopped onion
4 garlic cloves, chopped
2 cups thawed and well-drained
  frozen chopped spinach
2 tablespoons chopped fresh
  parsley
1 teaspoon Italian seasoning
⅛ teaspoon crushed red pepper
⅓ cup less 1 teaspoon grated
  Parmesan *or* Romano cheese
1 package refrigerated ready-to-
  bake pizza crust dough (10
  ounces)
1 tablespoon thawed frozen egg
  substitute

1. In 10-inch nonstick skillet heat oil; add onion and garlic and cook over medium-high heat, stirring frequently, until onion begins to soften, about 3 minutes. Add spinach, parsley, Italian seasoning, and red pepper and cook, stirring occasionally, until spinach is heated through, about 3 minutes. Let cool slightly; add cheese and stir to combine.

2. Preheat oven to 425°F. Stretch pizza dough into a 16 x 12-inch rectangle. Spread spinach mixture evenly over dough, leaving a 1½-inch border around edge of dough. Starting from the narrow end roll dough over spinach, jelly-roll fashion, to enclose filling; pinch seam well to seal.

3. Spray nonstick baking sheet with nonstick cooking spray and arrange roll, seam side down, on sheet. Brush egg substitute over roll and bake until golden brown, about 15 minutes.

4. Cut roll into 20 equal slices.

APPROXIMATE TOTAL TIME: 30 MINUTES (includes baking time)

MAKES 10 SERVINGS, 2 SLICES EACH

Each serving provides: ½ Fat; ½ Vegetable; 1 Bread; 15 Optional Calories
Per serving with Parmesan cheese: 120 calories; 5 g protein; 4 g fat; 16 g carbohydrate; 88 mg calcium; 219 mg sodium; 2 mg cholesterol; 1 g dietary fiber (this figure does not include pizza dough; nutrition analysis not available)
With Romano cheese: 118 calories; 5 g protein; 4 g fat; 16 g carbohydrate; 80 mg calcium; 202 mg sodium; 3 mg cholesterol; 1 g dietary fiber (this figure does not include pizza dough; nutrition analysis not available)

Apple, Walnut, and Cheddar Soup ⬇C ⬇S

1 teaspoon sweet margarine
½ pound Granny Smith apples, cored, pared, and chopped
½ cup chopped onion
½ ounce shelled walnuts
1 cup canned ready-to-serve low-sodium chicken broth
¾ ounce reduced-fat Cheddar cheese, shredded

1. In 1½-quart nonstick saucepan melt margarine; add apples, onion, and walnuts. Cover and cook over medium heat, stirring occasionally, until apples are soft, about 10 minutes. Let cool slightly.

2. Transfer mixture to blender; add broth and process until smooth. Return to saucepan; stir in cheese and cook over low heat, stirring constantly, until cheese melts, about 2 minutes.

APPROXIMATE TOTAL TIME: 25 MINUTES

MAKES 2 SERVINGS, ABOUT 1¼ CUPS EACH

Each serving provides: 1 Fat; 1 Protein; ½ Vegetable; 1 Fruit; 20 Optional Calories
Per serving: 181 calories; 6 g protein; 9 g fat; 20 g carbohydrate; 115 mg calcium; 103 mg sodium; 8 mg cholesterol; 3 g dietary fiber

Buttermilk-Walnut Soup ▽ⓒ

1½ cups low-fat buttermilk
  (1% milk fat)
1 ounce finely ground walnuts
½ teaspoon minced scallion
  (green onion)
1 garlic clove, minced
½ packet (about ½ teaspoon)
  instant chicken broth and
  seasoning mix
⅛ teaspoon salt
Dash white pepper
1½ teaspoons minced fresh dill

1. In blender combine all ingredients except dill and process until smooth; stir in dill. Cover and refrigerate until flavors blend, at least 1 hour.

APPROXIMATE TOTAL TIME: 10 MINUTES (does not include chilling time)

MAKES 2 SERVINGS, ABOUT ¾ CUP EACH

Each serving provides: ¾ Milk; 1 Fat; 1 Protein; 20 Optional Calories
Per serving: 170 calories; 8 g protein; 10 g fat; 12 g carbohydrate; 234 mg calcium; 581 mg sodium; 7 mg cholesterol; 1 g dietary fiber

Cheese and Broccoli Soup ▽C ▽F

2 teaspoons reduced-calorie
  margarine (tub)
2 tablespoons finely chopped
  onion
1 tablespoon plus 1½ teaspoons
  all-purpose flour
1 cup *each* skim *or* nonfat milk
  and broccoli florets
1 packet instant chicken broth
  and seasoning mix
½ teaspoon chopped fresh
  parsley
Dash white pepper
¾ ounce reduced-fat Cheddar *or*
  Monterey Jack cheese,
  shredded

1. In 2-quart nonstick saucepan melt margarine; add onion and sauté over medium-high heat, until softened, 1 to 2 minutes. Sprinkle flour over onion and stir quickly to combine. Continuing to stir, add *1 cup water* and the milk; add broccoli, broth mix, parsley, and pepper.

2. Reduce heat to low and cook, stirring occasionally, until broccoli is tender, 10 to 15 minutes (*do not boil*). Let cool slightly.

3. In blender process half of the soup until smooth; return to saucepan. Stir in cheese and cook over low heat until cheese is melted, about 5 minutes.

APPROXIMATE TOTAL TIME: 30 MINUTES

MAKES 2 SERVINGS, ABOUT 1¼ CUPS EACH

Each serving provides: ½ Milk; ½ Fat; ½ Protein; 1⅛ Vegetables; ¼ Bread; 5 Optional Calories
Per serving with Cheddar cheese: 142 calories; 11 g protein; 4 g fat; 16 g carbohydrate; 276 mg calcium; 690 mg sodium; 10 mg cholesterol; 0.3 g dietary fiber (this figure does not include broccoli florets; nutrition analysis not available)
With Monterey Jack cheese: 138 calories; 11 g protein; 4 g fat; 15 g carbohydrate; 276 mg calcium; 682 mg sodium; 10 mg cholesterol; 0.3 g dietary fiber (this figure does not include broccoli florets; nutrition analysis not available)

Fresh Tomato-Basil Soup ⛉ ⛉

2 teaspoons olive *or* vegetable oil
1 cup chopped onions
½ small garlic clove, mashed
6 large plum tomatoes, blanched, peeled, seeded, and chopped
1 cup canned ready-to-serve low-sodium chicken broth
2 tablespoons chopped fresh basil
Garnish: 2 basil sprigs

1. In 1½-quart nonstick saucepan heat oil; add onions and garlic and cook over medium-high heat until tender-crisp, about 2 minutes.

2. Stir in remaining ingredients and bring mixture to a boil. Reduce heat to low and let simmer, stirring occasionally, until flavors blend, about 15 minutes.

3. Pour soup into 2 soup bowls and garnish each portion with a basil sprig.

APPROXIMATE TOTAL TIME: 30 MINUTES

MAKES 2 SERVINGS, ABOUT 1¼ CUPS EACH

Each serving provides: 1 Fat; 4 Vegetables; 20 Optional Calories
Per serving: 114 calories; 4 g protein; 6 g fat; 14 g carbohydrate; 55 mg calcium; 41 mg sodium; 0 mg cholesterol; 3 g dietary fiber

Lima Bean Soup

½ cup chopped onion
¼ cup chopped carrot
2 teaspoons sweet margarine
1 cup *each* frozen green lima
    beans and canned ready-to-
    serve low-sodium chicken
    broth
Dash white pepper

1. In 1½-quart microwavable casserole combine first 3 ingredients. Microwave on High (100%) for 2 minutes until margarine is melted; add beans and broth. Cover and microwave on High for 5 minutes. Let cool slightly.

2. Transfer to blender and process until smooth. Return to casserole and microwave on High for 2 minutes, until thoroughly heated. Stir in pepper.

APPROXIMATE TOTAL TIME: 20 MINUTES

MAKES 2 SERVINGS, ABOUT 1 CUP EACH

Each serving provides: 1 Fat; 1 Bread; ¾ Vegetable; 20 Optional Calories
Per serving: 154 calories; 7 g protein; 5 g fat; 21 g carbohydrate; 34 mg calcium; 79 mg sodium; 0 mg cholesterol; 11 g dietary fiber

Microwave Vichyssoise ⬩C⬩ ⬩S⬩

2 teaspoons margarine
1 cup thoroughly washed thinly
  sliced leeks (white portion
  only)
1 cup canned ready-to-serve low-
  sodium chicken broth
6 ounces finely diced pared all-
  purpose potato
½ cup whole milk
1 tablespoon half-and-half (blend
  of milk and cream)
Dash *each* white pepper and
  ground nutmeg
2 teaspoons minced fresh chives
  or 1 teaspoon chopped chives

1. In 1-quart microwavable casserole microwave margarine on High (100%) for 30 seconds until melted. Add leeks and microwave on High for 1½ minutes, until slightly softened.

2. Add chicken broth and potato; cover and microwave on High for 5 minutes, until potato is tender, stirring halfway through cooking. Let stand for 1 minute. Uncover and let cool slightly, about 5 minutes.

3. Transfer potato-leek mixture to food processor and process until pureed. Return mixture to casserole.

4. Using a wire whisk, stir in milk, half-and-half, pepper, and nutmeg. Cover and refrigerate until chilled, at least 1 hour.

5. Divide soup into 4 soup bowls and sprinkle each portion with an equal amount of chives.

APPROXIMATE TOTAL TIME: 25 MINUTES (does not include chilling time)

MAKES 2 SERVINGS, ABOUT 1 CUP EACH

Each serving provides: ¼ Milk; 1 Fat; 1 Vegetable; 1 Bread; 50 Optional Calories
Per serving: 196 calories; 6 g protein; 8 g fat; 27 g carbohydrate; 120 mg calcium; 120 mg sodium; 11 mg cholesterol; 2 g dietary fiber

Oriental Hot Pot

1 tablespoon *each* rice vinegar and reduced-sodium soy sauce
1 packet instant beef broth and seasoning mix
1 teaspoon minced pared gingerroot
½ cup sliced carrot
1 cup thinly sliced Chinese chard (bok choy)
½ cup *each* bean sprouts, snow peas (Chinese pea pods), and sliced shiitake mushrooms *or* white mushrooms
¼ cup sliced scallions (green onions)
2 ounces uncooked cellophane noodles*

In this traditional Chinese dish, guests cook a selection of ingredients in hot broth in a pot set in the center of the table. Our version is completely prepared on the range prior to serving.

1. In 3-quart saucepan combine *3 cups water*, the vinegar, soy sauce, broth mix, and gingerroot; cover and cook over medium-high heat until mixture comes to a boil.

2. Reduce heat to low; add carrot and cook, uncovered, until tender, 8 to 10 minutes. Add remaining ingredients except noodles and stir to combine; cover and cook until vegetables are tender-crisp, about 5 minutes. Add noodles and stir to combine. Cook, uncovered, until noodles are transparent, about 3 minutes.

* Two ounces uncooked cellophane noodles yield about 1 cup cooked noodles.

APPROXIMATE TOTAL TIME: 30 MINUTES

MAKES 2 SERVINGS, ABOUT 2 CUPS EACH

Each serving provides: 3¼ Vegetables; 1 Bread; 5 Optional Calories
Per serving: 154 calories; 4 g protein; 0.4 g fat; 35 g carbohydrate; 79 mg calcium; 802 mg sodium; 0 mg cholesterol; 2 g dietary fiber (this figure does not include Chinese chard; nutrition analysis not available)

Puree of Green Bean Soup ⌄C⌄ ⌄F⌄ ⌄S⌄

2 cups sliced trimmed green
   beans
1 cup chopped onions
2 teaspoons reduced-calorie
   margarine (tub)
1 cup low-fat milk (1% milk fat)
¼ cup canned ready-to-serve
   low-sodium chicken broth
1 teaspoon all-purpose flour
Garnish: 6 trimmed chives

1. In 1-quart microwavable casserole combine first 3 ingredients; microwave on High (100%) for 2 minutes, until margarine is melted. Add ½ *cup water* and microwave on High for 5 minutes, until beans are tender. Let cool slightly.

2. Transfer mixture to blender and process until smooth; add remaining ingredients and process until combined. Return to casserole and microwave on High for 1 minute, until mixture thickens slightly and is thoroughly heated.

3. Pour soup into 2 soup bowls and garnish each portion with 3 trimmed chives.

APPROXIMATE TOTAL TIME: 20 MINUTES

MAKES 2 SERVINGS, ABOUT 2 CUPS EACH

Each serving provides: ½ Milk; ½ Fat; 3 Vegetables; 20 Optional Calories
Per serving: 138 calories; 7 g protein; 4 g fat; 21 g carbohydrate; 211 mg calcium; 116 mg sodium; 5 mg cholesterol; 3 g dietary fiber

Black Bean Dip ▽C ▽F

4 ounces rinsed drained canned
  black (turtle) beans
1 small garlic clove, chopped
1 cup prepared thick and chunky
  mild salsa

*Serve this nutritious dip with vege-
table crudités or toasted tortilla
pieces.*

1. In food processor combine beans and garlic and
process, using on-off motion, until smooth *(do not
puree)*. Transfer to bowl and stir in salsa.

APPROXIMATE TOTAL TIME: 10 MINUTES

MAKES 4 SERVINGS, ABOUT ½ CUP EACH

Each serving provides: ½ Protein; ½ Vegetable
Per serving: 49 calories; 2 g protein; 0.1 g fat; 10 g carbohydrate; 12 mg calcium; 456 mg sodium (estimated);
0 mg cholesterol; 1 g dietary fiber

Italian Herbed Dip

2 tablespoons thawed frozen egg
  substitute
1 teaspoon balsamic *or* red wine
  vinegar
1 small garlic clove
¼ cup *each* olive oil and finely
  chopped scallions (green
  onions)
1 tablespoon *each* finely chopped
  fresh basil and Italian
  (flat-leaf) parsley
¼ teaspoon oregano leaves

*This party dip is also great as a salad
dressing.*

1. In blender combine first 3 ingredients and process until combined. With motor running, gradually add oil in a steady stream until mixture thickens.

2. Transfer mixture to bowl; stir in remaining ingredients. Cover and refrigerate until chilled, at least 15 minutes.

APPROXIMATE TOTAL TIME: 10 MINUTES (does not include chilling time)

MAKES 12 SERVINGS, ABOUT 2 TEASPOONS EACH

Each serving provides: 1 Fat; 3 Optional Calories
Per serving: 42 calories; 0.3 g protein; 5 g fat; 0.3 g carbohydrate; 6 mg calcium; 5 mg sodium; 0 mg cholesterol; 0.1 g dietary fiber

Salmon Mousse ▽C

7 ounces drained canned salmon (packed in water), mashed

3 tablespoons whipped cream cheese, softened

2 tablespoons plus 2 teaspoons reduced-calorie mayonnaise

2 tablespoons *each* finely diced red onion, rinsed drained capers, and chopped fresh parsley

1 teaspoon lemon juice

1 teaspoon unflavored gelatin

½ packet (about ½ teaspoon) instant chicken broth and seasoning mix

3 egg whites

If canned salmon is too costly for your budget, substitute canned tuna.

1. Spray a 7⅜ x 3⅝ x 2¼-inch nonstick loaf pan with nonstick cooking spray. Cut a sheet of wax paper 7½ inches long and set in pan, folding excess paper over wide sides of pan; spray pan again with cooking spray. Set aside.

2. In large mixing bowl combine salmon, cream cheese, mayonnaise, onion, capers, parsley, and lemon juice; mix well and set aside.

3. In 1-quart saucepan sprinkle gelatin over ¼ *cup water*; let stand 1 minute to soften. Cook over medium heat, stirring constantly, until gelatin is completely dissolved, about 1 minute. Stir in broth mix. Remove from heat and let stand for 5 minutes.

4. Using mixer on medium-high speed, beat egg whites until stiff.

5. Add gelatin mixture to salmon mixture and stir to thoroughly combine. Add ⅓ of the egg whites to salmon-gelatin mixture and stir to combine; fold in remaining egg whites.

6. Spoon salmon mixture into prepared pan, spreading top smooth. Cover pan with plastic wrap and refrigerate until set, at least 2 hours or overnight.

7. To serve, invert pan onto serving platter and cut crosswise into 8 equal slices.

APPROXIMATE TOTAL TIME: 20 MINUTES (does not include chilling time)

MAKES 8 SERVINGS

Each serving provides: ½ Fat; 1 Protein; 15 Optional Calories
Per serving: 69 calories; 7 g protein; 4 g fat; 1 g carbohydrate; 67 mg calcium; 310 mg sodium; 15 mg cholesterol; 0.1 g dietary fiber

Spinach Dip

½ cup evaporated skimmed milk
2 teaspoons all-purpose flour
3 tablespoons whipped cream cheese
2 tablespoons sour cream
½ cup frozen chopped spinach, thawed and well drained
2 tablespoons finely chopped onion
1 small garlic clove, minced
1 teaspoon *each* grated Parmesan cheese and Worcestershire sauce
⅛ teaspoon *each* salt and pepper
Dash hot sauce

Serve with melba rounds, flatbreads, or vegetable crudités.

1. Using a wire whisk, in 1-quart shallow microwavable casserole combine milk and flour, stirring until flour is dissolved. Microwave on Medium (50%) for 1½ minutes, stirring once halfway through cooking, until mixture thickens.

2. Stir in cream cheese and sour cream; microwave on Medium for 2½ minutes, stirring once after every minute.

3. Stir in spinach, onion, and garlic and microwave on Medium for 2 minutes, stirring once halfway through cooking.

4. Stir in remaining ingredients until thoroughly combined.

5. Transfer to serving bowl and serve immediately.

APPROXIMATE TOTAL TIME: 10 MINUTES

MAKES 4 SERVINGS

Each serving provides: ¼ Milk; ¼ Vegetable; 50 Optional Calories
Per serving: 121 calories; 6 g protein; 5 g fat; 15 g carbohydrate; 146 mg calcium; 180 mg sodium; 12 mg cholesterol; 1 g dietary fiber

Tofu-Tahini Dip ▽

2 ounces firm-style tofu
1 tablespoon *each* tahini (sesame paste) and chopped scallion (green onion)
2 teaspoons ketchup
1 teaspoon *each* lemon juice and reduced-sodium soy sauce
½ garlic clove, chopped
1 teaspoon sesame seed, toasted
2 small pitas (1 ounce each), heated and cut into quarters

1. In blender combine all ingredients except sesame seed and pitas and process until pureed, about 1 minute. Transfer to serving bowl. Sprinkle with sesame seed and serve with pitas.

APPROXIMATE TOTAL TIME: 5 MINUTES

MAKES 2 SERVINGS

Each serving provides: ½ Fat; 1 Protein; 1 Bread; 15 Optional Calories
Per serving: 191 calories; 9 g protein; 7 g fat; 24 g carbohydrate; 116 mg calcium; 355 mg sodium; 0 mg cholesterol; 1 g dietary fiber

Breakfasts and Brunches

Breakfast is coming into its own. Nutrition-conscious people recognize that it's important to fuel up for the day with a nourishing meal. Our recipes make this easy with quickly prepared tasty dishes, many of them complete meals in themselves. How about Polenta with Blueberries in Syrup, microwaved in a nifty five minutes? Or a tasty Basil-Vegetable Quiche for brunch? Those who race off to work will find many of our items conveniently totable. (Pack an Apple-Cheddar Muffin for an energizing way to start your workday.)

Apple-Cheddar Muffins ⬥C ⬥S

1¾ cups all-purpose flour
½ pound apples, cored, pared, and finely chopped
½ cup rye flour
2 ounces reduced-fat Cheddar cheese, shredded
1½ ounces chopped walnuts
¼ cup granulated sugar
2 tablespoons dark raisins
2 teaspoons double-acting baking powder
¼ teaspoon ground allspice *or* ground cinnamon
½ cup skim *or* nonfat milk
⅓ cup plus 2 teaspoons reduced-calorie margarine (tub)
¼ cup thawed frozen egg substitute

These muffins are great for toting to the office when you want breakfast in a hurry. Enjoy with skim milk, yogurt, or cottage cheese.

1. Preheat oven to 375°F. In medium mixing bowl combine first 9 ingredients; stir to combine and set aside.

2. In blender combine remaining ingredients and process until smooth. Pour into dry ingredients and stir until moistened (*do not beat or overmix*).

3. Spray twelve 2½-inch nonstick muffin-pan cups with nonstick cooking spray; fill each cup with an equal amount of batter (each will be about ¾ full). Bake in middle of center oven rack for 20 minutes (until muffins are golden and a toothpick, inserted in center, comes out dry).

4. Invert muffins onto wire rack and let cool.

APPROXIMATE TOTAL TIME: 30 MINUTES (includes baking time)

MAKES 12 SERVINGS, 1 MUFFIN EACH

Each serving provides: 1 Fat; ½ Protein; 1 Bread; ¼ Fruit; 30 Optional Calories
Per serving: 181 calories; 5 g protein; 6 g fat; 26 g carbohydrate; 101 mg calcium; 180 mg sodium; 4 mg cholesterol; 2 g dietary fiber

Blueberry-Oat Bran Loaf ▽ⓢ

1¼ cups plus 1 tablespoon cake
  flour, sifted
2¼ ounces uncooked unprocessed
  oat bran
1½ ounces uncooked quick-
  cooking oats
1 teaspoon *each* ground
  cinnamon and baking soda
¼ teaspoon ground nutmeg
1 cup part-skim ricotta cheese
¾ cup low-fat buttermilk (1%
  milk fat)
2 eggs, lightly beaten
¼ cup *each* granulated sugar and
  vegetable oil
1½ cups fresh *or* frozen
  blueberries (no sugar added)

*Loaf can be cut into slices and each
slice individually wrapped and
stored in the freezer. Thaw slices at
room temperature. A slice of this nutritious loaf is delicious with a glass
of skim milk for breakfast.*

1. Preheat oven to 350°F. In medium mixing bowl combine flour, oat bran, oats, cinnamon, baking soda, and nutmeg, stirring to combine.

2. In separate medium mixing bowl combine remaining ingredients except blueberries and stir to combine. Add to flour mixture and stir until moistened; fold in blueberries.

3. Spray a 9 × 5 × 3-inch loaf pan with nonstick cooking spray and spread batter evenly in pan. Bake in middle of center oven rack for 55 minutes (until a cake tester, inserted in center, comes out dry). Set loaf pan on wire rack and let cool for 5 minutes; invert onto wire rack and let cool completely.

APPROXIMATE TOTAL TIME: 45 MINUTES (in-cludes baking time)

MAKES 12 SERVINGS

Each serving provides: 1 Fat; ½ Protein; 1 Bread; ¼ Fruit; 25 Optional Calories
Per serving: 195 calories; 7 g protein; 8 g fat; 24 g carbohydrate; 89 mg calcium; 122 mg sodium; 42 mg cholesterol; 2 g dietary fiber

Cranberry-Wheat Muffins ▽c ▽F

3 tablespoons granulated sugar
2 tablespoons thawed frozen
   concentrated apple juice
   (no sugar added)
½ cup cranberries
¼ cup plus I tablespoon golden
   or dark raisins
¾ cup low-fat buttermilk
   (1% milk fat)
¼ cup thawed frozen egg
   substitute
2 tablespoons plus 2 teaspoons
   margarine, melted
I cup all-purpose flour
½ cup buckwheat flour
2 teaspoons double-acting baking
   powder
½ teaspoon baking soda

Store muffins in the freezer. They taste as fresh as the day they were baked when thawed at room temperature. To make this meal complete, try a cup of reduced-calorie hot cocoa.

1. Preheat oven to 425°F. In small mixing bowl combine sugar, *2 tablespoons water*, and the apple juice concentrate, stirring to dissolve sugar. Add cranberries and raisins; stir to combine and set aside.

2. Using a fork, in separate small mixing bowl beat together buttermilk, egg substitute, and margarine; set aside.

3. In medium mixing bowl combine remaining ingredients; stir in buttermilk mixture, stirring until moistened. Stir in cranberry mixture.

4. Spray eight 2½-inch nonstick muffin-pan cups with nonstick cooking spray; fill each cup with an equal amount of batter and partially fill remaining cups with water (this will prevent pan from burning and/ or warping). Bake in middle of center oven rack for 20 minutes (until muffins are lightly browned and a toothpick, inserted in center, comes out dry). Transfer muffins to wire rack and let cool.

APPROXIMATE TOTAL TIME: 30 MINUTES (includes baking time)

MAKES 8 SERVINGS, I MUFFIN EACH

Each serving provides: I Fat; I Bread; ½ Fruit; 40 Optional Calories
Per serving: 167 calories; 4 g protein; 4 g fat; 29 g carbohydrate; 98 mg calcium; 242 mg sodium; I mg cholesterol; I g dietary fiber (this figure does not include cranberries and buckwheat flour; nutrition analyses not available)

Applesauce-Cheese Toast ▽Ⓒ ▽Ⓢ

¼ cup applesauce (no sugar added)
½ teaspoon maple syrup
¼ teaspoon ground cinnamon
¼ cup part-skim ricotta cheese
2 tablespoons whipped cream cheese
2 slices reduced-calorie raisin bread (40 calories per slice), lightly toasted
½ ounce chopped walnuts

1. In small mixing bowl combine first 3 ingredients; stir to combine and set aside.

2. In separate small mixing bowl combine cheeses, stirring to combine.

3. Onto each slice of bread spread half of the cheese mixture; top each with half of the applesauce mixture and half of the walnuts. Arrange bread slices on oven tray or baking sheet and bake at 425°F in toaster-oven or oven until applesauce mixture is heated through, 2 to 3 minutes.

APPROXIMATE TOTAL TIME: 10 MINUTES (includes baking time)

MAKES 2 SERVINGS

Each serving provides: ½ Fat; 1 Protein; ½ Bread; ¼ Fruit; 40 Optional Calories
Per serving: 178 calories; 7 g protein; 10 g fat; 17 g carbohydrate; 123 mg calcium; 170 mg sodium; 19 mg cholesterol; 1 g dietary fiber

English Muffin with Date-Nut Topping ⊽ⓒ ⊽ⓢ

¼ cup part-skim ricotta cheese
2 tablespoons whipped cream
  cheese
½ ounce shelled walnuts, toasted
  and chopped
2 pitted dates, chopped
1 cinnamon-raisin English muffin
  (2 ounces), split in half and
  toasted
Dash ground cinnamon

1. In small mixing bowl combine cheeses, mixing well; stir in nuts and dates.

2. Onto each muffin half spread half of the cheese mixture; sprinkle each with cinnamon.

3. Arrange muffin halves on oven tray of toaster-oven* and broil or top brown until cheese is heated through, 1 to 2 minutes.

* Broiler may be substituted for toaster-oven.

APPROXIMATE TOTAL TIME: 10 MINUTES

MAKES 2 SERVINGS

Each serving provides: ½ Fat; 1 Protein; 1 Bread; ½ Fruit; 35 Optional Calories
Per serving: 213 calories; 8 g protein; 11 g fat; 22 g carbohydrate; 119 mg calcium; 158 mg sodium; 19 mg cholesterol; 1 g dietary fiber

Apple-Cinnamon Popovers ▽ᶜ ▽ᶠ

1 cup thawed frozen egg
   substitute
¾ cup all-purpose flour
½ cup applesauce (no sugar
   added)
⅓ cup low-fat buttermilk
   (1% milk fat)
2 tablespoons plus 2 teaspoons
   reduced-calorie margarine
   (tub), melted and cooled
1 teaspoon ground cinnamon
¾ teaspoon granulated sugar
¼ teaspoon baking soda

*Start the weekend off right with a
breakfast of warm popovers and
fruit-topped yogurt.*

1. Preheat oven to 425°F. Spray four 10-ounce custard cups with nonstick cooking spray; set aside.

2. In blender process all ingredients until smooth. Pour ¼ of batter into each prepared cup. Set cups on baking sheet and bake in middle of center oven rack for 25 minutes, until puffed and golden brown.

3. Using a knife, pierce the top of each popover to allow steam to escape; bake 5 minutes longer.

APPROXIMATE TOTAL TIME: 35 MINUTES (includes baking time)

MAKES 4 SERVINGS, 1 POPOVER EACH

Each serving provides: 1 Fat; 1 Protein; 1 Bread; ¼ Fruit; 15 Optional Calories
Per serving: 178 calories; 10 g protein; 4 g fat; 25 g carbohydrate; 62 mg calcium; 260 mg sodium; 1 mg cholesterol; 1 g dietary fiber

Hawaiian Oatmeal ▽ᶜ ▽ᶠ ▽ˢ

¾ ounce uncooked instant
  oatmeal
¼ cup drained canned pineapple
  chunks (no sugar added)
¼ ounce macadamia nuts, sliced
½ teaspoon *each* firmly packed
  light brown sugar and shredded
  coconut
½ cup skim *or* nonfat milk

*Serve this island treat with skim milk
or reduced-calorie hot cocoa for a
complete breakfast.*

1. In medium microwavable bowl combine oatmeal and *½ cup water*, stirring to combine; microwave on High (100%) for 1 minute, stirring once halfway through cooking.

2. Add pineapple and microwave on High for 30 seconds.

3. To serve, divide cereal into 2 serving bowls and top each portion with half of the nuts, sugar, and coconut; pour half of the milk over each portion of cereal.

APPROXIMATE TOTAL TIME: 5 MINUTES

MAKES 2 SERVINGS

Each serving provides: ¼ Milk; ¼ Protein; ½ Bread; ¼ Fruit; 20 Optional Calories
Per serving: 112 calories; 4 g protein; 4 g fat; 17 g carbohydrate; 89 mg calcium; 34 mg sodium; 1 mg cholesterol; 1 g dietary fiber (this figure does not include macadamia nuts; nutrition analysis not available)

Maple-Spice Oat Bran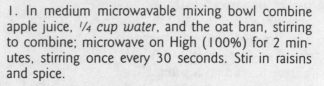

½ cup apple juice (no sugar added)

¾ ounce uncooked unprocessed oat bran

1 tablespoon dark raisins

¼ teaspoon apple pie spice

1 teaspoon maple syrup

¼ cup skim *or* nonfat milk

Hot cereal cooks in minutes in the microwave oven. Team it up with a glass of skim milk for a complete breakfast.

1. In medium microwavable mixing bowl combine apple juice, *¼ cup water,* and the oat bran, stirring to combine; microwave on High (100%) for 2 minutes, stirring once every 30 seconds. Stir in raisins and spice.

2. To serve, transfer to serving bowl and top with syrup and milk.

APPROXIMATE TOTAL TIME: 10 MINUTES

MAKES 1 SERVING

Each serving provides: ¼ Milk; 1 Bread; 1½ Fruits; 20 Optional Calories
Per serving: 206 calories; 7 g protein; 2 g fat; 42 g carbohydrate; 119 mg calcium; 38 mg sodium; 1 mg cholesterol; 4 g dietary fiber

Polenta with Blueberries in Syrup ⬇C ⬇F ⬇S

¾ ounce instant polenta (quick
  cooking yellow cornmeal)
½ cup blueberries
1 tablespoon reduced-calorie
  pancake syrup (30 calories per
  fluid ounce)

*Top off this unusual breakfast with
a serving of reduced-calorie hot cocoa, yogurt, or a glass of skim milk.*

1. In medium microwavable bowl microwave ¾ cup *water* on High (100%) for 3 minutes, until boiling. Stir in polenta and microwave on High for 1 minute, stirring halfway through cooking.

2. In small microwavable mixing bowl combine blueberries and syrup. Microwave on Medium (50%) for 1 minute, until hot.

3. Serve polenta topped with blueberry mixture.

APPROXIMATE TOTAL TIME: 5 MINUTES

MAKES 1 SERVING

Each serving provides: 1 Bread; 1 Fruit; 15 Optional Calories
Per serving: 131 calories; 2 g protein; 1 g fat; 31 g carbohydrate; 5 mg calcium; 5 mg sodium; 0 mg cholesterol; 3 g dietary fiber

Raisin-Nut Breakfast ⬇C ⬇F ⬇S

1½ ounces uncooked quick-
    cooking farina
¼ cup golden raisins
Dash ground cinnamon
1 cup skim *or* nonfat milk
½ ounce sliced almonds,
    toasted

1. In 1-quart saucepan bring *1½ cups water* to a boil; gradually stir in farina. Add raisins and cinnamon and cook, stirring constantly, for 2 to 3 minutes.

2. Into each of 2 serving bowls spoon half of the farina mixture; top each with ½ cup milk and ¼ ounce almonds.

APPROXIMATE TOTAL TIME: 5 MINUTES

MAKES 2 SERVINGS

Each serving provides: ½ Milk; ½ Fat; ½ Protein; 1 Bread; 1 Fruit;
Per serving: 218 calories; 8 g protein; 4 g fat; 39 g carbohydrate; 184 mg calcium; 67 mg sodium; 2 mg cholesterol; 2 g dietary fiber (this figure does not include almonds; nutrition analysis not available)

Egg in a Nest

2 slices reduced-calorie wheat
   bread (40 calories per slice)
1 teaspoon reduced-calorie sweet
   margarine (tub), divided
¼ cup thawed frozen egg
   substitute, divided

1. Using a 3-inch round cookie-cutter, cut a circle in center of each bread slice. Remove circles and reserve.

2. In 9-inch nonstick skillet melt ½ teaspoon margarine; add 1 bread slice and 1 bread circle. Pour 2 tablespoons egg substitute into hole in center of bread slice. Cook until bottom of bread is lightly browned, about 1 minute. Carefully turn over bread slice and bread circle and cook until other side is browned, about 1 minute longer. Transfer bread slice to plate and top with bread circle; keep warm.

3. Repeat procedure using remaining margarine, bread slice, bread circle, and egg substitute.

APPROXIMATE TOTAL TIME: 10 MINUTES

MAKES 1 SERVING

Each serving provides: ½ Fat; 1 Protein; 1 Bread
Per serving: 121 calories; 9 g protein; 2 g fat; 19 g carbohydrate; 60 mg calcium; 270 mg sodium; 0 mg cholesterol; dietary fiber data not available

Frittata Monterey ▽C

2 teaspoons margarine, divided
½ cup *each* sliced onion, sliced
   red bell pepper, and sliced
   zucchini
2 small plum tomatoes, diced
1 tablespoon chopped fresh basil
Dash pepper
½ cup thawed frozen egg
   substitute
⅓ cup low-fat cottage cheese
   (1% milk fat)
¼ cup evaporated skimmed milk
¾ ounce reduced-fat Monterey
   Jack cheese, shredded

1. In 10-inch nonstick skillet melt 1 teaspoon margarine; add onion, bell pepper, and zucchini and sauté over medium-high heat, until vegetables are lightly browned, 2 to 3 minutes.

2. Add tomatoes, basil, and pepper to skillet and stir to combine. Reduce heat to medium-low and cook until flavors blend, 2 to 3 minutes. Transfer vegetables to plate and keep warm.

3. Preheat broiler. In blender combine egg substitute, cottage cheese, and milk and process until smooth, scraping down sides of container as necessary; set aside.

4. In 10-inch nonstick skillet that has a metal or removable handle melt remaining margarine; add egg mixture and cook over medium-high heat until bottom begins to brown, about 1 minute. Transfer skillet to broiler and broil until top is set, 2 to 3 minutes.

5. Spread vegetable mixture over egg mixture and then sprinkle with cheese; broil until cheese melts, 1 to 2 minutes.

APPROXIMATE TOTAL TIME: 20 MINUTES

MAKES 2 SERVINGS

Each serving provides: ¼ Milk; 1 Fat; 2 Proteins; 2 Vegetables
Per serving: 181 calories; 18 g protein; 6 g fat; 13 g carbohydrate; 268 mg calcium; 412 mg sodium; 10 mg cholesterol; 2 g dietary fiber

Spanish Omelet ▽

1 teaspoon vegetable oil
¼ cup *each* diced green bell
   pepper and chopped onion
2 garlic cloves, minced
½ cup canned Italian tomatoes
   (reserve liquid), seeded and
   finely chopped
2 eggs
1 teaspoon margarine
1½ ounces reduced-fat Monterey
   Jack cheese, shredded

1. In small saucepan heat oil; add pepper, onion, and garlic and cook over medium heat, stirring frequently, until pepper is softened, 1 to 2 minutes.

2. Add tomatoes with reserved liquid and stir to combine. Reduce heat to low and let simmer, stirring occasionally, until mixture is reduced by half, 5 to 10 minutes.

3. While tomato mixture cooks prepare omelet. Using a fork, in small mixing bowl beat together eggs and 2 *tablespoons water*.

4. Preheat broiler. In 9-inch nonstick skillet that has a metal or removable handle melt margarine; add eggs and cook over medium-high heat, tilting pan, until bottom of omelet is set and lightly browned, about 1 minute. Sprinkle cheese over omelet.

5. Transfer skillet to broiler and broil 5 inches from heat source until omelet is cooked through, 2 to 3 minutes.

6. To serve, fold omelet in half and arrange on serving platter; spoon tomato mixture over center of omelet.

APPROXIMATE TOTAL TIME: 20 MINUTES

MAKES 2 SERVINGS

Each serving provides: 1 Fat; 2 Proteins; 1 Vegetable
Per serving: 198 calories, 13 g protein; 13 g fat; 6 g carbohydrate; 239 mg calcium; 319 mg sodium; 228 mg cholesterol; 1 g dietary fiber

Western Omelet ⬦ ⬦

¼ cup finely diced onion
2 tablespoons *each* finely diced
  red and green bell pepper
3 ounces diced cooked potato
1 ounce finely diced turkey-ham
¾ ounce reduced-fat Cheddar
  cheese, shredded
Dash pepper
2 teaspoons margarine
¾ cup thawed frozen egg
  substitute
1 cherry tomato, cut in half
¼ cup alfalfa sprouts

Enjoy the taste of an omelet for breakfast without a large amount of cholesterol, thanks to egg substitute, reduced-fat Cheddar cheese, and turkey-ham.

1. Spray 10-inch nonstick skillet with nonstick cooking spray and heat; add onion and bell peppers and cook over medium-high heat, stirring frequently, until onion is translucent, about 2 minutes. Add potato and turkey-ham; continuing to stir, cook until potato is heated through, about 1 minute. Remove from heat; stir in cheese and pepper. Transfer to plate; set aside and keep warm.

2. Wipe skillet clean. Melt margarine in skillet; add egg substitute and cook over medium heat, stirring occasionally, for 30 seconds. Continue cooking without stirring until egg substitute is set, about 1½ minutes.

3. Spoon potato mixture onto center of omelet; fold in half to enclose filling and transfer to serving platter. Garnish platter with tomato halves and sprouts.

APPROXIMATE TOTAL TIME: 15 MINUTES

MAKES 2 SERVINGS

Each serving provides: 1 Fat; 2½ Proteins; ¾ Vegetable; ½ Bread
Per serving: 172 calories; 14 g protein; 7 g fat; 13 g carbohydrate; 138 mg calcium; 384 mg sodium; 8 mg cholesterol; 1 g dietary fiber

Basil-Vegetable Quiche ∇ ∇ ∇

1 cup thinly sliced onions
1½ medium red bell peppers, seeded and cut into 6 strips and 12 diamonds; dice remaining pepper
¾ cup sliced mushrooms
1 small garlic clove, minced
1½ cups thawed frozen egg substitute
1½ ounces reduced-fat Swiss cheese, shredded
½ cup fresh basil, chopped
2 medium zucchini (about 10 ounces), cut lengthwise into thin slices and steamed
Garnish: basil sprigs

1. Preheat oven to 350°F. Spray 9-inch nonstick skillet with nonstick cooking spray; add onions, all of the peppers, the mushrooms, and garlic and cook over medium heat, stirring frequently, until onions are lightly browned, 1 to 2 minutes. Add *1 tablespoon water*; cover and cook until vegetables are tender, about 1 minute longer.

2. Remove pepper strips, pepper diamonds, and ¼ cup mushrooms to plate and set aside. Transfer remaining vegetable mixture to medium mixing bowl; add egg substitute, cheese, and chopped basil and stir to combine. Carefully pour into 9-inch quiche dish or pie plate. Decoratively arrange zucchini over egg substitute mixture.

3. Bake for 15 to 20 minutes (until a knife, inserted in center, comes out dry).

4. Garnish quiche with the reserved pepper strips and diamonds, mushrooms, and the basil sprigs.

APPROXIMATE TOTAL TIME: 40 MINUTES (includes baking time; does not include cooling time)

MAKES 4 SERVINGS

Each serving provides: 2 Proteins; 2½ Vegetables
Per serving: 111 calories; 13 g protein; 2 g fat; 10 g carbohydrate; 233 mg calcium; 142 mg sodium; 8 mg cholesterol; 2 g dietary fiber

Broccoli and Cheese Stratas

2 slices white bread (1 ounce each)
¾ ounce reduced-fat Cheddar cheese, shredded
1 cup thawed frozen chopped broccoli
3 eggs
½ cup low-fat milk (1% milk fat)
¼ cup evaporated skimmed milk
½ teaspoon Dijon-style mustard
Dash white pepper

For convenience, you can prepare this recipe ahead (except for the baking) and store it in the refrigerator for several hours or overnight.

1. Preheat oven to 350°F. Using a 3-inch round biscuit-cutter, cut out a circle from the center of each slice of bread and set aside. Cut remaining bread into ½-inch cubes.

2. Into each of two 10-ounce custard cups arrange half of the bread cubes. Sprinkle each portion with half of the cheese and broccoli, then top each with a reserved bread circle. Set aside.

3. Using a wire whisk, in medium mixing bowl beat together remaining ingredients; pour half of mixture into each custard cup, making sure bread circles are moistened.

4. Bake in middle of center oven rack for 30 minutes (until a knife, inserted in center, comes out dry).

APPROXIMATE TOTAL TIME: 45 MINUTES (includes baking time)

MAKES 2 SERVINGS

Each serving provides: ½ Milk; 2 Proteins; 1 Vegetable; 1 Bread; 5 Optional Calories
Per serving: 286 calories; 20 g protein; 11 g fat; 24 g carbohydrate; 347 mg calcium; 428 mg sodium; 331 mg cholesterol; 1 g dietary fiber

Savory Orzo Custards ⱱ̲C̲ ⱱ̲S̲

1 teaspoon margarine
2 cups finely chopped onions
1 small garlic clove, minced
1½ ounces orzo (rice-shaped pasta), cooked according to package directions
½ cup *each* thawed frozen egg substitute and skim *or* nonfat milk
2 ounces Fontina cheese, shredded
1 tablespoon chopped fresh basil

This custard, made the cholesterol-reduced way, uses egg substitute rather than eggs.

1. Preheat oven to 400°F. In 9-inch nonstick skillet melt margarine; add onions and garlic and sauté over medium heat, until tender-crisp, 2 to 3 minutes.

2. Transfer onion mixture to medium mixing bowl; add remaining ingredients and stir to combine. Spray two 10-ounce custard cups with nonstick cooking spray; spoon half of the orzo-onion mixture into each cup.

3. Bake for 20 minutes (until a knife, inserted in center, comes out dry). Set aside and let cool slightly.

4. To serve, invert custards onto serving plates.

APPROXIMATE TOTAL TIME: 40 MINUTES (includes baking time)

MAKES 2 SERVINGS, 1 CUSTARD EACH

Each serving provides: ¼ Milk; ½ Fat; 2 Proteins; 2 Vegetables; 1 Bread; 25 Optional Calories
Per serving: 309 calories; 19 g protein; 12 g fat; 33 g carbohydrate; 311 mg calcium; 138 mg sodium; 34 mg cholesterol; 3 g dietary fiber

German Egg Cakes ▽⟨S⟩

⅓ cup plus 2 teaspoons all-purpose flour

½ teaspoon double-acting baking powder

¼ teaspoon baking soda

⅓ cup plus 2 teaspoons low-fat buttermilk (1% milk fat)

4 eggs, separated

1 teaspoon vanilla extract

¼ teaspoon cream of tartar

¼ cup reduced-calorie raspberry spread (16 calories per 2 teaspoons), melted

1 tablespoon plus 1 teaspoon sour cream

1. In large mixing bowl combine first 3 ingredients; stir in buttermilk, egg yolks, and vanilla, stirring until smooth. Set aside.

2. Using mixer on high speed, in separate large mixing bowl beat egg whites until foamy; add cream of tartar and continue beating until whites are stiff but not dry.

3. Gently fold beaten whites into flour mixture.

4. Spray nonstick griddle or 12-inch nonstick skillet with nonstick cooking spray and heat. Using ¼ of batter, drop batter on griddle, forming 4 cakes. Cook over medium-high heat until bottom is lightly browned, 3 to 4 minutes; using pancake turner, turn cakes over and cook until the other side is browned, 2 to 3 minutes longer.

5. Remove cakes to plate and keep warm. Repeat procedure 3 more times, spraying griddle with cooking spray and making 12 more cakes.

6. Serve each portion of cakes topped with 1 tablespoon spread and 1 teaspoon sour cream.

APPROXIMATE TOTAL TIME: 45 MINUTES

MAKES 4 SERVINGS, 4 CAKES EACH

Each serving provides: 1 Protein; ½ Bread; 45 Optional Calories
Per serving: 165 calories; 8 g protein; 6 g fat; 17 g carbohydrate; 85 mg calcium; 193 mg sodium; 216 mg cholesterol; 0.3 g dietary fiber

Oat-Raisin Pancakes with Sausages

3 ounces uncooked quick-cooking oats

1 cup skim *or* nonfat milk

1 egg *or* ¼ cup thawed frozen egg substitute

1 tablespoon *each* all-purpose flour and granulated sugar

¼ teaspoon *each* double-acting baking powder and baking soda

½ cup dark raisins, plumped

1 tablespoon plus 1 teaspoon vegetable oil, divided

16 mild fresh turkey breakfast sausage links (1 ounce each)*

¼ cup reduced-calorie pancake syrup (60 calories per fluid ounce)

1 small orange (about 6 ounces), cut into 8 wedges

Mint sprigs

1. In blender process oats into powder; add milk, egg, flour, sugar, baking powder, and baking soda and process until combined. Transfer to medium mixing bowl; add raisins and stir to combine. Let batter stand for 10 minutes.

2. In 12-inch nonstick skillet or griddle heat 2 teaspoons oil. Using half of batter, drop batter by scant ¼-cup measures, making 4 pancakes, each 3 inches in diameter. Cook over medium heat until bubbles appear on surface and bottom is golden brown, 2 to 3 minutes. Using pancake turner, turn pancakes over and cook until the other side is browned. Remove pancakes to plate and keep warm. Repeat procedure, using remaining oil and making 4 more pancakes.

3. Spray 9-inch nonstick skillet with nonstick cooking spray; add sausages and cook over medium heat until browned on all sides, 4 to 5 minutes.

4. To serve, on serving platter arrange pancakes and sausages and top pancakes with syrup. Decoratively arrange orange wedges and mint sprigs on platter.

* A 1-ounce turkey breakfast sausage will yield about ½ ounce cooked sausage.

APPROXIMATE TOTAL TIME: 40 MINUTES

MAKES 4 SERVINGS, 2 PANCAKES AND 4 SAUSAGES EACH

Each serving provides: ¼ Milk; 1 Fat; 2¼ Proteins; 1 Bread; 1¼ Fruits; 55 Optional Calories
Per serving with egg: 531 calories; 33 g protein; 24 g fat; 46 g carbohydrate; 151 mg calcium; 938 mg sodium; 146 mg cholesterol; 3 g dietary fiber
With egg substitute: 518 calories; 33 g protein; 23 g fat; 46 g carbohydrate; 149 mg calcium; 942 mg sodium; 93 mg cholesterol; 3 g dietary fiber

Orange-Pecan French Toast ⊽_C ⊽_F

½ cup thawed frozen egg
   substitute
1 teaspoon vanilla extract
¼ teaspoon *each* grated orange
   peel and ground cinnamon
2 teaspoons reduced-calorie
   margarine (tub)
4 slices reduced-calorie raisin
   bread (40 calories per slice)
½ cup orange juice (no sugar
   added)
1 tablespoon maple syrup
1½ teaspoons cornstarch
½ ounce shelled pecans, toasted
   and chopped

This French toast is made the cholesterol-reduced way, with egg substitute rather than eggs.

1. Using a fork, in medium mixing bowl beat together egg substitute, vanilla, orange peel, and cinnamon; set aside.

2. Spray 10-inch nonstick skillet with nonstick cooking spray; add margarine and melt. Dip bread slices into egg mixture, coating both sides; add to skillet and pour an equal amount of any remaining egg mixture over each slice. Cook until lightly browned, 2 to 3 minutes on each side. Cut each slice of French toast in half diagonally, making 8 triangles. Transfer to serving platter and keep warm.

3. In small saucepan combine juice, syrup, and cornstarch; cook over medium-high heat until mixture comes to a boil. Reduce heat to low, stir in pecans, and let simmer until mixture thickens slightly, 3 to 4 minutes. Pour over French toast.

APPROXIMATE TOTAL TIME: 15 MINUTES

MAKES 2 SERVINGS

Each serving provides: 1 Fat; 1½ Proteins; 1 Bread; ½ Fruit; 40 Optional Calories
Per serving: 246 calories; 12 g protein; 7 g fat; 36 g carbohydrate; 8 mg calcium; 338 mg sodium; 0 mg cholesterol; 1 g dietary fiber

Fruit and Nut Breakfast Bars $\triangledown\!\!\!{}_C$ $\triangledown\!\!\!{}_S$

1½ cups golden raisins, plumped and drained
1 tablespoon all-purpose flour
9 ounces uncooked quick *or* old-fashioned oats
5 ounces coarsely chopped almonds
½ cup *each* firmly packed light brown sugar and thawed frozen egg substitute
⅓ cup reduced-calorie magarine (tub), melted
½ teaspoon vanilla extract
⅛ teaspoon almond extract

1. Preheat oven to 350°F. Spray 13 × 9 × 2-inch nonstick baking pan with nonstick cooking spray. Line pan with a sheet of wax paper over bottom and up sides of pan; set aside.

2. In medium mixing bowl combine raisins with flour, tossing to coat. Add oats, almonds, and sugar and stir to combine; set aside.

3. In 1-cup liquid measure combine remaining ingredients; add to dry ingredients and stir until moistened.

4. Press mixture into prepared pan. Bake until golden brown, about 25 minutes. Set pan on wire rack and let cool for 30 minutes. Invert pan onto clean work surface, discarding wax paper; let cool completely.

5. Cut in half lengthwise, then cut each half into 12 equal bars, making 24 bars. Wrap each bar in plastic wrap and freeze for future use.

APPROXIMATE TOTAL TIME: 35 MINUTES (includes baking time; does not include cooling time)

MAKES 12 SERVINGS, 2 BARS EACH

Each serving provides: 1½ Fats; 1 Protein; 1 Bread; 1 Fruit; 45 Optional Calories
Per serving: 269 calories; 7 g protein; 10 g fat; 41 g carbohydrate; 63 mg calcium; 69 mg sodium; 0 mg cholesterol; 3 g dietary fiber

Egg Substitutes and Cheeses

Egg lovers look out! Now there's egg substitutes. All the flavor of eggs but usually little or no cholesterol. Keep them on hand in your freezer for added convenience. Enjoy them in our delectable puddings and cholesterol-reduced "Hollandaise" Sauce. When it comes to cheeses, select those that are reduced-fat; they're often lower in sodium as well. (Remember to read package labels.) Our cheese-topped Eggplant Pizzas keep the calorie count down even further by using eggplant slices for a unique "crust."

Blueberry-Corn Pudding ▽C ▽F

½ cup *each* low-fat milk (1% milk fat) and thawed frozen egg substitute

1 tablespoon plus 1 teaspoon reduced-calorie margarine (tub), melted and cooled

1 tablespoon *each* all-purpose flour and granulated sugar

1 cup *each* fresh *or* frozen blueberries and thawed frozen whole-kernel corn

1. Preheat oven to 375°F. In medium mixing bowl combine all ingredients except blueberries and corn and stir until thoroughly blended. Gently fold in blueberries and corn.

2. Spray two 10-ounce custard cups with nonstick cooking spray and fill each cup with half of the blueberry-corn mixture. Set cups in 8 × 8 × 2-inch baking pan and fill with water to a depth of about 1 inch.

3. Bake for 20 minutes (until a knife, inserted in center, comes out dry).

APPROXIMATE TOTAL TIME: 30 MINUTES

MAKES 2 SERVINGS

Each serving provides: ¼ Milk; 1 Fat; 1 Protein; 1 Bread; 1 Fruit; 50 Optional Calories
Per serving: 243 calories; 12 g protein; 6 g fat; 41 g carbohydrate; 110 mg calcium; 224 mg sodium; 2 mg cholesterol; 3 g dietary fiber

Tomato-Bread Pudding ⩔ ⩔

1½ cups drained canned stewed
  tomatoes (reserve ½ cup
  liquid), chopped
2 ounces *each* seasoned croutons
  and reduced-fat Swiss *or*
  Cheddar cheese, shredded,
  divided
½ cup thawed frozen egg
  substitute

1. In medium mixing bowl combine tomatoes with reserved liquid, the croutons, 1 ounce cheese, and the egg substitute, stirring to combine.

2. Spray four 10-ounce microwavable custard cups with nonstick cooking spray and fill each cup with ¼ of the tomato mixture. Top each with an equal amount of the remaining cheese.

3. Set cups in 8 × 8 × 2-inch baking dish and pour water into dish to a depth of about 2 inches. Cover and microwave on Medium (50%) for 8 minutes, rotating cups every 2 minutes. Let cool slightly.

APPROXIMATE TOTAL TIME: 20 MINUTES

MAKES 4 SERVINGS

Each serving provides: 1 Protein; ¾ Vegetable; 1 Bread; 10 Optional Calories
Per serving with Swiss cheese: 165 calories; 11 g protein; 6 g fat; 18 g carbohydrate; 250 mg calcium; 600 mg sodium; 10 mg cholesterol; dietary fiber data not available
With Cheddar cheese: 165 calories; 11 g protein; 6 g fat; 18 g carbohydrate; 200 mg calcium; 677 mg sodium; 10 mg cholesterol; dietary fiber data not available

"Hollandaise" Sauce �{C} �{S}

¼ cup thawed frozen egg
   substitute
1 tablespoon plus 1 teaspoon
   reduced-calorie margarine (tub)
1 teaspoon lemon juice
½ teaspoon Dijon-style mustard
Dash ground red pepper

*This cholesterol-reduced version of
a classic sauce is made the easy way,
in the microwave oven. Serve it over
cooked vegetables, fish, chicken, or
roast beef.*

1. In 1-cup microwavable liquid measure combine first 2 ingredients; microwave on Low (20%) for 1 minute, stirring once halfway through cooking, until margarine is softened.

2. Stir juice and mustard into egg substitute mixture; microwave on Low for 3 minutes, stirring every 30 seconds, until thickened. Stir in pepper. (If mixture curdles, transfer to blender and process on low speed for 30 seconds, until smooth.)

APPROXIMATE TOTAL TIME: 10 MINUTES

MAKES 2 SERVINGS, ABOUT 3 TABLESPOONS EACH

Each serving provides: 1 Fat; ½ Protein
Per serving: 52 calories; 3 g protein; 4 g fat; 1 g carbohydrate; 14 mg calcium; 171 mg sodium; 0 mg cholesterol; dietary fiber data not available

Baked Cauliflower Casserole ▽C

4 cups cauliflower florets,
   blanched
½ cup tomato sauce
1½ ounces mozzarella cheese,
   shredded
2 tablespoons grated Parmesan
   cheese

*It takes only four ingredients to
make this sensational dish.*

1. Preheat oven to 375°F. Spray 9-inch glass pie plate with nonstick cooking spray. Arrange cauliflower in pie plate and spoon tomato sauce over cauliflower.

2. In small mixing bowl combine cheeses; sprinkle over tomato sauce.

3. Bake until cauliflower is thoroughly heated, about 15 minutes.

APPROXIMATE TOTAL TIME: 30 MINUTES (includes baking time)

MAKES 4 SERVINGS

Each serving provides: ½ Protein; 2¼ Vegetables; 15 Optional Calories
Per serving: 74 calories; 5 g protein; 3 g fat; 7 g carbohydrate; 123 mg calcium; 286 mg sodium; 10 mg cholesterol; 3 g dietary fiber

Cheese Crisp

1 flour tortilla (6-inch diameter)
¼ cup chopped drained canned
mild chili *or* jalapeño pepper
1½ ounces reduced-fat Colby *or*
Cheddar cheese, shredded
1 tablespoon sour cream

1. Preheat broiler. Arrange tortilla directly on oven rack, 6 inches from heat source, and broil until lightly toasted, 1 to 2 minutes on each side.

2. Transfer tortilla to baking sheet; top with pepper and sprinkle with cheese. Broil until cheese is melted, 1 to 2 minutes.

3. To serve, arrange tortilla on serving plate and top with sour cream.

APPROXIMATE TOTAL TIME: 10 MINUTES

MAKES 1 SERVING

Each serving provides: 2 Proteins; ½ Vegetable; 1 Bread; 35 Optional Calories
Per serving with Colby cheese: 229 calories; 15 g protein; 13 g fat; 16 g carbohydrate; 359 mg calcium; 595 mg sodium, 36 mg cholesterol; 1 g dietary fiber
With Cheddar cheese: 244 calories; 15 g protein; 13 g fat; 16 g carbohydrate; 434 mg calcium; 655 mg sodium; 36 mg cholesterol; 1 g dietary fiber

Eggplant Pizzas ▽C

6 ounces eggplant, cut crosswise into four ¼-inch-thick round slices

¼ teaspoon salt

¼ cup thawed frozen egg substitute

¼ teaspoon garlic powder

3 tablespoons plain dried bread crumbs

¾ ounce (2 tablespoons) uncooked yellow cornmeal

1 teaspoon olive *or* vegetable oil

4 slices Provolone cheese (½ ounce each)

2 tablespoons drained julienne-cut (matchstick pieces) pimiento

2 teaspoons grated Parmesan cheese

Eggplant slices provide a nutritious low-calorie crust for these tasty pizzas.

1. On paper towels arrange eggplant slices in a single layer; sprinkle both sides of each eggplant slice with salt and let stand for 10 minutes.

2. In small mixing bowl combine egg substitute, *½ teaspoon water*, and the garlic powder and, using a fork, beat until combined. On sheet of wax paper combine bread crumbs and cornmeal.

3. Pat eggplant dry. Dip each eggplant slice in egg substitute mixture, then in crumb mixture, coating both sides and using all of egg substitute and crumb mixtures.

4. In 10-inch nonstick skillet heat oil; add eggplant slices and cook over medium-high heat, until golden, 7 minutes on each side *(being careful not to burn crumb mixture)*.

5. Preheat broiler. Arrange eggplant slices on broiler pan. Top each eggplant slice with 1 slice Provolone cheese, ¼ of the pimiento, and ¼ of the Parmesan cheese. Broil until cheeses are golden, about 2 minutes.

APPROXIMATE TOTAL TIME: 30 MINUTES

MAKES 2 SERVINGS, 2 PIZZAS EACH

Each serving provides: ½ Fat; 1½ Proteins; 1¼ Vegetables; 1 Bread; 35 Optional Calories
Per serving: 241 calories; 14 g protein; 11 g fat; 23 g carbohydrate; 293 mg calcium; 665 mg sodium; 21 mg cholesterol; 2 g dietary fiber

Italian Grilled Cheese Sandwich 〖C〗

¾ ounce mozzarella cheese, shredded
Dash oregano leaves
2 slices reduced-calorie white bread (40 calories per slice)
2 teaspoons reduced-calorie margarine (tub), melted
3 fresh basil leaves *or* dash dried basil
½ medium tomato, cut into 3 slices

Fresh basil and mozzarella cheese add a boost of flavor to the familiar grilled cheese sandwich.

1. In small mixing bowl combine cheese and oregano; set aside.

2. Brush both sides of each slice of bread with margarine; top 1 slice of bread with cheese mixture, the basil, tomato, and remaining bread slice.

3. Spray 6-inch nonstick skillet with nonstick cooking spray and heat; add sandwich and cook over low heat, turning frequently, until cheese is melted, about 5 minutes.

APPROXIMATE TOTAL TIME: 10 MINUTES

MAKES 1 SERVING

Each serving provides: 1 Fat; 1 Protein; 1 Vegetable; 1 Bread
Per serving: 185 calories; 9 g fat; 9 g protein; 21 g carbohydrate; 157 mg calcium; 354 mg sodium; 17 mg cholesterol; 1 g dietary fiber

Vegetable Quesadillas ▽C

¼ cup *each* seeded and diced tomato and diced yellow *or* red bell pepper
2 tablespoons chopped scallion (green onion)
1 teaspoon *each* seeded and chopped hot chili pepper and chopped fresh cilantro (Chinese parsley) *or* Italian (flat-leaf) parsley
2 flour tortillas (6-inch diameter each)
1½ ounces reduced-fat Monterey Jack cheese, shredded
1 teaspoon vegetable oil

1. In small mixing bowl combine tomato, bell pepper, scallion, chili pepper, and cilantro; set aside.

2. In 10-inch nonstick skillet cook 1 tortilla over medium heat until flexible, about 1 minute on each side. Transfer tortilla to a plate.

3. Top half of tortilla with half of the cheese and then with half of the vegetable mixture; fold tortilla in half to cover filling. Repeat procedure with remaining tortilla, cheese, and vegetable mixture.

4. In same skillet heat oil; add tortillas and cook until cheese is melted, 1 to 2 minutes on each side. Cut each tortilla in half.

APPROXIMATE TOTAL TIME: 15 MINUTES

MAKES 2 SERVINGS

Each serving provides: ½ Fat; 1 Protein; ¾ Vegetable; 1 Bread
Per serving: 160 calories; 8 g protein; 8 g fat; 14 g carbohydrate; 234 mg calcium; 278 mg sodium; 15 mg cholesterol; 1 g dietary fiber

Warm Cheese-Walnut Pitas ⓥ

2 ounces reduced-fat Swiss
    cheese, shredded
½ cup grated seeded pared
    cucumber
½ ounce chopped walnuts
1 teaspoon olive *or* vegetable oil
½ teaspoon country Dijon-style
    mustard
Dash *each* oregano leaves, basil
    leaves, and garlic powder
2 small pitas (1 ounce each);
    each cut in half horizontally

*Here's a special brown-bag meal if
your office is equipped with a toaster
oven. Prepare this recipe at home but
bake it at the office.*

1. Preheat oven to 400°F. In small mixing bowl combine all ingredients except pitas.

2. Onto bottom half of each pita spread half of the cheese-walnut mixture; top each with remaining half of pita.

3. Arrange pitas on baking sheet and bake until cheese is melted, about 15 minutes. Cut each pita in half.

APPROXIMATE TOTAL TIME: 25 MINUTES (includes baking time)

MAKES 2 SERVINGS, 1 PITA EACH

Each serving provides: 1 Fat; 1½ Proteins; ½ Vegetable; 1 Bread; 25 Optional Calories
Per serving: 249 calories; 14 g protein; 12 g fat; 22 g carbohydrate; 369 mg calcium; 267 mg sodium; 20 mg cholesterol; 1 g dietary fiber

"Pizza" Stuffed Potato

1 baking potato (6 ounces),
   baked
1½ ounces mozzarella cheese,
   shredded, divided
¼ cup *each* tomato sauce and
   part-skim ricotta cheese
⅛ teaspoon *each* oregano leaves
   and garlic powder
2 teaspoons grated Parmesan
   cheese

You'll need a baked potato for this recipe. Do the baking in your microwave oven or plan ahead and do it the night before.

1. Preheat oven to 450°F. Cut potato in half lengthwise. Scoop out pulp from potato halves into a bowl, leaving ¼-inch-thick shells; mash pulp and reserve shells.

2 Add 1 ounce mozzarella cheese, the tomato sauce, ricotta cheese, oregano, and garlic powder to potato pulp and stir to combine.

3. Spoon half of potato mixture into each reserved shell; top each with half of the remaining mozzarella cheese and half of the Parmesan cheese. Set potato shells in 1-quart casserole and bake until thoroughly heated, about 10 minutes.

APPROXIMATE TOTAL TIME: 30 MINUTES (includes baking time)

MAKES 2 SERVINGS

Each serving provides: 1½ Proteins; ¼ Vegetable; 1 Bread; 10 Optional Calories
Per serving: 183 calories; 11 g protein; 8 g fat; 19 g carbohydrate; 233 mg calcium; 339 mg sodium; 27 mg cholesterol; 2 g dietary fiber

Cheese and Vegetable Manicotti ▽ⓒ

1 tablespoon plus 1 teaspoon
  olive oil, divided
½ cup *each* finely chopped onion,
  mushrooms, and red bell
  pepper
1 small garlic clove, minced
1 package (10 ounces) frozen
  chopped spinach *or* broccoli,
  thawed
1 cup part-skim ricotta cheese
¼ cup thawed frozen egg
  substitute
2 tablespoons chopped fresh basil
  or 1 teaspoon basil leaves
1½ ounces *each* grated Parmesan
  cheese and shredded
  mozzarella cheese
8 manicotti shells (¾ ounce
  each), cooked according to
  package directions
1 cup canned Italian tomatoes
  (reserve liquid), finely chopped

1. Preheat oven to 350°F. In 9-inch nonstick skillet heat 2 teaspoons oil; add onion, mushrooms, pepper, and garlic and cook over medium-high heat until pepper is softened, about 2 minutes.

2. Add spinach and cook, stirring constantly, until moisture has evaporated, about 2 minutes. Transfer to large mixing bowl; add ricotta cheese, egg substitute, and basil and stir to combine. Set aside.

3. In small mixing bowl combine Parmesan and mozzarella cheeses; add ⅔ of cheese mixture to spinach-ricotta mixture and stir to combine.

4. Spray a 13 × 9 × 2-inch baking dish with nonstick cooking spray. Fill each manicotti shell with an equal amount of spinach-cheese mixture and set shells in baking dish. Brush manicotti shells evenly with remaining oil. Cover with foil and bake for 15 minutes.

5. Spoon tomatoes with reserved liquid over top of manicotti shells and sprinkle with remaining cheese mixture. Bake, uncovered, until cheeses melt, about 5 minutes longer.

APPROXIMATE TOTAL TIME: 35 MINUTES (includes baking time)

MAKES 4 SERVINGS, 2 MANICOTTI EACH

Each serving provides: 1 Fat; 2¼ Proteins; 2¼ Vegetables; 2 Breads
Per serving: 412 calories; 24 g protein; 16 g fat; 44 g carbohydrate; 492 mg calcium; 496 mg sodium; 36 mg cholesterol; 4 g dietary fiber

Spinach and Pasta Casserole ⟨C⟩

1 tablespoon *each* reduced-calorie
  margarine (tub) and all-
  purpose flour
½ cup skim *or* nonfat milk
¼ cup canned ready-to-serve
  low-sodium chicken broth
2¼ ounces ditalini *or* other small
  tubular pasta, cooked according
  to package directions
½ cup *each* well-drained cooked
  chopped spinach and part-skim
  ricotta cheese
1½ ounces mozzarella cheese,
  shredded, divided
¼ cup thawed frozen egg
  substitute
2 tablespoons grated Parmesan *or*
  Romano cheese, divided

1. In 1-quart saucepan melt margarine over high heat; sprinkle with flour and stir quickly to combine. Continuing to stir, cook for 30 seconds. Gradually stir in milk and chicken broth. Reduce heat to medium-high and cook, stirring constantly, until mixture thickens slightly, about 3 minutes.

2. Add pasta and spinach and stir well to combine; set aside.

3. Preheat oven to 350°F. In medium mixing bowl combine ricotta cheese, 1 ounce mozzarella cheese, the egg substitute, and 1 tablespoon Parmesan cheese; add spinach mixture and stir to combine.

4. Spray 1-quart casserole with nonstick cooking spray and add spinach-cheese mixture to casserole. Sprinkle with remaining mozzarella and Parmesan cheeses and bake until cheeses are melted, about 20 minutes.

APPROXIMATE TOTAL TIME: 35 MINUTES (includes baking time)

MAKES 2 SERVINGS

Each serving provides: ¼ Milk; ¾ Fat; 2½ Proteins; ½ Vegetable; 1½ Breads; 50 Optional Calories
Per serving with Parmesan cheese: 372 calories; 24 g protein; 15 g fat; 36 g carbohydrate; 501 mg calcium; 503 mg sodium; 41 mg cholesterol; 2 g dietary fiber
With Romano cheese: 368 calories; 23 g protein; 15 g fat; 36 g carbohydrate; 485 mg calcium; 470 mg sodium; 42 mg cholesterol; 2 g dietary fiber

Beet and Feta Salad ▽ᶜ ▽ˢ

2 cups watercress
½ cup *each* thinly sliced cucumber
    and julienne-cut (matchstick
    pieces) cooked beet
¼ cup thinly sliced red onion
¾ ounce feta cheese, crumbled
½ ounce chopped walnuts
1 tablespoon plus 1 teaspoon red
    wine vinegar
1 teaspoon *each* walnut* and
    olive oil
⅛ teaspoon pepper

*Cook the beet for this colorful salad
in your microwave oven . . . it's a
real timesaver!*

1. Line serving platter with watercress. Decoratively arrange cucumber, beet, and onion on watercress; top with cheese and sprinkle with walnuts.

2. In small mixing bowl combine *1 tablespoon water* and the remaining ingredients, mixing well. Pour over salad.

* Olive oil may be substituted for the walnut oil.

APPROXIMATE TOTAL TIME: 15 MINUTES

MAKES 2 SERVINGS

Each serving provides: 1½ Fats; 1 Protein; 3¼ Vegetables
Per serving: 130 calories; 4 g protein; 10 g fat; 8 g carbohydrate; 115 mg calcium; 155 mg sodium; 9 mg cholesterol; 3 g dietary fiber

Fish and Shellfish

Look to fish for good nutrition. Many species, including so-called fatty fish and shellfish, are prime sources of omega-3 fatty acids, which may help maintain cardiovascular health. Among the best sources of omega-3 fatty acids are salmon, tuna, bluefish, anchovy, catfish, bass, and trout. Salmon becomes a stand-in for clams in an innovative Salmon Chowder. Trout, a gourmet favorite, takes on easy elegance in our Pecan Trout, and the world will be your oyster when you serve Spinach Salad with Oysters.

Clams Fra Diavolo

1½ cups canned Italian tomatoes (reserve liquid), divided
¼ cup minced onion
2 teaspoons olive *or* vegetable oil
2 garlic cloves, minced
2 dozen littleneck clams*
1 tablespoon chopped fresh basil *or* 1 teaspoon basil leaves
⅛ teaspoon *each* crushed red pepper and black pepper

To ensure that clams are free of sand, the night before preparing this dish, place them in a large bowl and cover with uncooked cornmeal and some water; refrigerate overnight. Before preparing, discard the cornmeal mixture and thoroughly scrub the clams, rinsing them under running cold water.

1. In blender process 1 cup tomatoes with reserved liquid until pureed; set aside. Seed and chop remaining tomatoes; set aside.

2. In 10-inch round microwavable shallow baking dish combine onion, oil, and garlic and stir to combine. Microwave on High (100%) for 1 minute, until onion is translucent.

3. Set sieve over onion mixture and press pureed tomatoes through sieve into dish, discarding solids; add chopped tomatoes and stir to combine. Microwave on High for 8 minutes, stirring halfway through cooking.

4. Arrange clams over tomato mixture with hinged sides facing toward center of dish. Cover and microwave on High for 5 minutes, until clam shells open. Sprinkle with basil and peppers.

* Two dozen littleneck clams will yield about ¼ pound cooked seafood.

APPROXIMATE TOTAL TIME: 25 MINUTES

MAKES 2 SERVINGS

Each serving provides: 1 Fat; 2 Proteins; 1¾ Vegetables
Per serving: 174 calories; 17 g protein; 6 g fat; 14 g carbohydrate; 126 mg calcium; 358 mg sodium; 38 mg cholesterol; 2 g dietary fiber

Mussels with Pepper Vinaigrette ⊽ᶜ ⊽ˢ

1 dozen medium mussels,*
  scrubbed
1 teaspoon Dijon-style mustard
2 teaspoons *each* white wine
  vinegar and olive oil
1 tablespoon *each* finely chopped
  red and yellow bell pepper
1 tablespoon chopped fresh
  Italian (flat-leaf) parsley
Garnish: Italian (flat-leaf) parsley
  sprigs

1. In 2-quart microwavable casserole microwave ½ *cup water* on High (100%) for 3 minutes, until boiling.

2. Add mussels to casserole; cover and microwave on High for 2 minutes, rotating casserole ½ turn halfway through cooking, until shells open. Uncover and set aside until mussels are cool enough to handle.

3. Using a wire whisk, in small mixing bowl beat together *1 tablespoon water*, the mustard, and vinegar. Gradually beat in oil, a few drops at a time. Stir in peppers and chopped parsley.

4. Remove mussels from cooking liquid, discarding liquid. Remove and discard top shell from each mussel. Loosen meat in remaining shell and arrange on serving platter. Top each mussel with an equal amount of pepper mixture (about 1 teaspoon). Garnish with parsley sprigs.

* One dozen medium mussels will yield about ¼ pound cooked seafood.

APPROXIMATE TOTAL TIME: 15 MINUTES

MAKES 2 SERVINGS

Each serving provides: 1 Fat; 2 Proteins; ⅛ Vegetable
Per serving: 143 calories; 14 g protein; 7 g fat; 5 g carbohydrate; 20 mg calcium; 285 mg sodium; 32 mg cholesterol; 0.1 g dietary fiber

Spinach Salad with Oysters ▽ⓒ

4 cups spinach leaves, trimmed, thoroughly washed, and drained

1 teaspoon vegetable oil

½ cup *each* julienne-cut (matchstick pieces) red and yellow bell pepper

¼ cup thinly sliced onion

1 garlic clove, minced

5 ounces shucked oysters (drain and reserve liquid)

1 tablespoon *each* reduced-sodium soy sauce, balsamic vinegar, and dry sherry

1 teaspoon Worcestershire sauce

1. On serving platter arrange spinach leaves; set aside.

2. In 10-inch nonstick skillet heat oil; add peppers, onion, and garlic and cook, stirring frequently, until peppers are tender-crisp, 2 to 3 minutes. Spoon over spinach leaves; keep warm.

3. In same skillet cook oysters over high heat, turning once, until lightly browned, 1 to 2 minutes.

4. In small bowl combine reserved oyster liquid and remaining ingredients; stir into skillet and cook, stirring frequently, until liquid is reduced by half, 2 to 3 minutes.

5. Using a slotted spoon, arrange oysters over vegetables on serving platter; pour oyster liquid mixture over salad.

APPROXIMATE TOTAL TIME: 20 MINUTES

MAKES 2 SERVINGS

Each serving provides: ½ Fat; 2 Proteins; 5¼ Vegetables; 5 Optional Calories
Per serving: 135 calories, 10 g protein; 5 g fat; 14 g carbohydrate; 156 mg calcium; 498 mg sodium; 39 mg cholesterol; 4 g dietary fiber

Buttery Braised Scallops ▽c

4 cups broccoli rabe, chopped
1 tablespoon whipped butter
¼ teaspoon salt
⅛ teaspoon pepper
2 teaspoons olive oil
2 garlic cloves, minced
½ pound sea scallops
3 tablespoons dry white
　table wine
1 slice crisp bacon, crumbled
1 tablespoon balsamic *or* red
　wine vinegar
2 teaspoons lemon juice

If you prefer, broccoli florets can be substituted for the broccoli rabe.

1. In 10-inch nonstick skillet bring ¼ *cup water* to a boil; add broccoli rabe, cover, and cook over medium-high heat, stirring occasionally, until broccoli rabe is tender-crisp, 3 to 4 minutes.

2. Remove from heat; stir in butter, salt, and pepper. Transfer to serving platter; keep warm.

3. In same skillet heat oil; add garlic and cook over medium-high heat, stirring occasionally, until lightly golden, about 1 minute. Add scallops and cook, stirring occasionally, until scallops are slightly opaque, 2 to 3 minutes.

4. Add remaining ingredients and stir to combine; cook until liquid is reduced by half, 2 to 3 minutes.

5. Using a slotted spoon, arrange scallop mixture over broccoli rabe; pour cooking liquid over broccoli rabe and scallop mixture.

APPROXIMATE TOTAL TIME: 20 MINUTES

MAKES 2 SERVINGS

Each serving provides: 1 Fat; 3 Proteins; 4 Vegetables; 65 Optional Calories
Per serving: 243 calories; 24 g protein; 10 g fat; 11 g carbohydrate; 136 mg calcium; 603 mg sodium; 48 mg cholesterol; 4 g dietary fiber

Variation: Braised Scallops—Omit whipped butter and bacon from recipe. In Serving Information decrease Optional Calories to 20.
Per serving: 199 calories; 24 g protein; 6 g fat; 11 g carbohydrate; 135 mg calcium; 524 mg sodium; 37 mg cholesterol; 4 g dietary fiber

Greek-Style Scallops

2 teaspoons olive *or* vegetable oil
1 cup chopped onions
1 small garlic clove, minced
4 large plum tomatoes, blanched,
    peeled, seeded, and chopped
2 tablespoons *each* chopped fresh
    dill and fresh basil
7 ounces bay *or* sea scallops
    (cut into quarters)
1½ ounces uncooked orzo
    (rice-shaped pasta), cooked
    according to package directions
2 teaspoons lemon juice
¾ ounce feta cheese, crumbled

1. In 9-inch nonstick skillet heat oil; add onions and garlic and cook over medium-high heat, stirring occasionally, until tender-crisp, about 2 minutes. Stir in tomatoes, dill, and basil and bring mixture to a boil. Reduce heat to low; add scallops and stir to combine. Cook, stirring constantly, until scallops turn opaque. Set aside.

2. Preheat broiler. Spray 2 individual flameproof casseroles with nonstick cooking spray and spread half of the orzo over bottom of each casserole. Drizzle half of the lemon juice over each portion of ozro and then top each with half of the scallop-tomato mixture. Top each portion with half of the cheese.

3. Broil until cheese melts, about 2 minutes.

APPROXIMATE TOTAL TIME: 35 MINUTES

MAKES 2 SERVINGS

Each serving provides: 1 Fat; 3 Proteins; 3 Vegetables;
1 Bread
Per serving: 288 calories; 23 g protein; 8 g fat; 31 g carbohydrate; 147 mg calcium; 293 mg sodium; 42 mg cholesterol; 3 g dietary fiber

Oven-"Fried" Scallops ▽C ▽F

15 ounces sea scallops, cut into quarters
3 tablespoons low-fat buttermilk (1% milk fat)
⅓ cup plus 2 teaspoons seasoned dried bread crumbs
½ teaspoon ground thyme

Here's a way to have crispy-coated scallops without the fat and calories associated with frying.

1. Preheat oven to 500°F. Spray baking sheet with nonstick cooking spray and set aside.

2. In medium mixing bowl combine scallops and buttermilk, turning to coat; let stand at room temperature for 15 minutes to marinate.

3. In small mixing bowl combine bread crumbs and thyme. Dredge each scallop in bread crumb mixture, coating both sides, and arrange scallops on prepared baking sheet.

4. Bake, carefully turning scallops over until browned on all sides, about 5 minutes.

APPROXIMATE TOTAL TIME: 10 MINUTES (includes baking time; does not include marinating time)

MAKES 4 SERVINGS

Each serving provides: 3 Proteins; ½ Bread; 5 Optional Calories
Per serving: 139 calories; 20 g protein; 1 g fat; 11 g carbohydrate; 52 mg calcium; 481 mg sodium; 36 mg cholesterol; 0.5 g dietary fiber

Scallops with Cucumbers ⟨C⟩ ⟨S⟩

1 medium cucumber (about ½
   pound), scored, cut lengthwise
   into quarters, seeded, and
   sliced
½ cup sliced scallions (green
   onions)
2 teaspoons peanut *or* vegetable
   oil
½ pound bay *or* sea scallops
   (cut into quarters)
2 tablespoons rice wine vinegar
½ teaspoon granulated sugar
1 teaspoon sesame seed, toasted

Cucumbers are more than just for
salads. Here we've combined them
with scallops and cooked them in the
microwave oven. It's a dish well
worth a try.

1. In 1-quart microwavable casserole combine cucumber, scallions, and oil and stir to coat; microwave on High (100%) for 2 minutes, stirring once halfway through cooking, until scallions are softened.

2. Add scallops and stir to combine; microwave on High for 2 minutes, stirring once halfway through cooking.

3. Add vinegar and sugar and stir to combine; microwave on High for 1 minute, until scallops are opaque.

4. Sprinkle with sesame seed.

APPROXIMATE TOTAL TIME: 15 MINUTES

MAKES 2 SERVINGS

Each serving provides: 1 Fat; 3 Proteins; 1½ Vegetables; 15 Optional Calories
Per serving: 174 calories; 20 g protein; 6 g fat; 9 g carbohydrate; 60 mg calcium; 189 mg sodium; 37 mg cholesterol; 2 g dietary fiber (this figure does not include sesame seed; nutrition analysis not available)

Southwest Scallops and Pasta $\triangledown$C $\triangledown$F $\triangledown$S

¼ cup *each* sliced scallions (green onions), diced green bell pepper, and diced red bell pepper
2 teaspoons olive *or* vegetable oil
½ small jalapeño pepper, seeded and minced
I small garlic clove, minced
5 ounces bay *or* sea scallops (cut into quarters)
½ cup frozen whole-kernel corn
I cup cooked thin spaghetti
2 tablespoons *each* chopped cilantro (Chinese parsley) *or* Italian (flat-leaf) parsley and lime juice (no sugar added)
Dash hot sauce (optional)

To save time use leftover spaghetti in this colorful dish.

1. In I-quart microwavable casserole combine scallions, bell peppers, oil, jalapeño pepper, and garlic and stir to coat with oil. Microwave on High (100%) for 2 minutes, stirring once halfway through cooking, until bell peppers are tender-crisp.

2. Add scallops and corn and stir to combine; microwave on Medium (50%) for 4 minutes, stirring once every I ½ minutes.

3. Add remaining ingredients and stir to combine. Cover and microwave on Medium for I minute, stirring once halfway through cooking. Let stand for I minute until scallops are opaque and cooking is completed.

APPROXIMATE TOTAL TIME: 20 MINUTES

MAKES 2 SERVINGS

Each serving provides: I Fat; 2 Proteins; ¾ Vegetable; I ½ Breads
Per serving: 252 calories; 17 g protein; 6 g fat; 34 g carbohydrate; 38 mg calcium; 120 mg sodium; 23 mg cholesterol; 3 g dietary fiber

Creamy Scallop Salad ▽C ▽F ▽S

½ cup sliced scallions (green onions), white portion and some green
¼ cup *each* diced red bell pepper and sliced celery
½ pound bay *or* sea scallops (cut into quarters)
¼ cup plain low-fat yogurt
1 tablespoon *each* chopped fresh dill and tartar sauce
2 cups torn lettuce leaves

For a change of pace from the usual tuna salad, try this warm scallop salad.

1. In 1-quart microwavable casserole combine scallions, pepper, and celery; microwave on High (100%) for 1 minute, until scallions are softened.

2. Add scallops and stir to combine; microwave on Medium (50%) for 3 minutes, stirring once halfway through cooking, until scallops are opaque.

3. Add remaining ingredients except lettuce and stir to combine.

4. Onto each of 2 individual serving plates arrange 1 cup lettuce; top with half of the scallop mixture.

APPROXIMATE TOTAL TIME: 15 MINUTES

MAKES 2 SERVINGS

Each serving provides: ¼ Milk; 1 Fat; 3 Proteins; 3 Vegetables
Per serving: 179 calories; 22 g protein; 6 g fat; 10 g carbohydrate; 147 mg calcium; 274 mg sodium; 43 mg cholesterol; 2 g dietary fiber

Italian Seafood Stew ▽F▽

2 cups sliced carrots (1-inch pieces)

1 cup canned Italian tomatoes (with liquid), pureed

3 ounces diced pared all-purpose potato

½ cup thoroughly washed diced leeks (white portion and some green)

¼ cup dry white table wine

2 teaspoons all-purpose flour

2 garlic cloves, minced

¼ pound *each* sea scallops and shelled and deveined large shrimp

2 bay leaves

¼ teaspoon fennel seed

⅛ teaspoon crushed red pepper

1. In 3-quart microwavable casserole combine *1½ cups water*, the carrots, tomatoes, potato, leeks, wine, flour, and garlic, stirring to dissolve flour. Cover and microwave on High (100%) for 10 minutes, until carrots are tender.

2. Add scallops, shrimp, and bay leaves; cover and microwave on High for 3 minutes until shrimp turn pink.

3. Add fennel seed and pepper and stir to combine. Remove and discard bay leaves.

APPROXIMATE TOTAL TIME: 25 MINUTES

MAKES 2 SERVINGS

Each serving provides: 3 Proteins; 3½ Vegetables; ½ Bread; 35 Optional Calories
Per serving: 268 calories; 25 g protein; 2 g fat; 33 g carbohydrate; 138 mg calcium; 420 mg sodium; 105 mg cholesterol; 6 g dietary fiber

Lemon Scallops and Shrimp ⬦Ⓢ

¼ **pound** *each* **sea scallops and shelled and deveined large shrimp**

1 **tablespoon plus 1 teaspoon all-purpose flour**

2 **teaspoons olive** *or* **vegetable oil**

2 **garlic cloves, minced**

¼ **cup** *each* **dry white table wine and canned ready-to-serve low-sodium chicken broth**

2 **tablespoons lemon juice**

1 **teaspoon chopped fresh parsley**

1. On sheet of wax paper dredge scallops and shrimp in flour, coating all sides.

2. In 10-inch nonstick skillet heat oil; add scallops and shrimp and cook over medium-high heat, turning occasionally, until shrimp begin to turn pink, 2 to 3 minutes. Transfer to plate.

3. To same skillet add garlic and cook over medium heat, stirring frequently, until golden, about 1 minute. Add wine, broth, lemon juice, and parsley; return scallops and shrimp to skillet. Cook until flavors blend, 2 to 4 minutes.

APPROXIMATE TOTAL TIME: 20 MINUTES

MAKES 2 SERVINGS

Each serving provides: 1 Fat; 3 Proteins; 50 Optional Calories

Per serving: 201 calories; 22 g protein; 6 g fat; 8 g carbohydrate; 55 mg calcium; 188 mg sodium; 105 mg cholesterol; 0.2 g dietary fiber

Russian Shrimp Cocktail

1 cup shredded iceberg lettuce
2 tablespoons thinly sliced red
   onion
1 tablespoon plus 1 teaspoon
   reduced-calorie mayonnaise
1 tablespoon ketchup
1 teaspoon red wine vinegar
1 medium tomato, blanched,
   peeled, seeded, and chopped
3 ounces shelled and deveined
   cooked medium shrimp, chilled
   and cut lengthwise into halves

1. In medium mixing bowl combine lettuce and onion, tossing to combine; arrange on serving platter.

2. Using a wire whisk, in small mixing bowl beat together mayonnaise, ketchup, and vinegar; add tomato and stir to coat. Spoon tomato mixture onto center of lettuce-onion mixture; top with shrimp.

APPROXIMATE TOTAL TIME: 15 MINUTES

MAKES 2 SERVINGS

Each serving provides: 1 Fat; 1½ Proteins; 2⅛ Vegetables; 10 Optional Calories
Per serving: 98 calories; 10 g protein; 3 g fat; 7 g carbohydrate; 46 mg calcium; 268 mg sodium; 86 mg cholesterol; 1 g dietary fiber

Cinnamon-Pepper Shrimp ⏷ⓢ

2 teaspoons olive *or* vegetable oil
½ pound shelled and deveined
   shrimp (tail feathers left on)
1 cup diagonally thinly sliced
   scallions (green onions)
2 large plum tomatoes, seeded
   and cut into thin strips
1 small jalapeño pepper, seeded
   and thinly sliced
2 tablespoons freshly squeezed
   lime juice
½ teaspoon ground cinnamon
¼ teaspoon granulated sugar
1 tablespoon chopped fresh
   cilantro (Chinese parsley) *or*
   Italian (flat-leaf) parsley

1. In 9-inch nonstick skillet heat oil; add shrimp and scallions and cook over high heat, stirring frequently, until shrimp just turn pink, about 2 minutes.

2. Add remaining ingredients except cilantro and stir to combine; cook, stirring constantly, until flavors blend, about 2 minutes.

3. Sprinkle with cilantro.

APPROXIMATE TOTAL TIME: 15 MINUTES

MAKES 2 SERVINGS

Each serving provides: 1 Fat; 3 Proteins; 2¼ Vegetables; 3 Optional Calories
Per serving: 192 calories; 25 g protein; 7 g fat; 9 g carbohydrate; 102 mg calcium; 175 mg sodium; 173 mg cholesterol; 2 g dietary fiber

Open-Face Shrimp Melt

3 ounces shelled and deveined cooked small shrimp, cut lengthwise into halves
¼ cup finely chopped celery
2 tablespoons chopped scallion (green onion)
1 tablespoon plus 1 teaspoon reduced-calorie mayonnaise
1 tablespoon dry sherry
2 teaspoons lemon juice
1 teaspoon Dijon-style mustard
2 slices reduced-calorie wheat bread (40 calories per slice), lightly toasted
4 thin tomato slices
2 slices (¾ ounce each) reduced-fat Monterey Jack cheese

1. Preheat broiler. In small mixing bowl combine all ingredients except bread, tomato slices, and cheese; mix well.

2. Onto each slice of bread arrange 2 tomato slices and half of the shrimp mixture, then top with 1 cheese slice.

3. On nonstick baking sheet arrange sandwiches and broil 5 to 6 inches from heat source until cheese melts, about 1 minute.

APPROXIMATE TOTAL TIME: 15 MINUTES

MAKES 2 SERVINGS

Each serving provides: 1 Fat; 2½ Proteins; ¾ Vegetable; ½ Bread; 5 Optional Calories
Per serving: 192 calories; 17 g protein; 7 g fat; 13 g carbohydrate; 236 mg calcium; 492 mg sodium; 101 mg cholesterol; 1 g dietary fiber

Shrimp and Orzo Salad ⬡F ⬡S

¼ pound shelled and deveined cooked small shrimp, cut lengthwise into halves

1½ ounces orzo (rice-shaped pasta), cooked according to package directions

½ cup thawed frozen whole-kernel corn

¼ cup diced red bell pepper

2 tablespoons chopped scallion (green onion)

1 tablespoon *each* chopped fresh dill, lemon juice, and red wine vinegar

2 teaspoons olive oil

½ teaspoon Dijon-style mustard

⅛ teaspoon pepper

8 lettuce leaves

Use your microwave oven to cook the shrimp in minutes.

1. In medium mixing bowl combine first 5 ingredients; set aside.

2. In small bowl combine remaining ingredients except lettuce, mixing well. Pour over shrimp mixture and toss to coat.

3. To serve, line serving bowl with lettuce and top with shrimp mixture.

APPROXIMATE TOTAL TIME: 20 MINUTES

MAKES 2 SERVINGS

Each serving provides: 1 Fat; 2 Proteins; 1¼ Vegetables; 1½ Breads
Per serving: 226 calories; 16 g protein; 6 g fat; 28 g carbohydrate; 64 mg calcium; 172 mg sodium; 111 mg cholesterol; 2 g dietary fiber

Shrimp Salad Vinaigrette ⬇F⬇S

1 *each* medium red and green bell pepper

2 teaspoons olive *or* vegetable oil

½ pound shelled and deveined shrimp (tail feathers left on)

2 small garlic cloves, minced

1 package (9 ounces) frozen quartered artichoke hearts, cooked according to package directions; drained and cooled

½ cup thinly sliced scallions (green onions)

2 tablespoons balsamic *or* red wine vinegar

1 tablespoon *each* chopped Italian (flat-leaf) parsley and fresh basil

4 lettuce leaves

This colorful dish can be served warm or eaten chilled.

1. Preheat broiler. On baking sheet lined with heavy-duty foil broil peppers 3 inches from heat source, turning frequently, until charred on all sides; let stand until cool enough to handle. Peel peppers; remove and discard stem ends and seeds. Cut peppers into strips.

2. In 9-inch nonstick skillet heat oil; add shrimp and garlic and cook over high heat, stirring frequently, until shrimp just turn pink, about 2 minutes. Add bell pepper strips and remaining ingredients except lettuce and cook, stirring occasionally, until thoroughly heated, about 3 minutes.

3. Line serving platter with lettuce and top with shrimp mixture.

APPROXIMATE TOTAL TIME: 40 MINUTES

MAKES 2 SERVINGS

Each serving provides: 1 Fat; 3 Proteins; 5 Vegetables
Per serving: 243 calories; 28 g protein; 7 g fat; 18 g carbohydrate; 132 mg calcium; 234 mg sodium; 173 mg cholesterol; 7 g dietary fiber

Shrimp Salad with Pineapple and Pecans ⬦S⬦

3 ounces shelled and deveined
  cooked shrimp, cut lengthwise
  into halves
½ cup *each* drained canned
  pineapple chunks (no sugar
  added) and snow peas
  (Chinese pea pods), stem ends
  and strings removed, blanched
½ ounce pecan halves, toasted
1 tablespoon plus 1½ teaspoons
  sliced scallion (green onion)
2 tablespoons *each* plain low-fat
  yogurt and sour cream
2 teaspoons *each* reduced-calorie
  mayonnaise and white wine
  vinegar
Dash *each* salt and pepper

*Save time by cooking and shelling
the shrimp the night before you plan
to use them.*

1. In medium mixing bowl combine shrimp, pine-apple, snow peas, pecans, and scallion.

2. Using a wire whisk, in small mixing bowl beat together remaining ingredients; pour over shrimp mixture and toss to coat. Cover and refrigerate until ready to serve.

APPROXIMATE TOTAL TIME: 20 MINUTES

MAKES 2 SERVINGS

Each serving provides: 1 Fat; 2 Proteins; ½ Vegetable; ½ Fruit; 45 Optional Calories
Per serving: 197 calories; 12 g protein; 10 g fat; 16 g carbohydrate; 89 mg calcium; 219 mg sodium; 92 mg cholesterol; 2 g dietary fiber

Baked Fish in Cream Sauce ▽Ⓢ

½ pound bluefish *or* red snapper fillet, cut in half

½ cup chopped onion

½ medium tomato, chopped

Dash *each* garlic powder and pepper

¼ cup low-fat milk (1% milk fat)

2 teaspoons reduced-calorie margarine (tub), melted and cooled

1 teaspoon cornstarch

1 tablespoon *each* chopped fresh basil and Italian (flat-leaf) parsley

1. Preheat oven to 400°F. Spray 9-inch pie plate with nonstick cooking spray. Arrange fish in plate and top with onion, tomato, garlic powder, and pepper.

2. In 1-cup liquid measure combine milk, margarine, and cornstarch, stirring to dissolve cornstarch; pour over fish. Bake until fish flakes easily when tested with a fork, 12 to 15 minutes.

3. To serve, carefully transfer each fillet to a serving plate; stir pan juices to thoroughly combine and pour half over each fillet. Sprinkle each portion with half of the basil and parsley.

APPROXIMATE TOTAL TIME: 25 MINUTES

MAKES 2 SERVINGS

Each serving provides: ½ Fat; 3 Proteins; 1 Vegetable; 20 Optional Calories

Per serving with bluefish: 197 calories; 25 g protein; 7 g fat; 7 g carbohydrate; 72 mg calcium; 128 mg sodium; 68 mg cholesterol; 1 g dietary fiber

With red snapper: 170 calories; 25 g protein; 4 g fat; 7 g carbohydrate; 101 mg calcium; 132 mg sodium; 43 mg cholesterol; 1 g dietary fiber

Broiled Fish with Stewed Tomatoes

½ pound bluefish *or* red snapper fillet, cut in half

1 tablespoon plus 1 teaspoon reduced-calorie margarine (tub), divided

⅛ teaspoon *each* garlic powder and pepper, divided

1 cup canned stewed tomatoes

1 tablespoon *each* finely chopped fresh basil and Italian (flat-leaf) parsley

1. Preheat broiler. Spray 9-inch flameproof pie plate with nonstick cooking spray. Arrange fish in plate and brush with half of the margarine; sprinkle with half of the garlic powder and pepper.

2. Broil for 5 minutes; carefully turn each fillet over. Brush with remaining margarine and sprinkle with remaining garlic powder and pepper. Spoon tomatoes around fillets and sprinkle with basil and parsley. Broil until fish flakes easily when tested with a fork, about 5 minutes.

3. To serve, carefully transfer each fillet to a serving plate; stir tomato mixture and spoon half over each fillet.

APPROXIMATE TOTAL TIME: 20 MINUTES

MAKES 2 SERVINGS

Each serving provides: 1 Fat; 3 Proteins; 1 Vegetable
Per serving with bluefish: 210 calories; 24 g protein; 9 g fat; 9 g carbohydrate; 65 mg calcium; 473 mg sodium; 67 mg cholesterol; 0.1 g dietary fiber (this figure does not include stewed tomatoes; nutrition analysis not available)
With red snapper: 183 calories; 25 g protein; 6 g fat; 9 g carbohydrate; 93 mg calcium; 477 mg sodium; 42 mg cholesterol; 0.1 g dietary fiber (this figure does not include stewed tomatoes; nutrition analysis not available)

Fillets with Peppers and Tomatoes $\triangledown$ $\triangledown$

2 fish fillets (sole, flounder, *or* red snapper), ¼ pound each
2 tablespoons all-purpose flour
2 teaspoons olive *or* vegetable oil
½ cup *each* sliced onion and green bell pepper
1 garlic clove, minced
½ cup seeded and chopped drained canned Italian tomatoes
¼ cup dry white table wine
⅛ teaspoon pepper
Dash thyme leaves

1. On sheet of wax paper dredge fish in flour.

2. In 10-inch nonstick skillet heat oil; add fish and cook over medium-high heat until lightly browned and fish flakes easily when tested with a fork, 2 to 3 minutes on each side. Using a spatula, transfer fish to serving platter; keep warm.

3. In same skillet combine onion, bell pepper, and garlic; cook over medium-high heat, stirring frequently, until bell pepper is tender-crisp, 2 to 3 minutes. Stir in tomatoes, wine, pepper, and thyme. Reduce heat to low and cook, stirring occasionally, until mixture thickens, 5 to 6 minutes. Spoon over fish.

APPROXIMATE TOTAL TIME: 30 MINUTES

MAKES 2 SERVINGS

Each serving provides: 1 Fat; 3 Proteins; 1½ Vegetables; 55 Optional Calories
Per serving with sole or flounder: 226 calories; 24 g protein; 6 g fat; 14 g carbohydrate; 56 mg calcium; 193 mg sodium; 54 mg cholesterol; 2 g dietary fiber
With red snapper: 236 calories; 25 g protein; 6 g fat; 14 g carbohydrate; 71 mg calcium; 174 mg sodium; 42 mg cholesterol; 2 g dietary fiber

Golden Fish Meunière ⬡S⬡

1½ ounces (about ¼ cup) uncooked yellow cornmeal
¼ teaspoon grated lemon peel
2 sole *or* flounder fillets (¼ pound each)
1 tablespoon vegetable oil
¼ cup dry white table wine
2 tablespoons lemon juice
1 tablespoon chopped fresh parsley
1 teaspoon rinsed drained capers
1 tablespoon whipped butter

1. On sheet of wax paper combine cornmeal and lemon peel. Dredge fish in cornmeal mixture, coating both sides and using all of mixture.

2. In 10-inch nonstick skillet heat oil; add fish to skillet and cook until lightly browned and fish flakes easily when tested with a fork, 2 to 3 minutes on each side. Using a spatula, transfer fish to serving platter; keep warm.

3. In same skillet combine remaining ingredients except butter; cook until liquid is reduced by half, 1 to 2 minutes. Add butter and stir until melted; pour evenly over fish.

APPROXIMATE TOTAL TIME: 20 MINUTES

MAKES 2 SERVINGS

Each serving provides: 1½ Fats; 3 Proteins; 1 Bread; 50 Optional Calories
Per serving: 290 calories; 23 g protein; 11 g fat; 18 g carbohydrate; 30 mg calcium; 163 mg sodium; 62 mg cholesterol; 1 g dietary fiber (this figure does not include capers; nutrition analysis not available)

Sesame Flounder Fillets ⟨S⟩

⅓ cup plus 2 teaspoons plain
 dried bread crumbs
1 tablespoon sesame seed
1¾ teaspoons vegetable oil,
 divided
¼ teaspoon Chinese sesame oil
3 tablespoons low-fat buttermilk
 (1% milk fat)
1 teaspoon *each* reduced-sodium
 soy sauce and lemon juice
2 flounder fillets (¼ pound each)

1. Preheat broiler. In shallow mixing bowl combine bread crumbs, sesame seed, ¾ teaspoon vegetable oil, and the sesame oil; mix well until thoroughly combined. Set aside.

2. In shallow mixing bowl combine buttermilk, soy sauce, and lemon juice. Dip fillets in buttermilk mixture and dredge in crumb mixture, coating both sides and using all of the mixtures.

3. Arrange fillets on nonstick baking sheet. Drizzle each fillet with ¼ teaspoon vegetable oil. Broil 5 to 6 inches from heat source until lightly browned, 3 to 4 minutes.

4. Using spatula, carefully turn fillets over and drizzle each with ¼ teaspoon vegetable oil. Broil until fillets flake easily when tested with a fork, 3 to 4 minutes longer.

APPROXIMATE TOTAL TIME: 20 MINUTES

MAKES 2 SERVINGS
Each serving provides: 1 Fat; 3 Proteins; 1 Bread; 40 Optional Calories
Per serving: 254 calories; 25 g protein; 9 g fat; 16 g carbohydrate; 115 mg calcium; 355 mg sodium; 56 mg cholesterol; 1 g dietary fiber (this figure does not include sesame seed; nutrition analysis not available)

Sesame Monkfish

1 cup chopped onions
1 teaspoon vegetable oil
5 ounces monkfish fillet, cut into
  6 equal strips
Dash *each* salt and pepper
1 tablespoon *each* tahini (sesame
  paste) and finely chopped fresh
  parsley
1 teaspoon sesame seed, toasted

1. In 1-quart microwavable casserole combine onions and oil and stir to coat. Cover and microwave on High (100%) for 2 minutes, until onions are soft.

2. Sprinkle fish with salt and pepper and arrange over onions. Spread tahini over fish and then sprinkle with parsley.

3. Cover and microwave on High for 3 minutes. Let stand for 1 minute, until fish flakes easily when tested with a fork.

4. Sprinkle with sesame seed.

APPROXIMATE TOTAL TIME: 15 MINUTES

MAKES 2 SERVINGS

Each serving provides: 1 Fat; 2½ Proteins; 1 Vegetable; 10 Optional Calories
Per serving: 155 calories; 13 g protein; 8 g fat; 8 g carbohydrate; 75 mg calcium; 90 mg sodium; 18 mg cholesterol; 2 g dietary fiber (this figure does not include sesame seed; nutrition analysis not available)

Salmon Chowder

1 tablespoon plus 1 teaspoon
   margarine
½ cup chopped onion
1 tablespoon all-purpose flour
1 cup *each* bottled clam juice,
   seeded and diced drained
   canned Italian tomatoes, and
   low-fat milk (1% milk fat)
6 ounces diced pared all-purpose
   potato
½ cup thawed frozen whole-
   kernel corn
1 tablespoon chopped fresh
   parsley
⅛ teaspoon *each* white pepper
   and thyme leaves
5 ounces salmon fillet, cut into
   ½-inch cubes

*A little fish goes a long way when
added to this hearty chowder.*

1. In 3-quart saucepan melt margarine; add onion and sauté over medium-high heat, stirring frequently, until onion is softened, 1 to 2 minutes. Sprinkle flour over onion and stir quickly to combine. Continuing to stir, add *1 cup water*, the clam juice, and tomatoes. Reduce heat to medium-low and cook until mixture thickens, about 5 minutes.

2. Add remaining ingredients except salmon and stir to combine; cook until potato is tender, about 10 minutes. Add salmon and cook until opaque, about 5 minutes longer.

APPROXIMATE TOTAL TIME: 30 MINUTES

MAKES 4 SERVINGS, ABOUT 1¼ CUPS EACH

Each serving provides: ¼ Milk; 1 Fat; 1 Protein; ¾ Vegetable; ¾ Bread; 25 Optional Calories
Per serving: 189 calories; 12 g protein; 7 g fat; 21 g carbohydrate; 115 mg calcium; 321 mg sodium; 22 mg cholesterol; 2 g dietary fiber

Grilled Salmon with Lime Butter ⟨s⟩

2 tablespoons freshly squeezed
  lime juice
2 teaspoons mashed pared
  gingerroot
2 salmon fillets (¼ pound each)
1 tablespoon whipped sweet
  butter, softened
2 teaspoons fresh grated lime
  peel
Garnish: lemon and lime slices

*So easy to make, but a truly elegant
recipe. Serve it on a special occa-
sion.*

1. In glass or stainless-steel shallow bowl combine lime juice and gingerroot; add salmon fillets and let stand at room temperature for 15 minutes, turning fillets over every 5 minutes.

2. In small bowl combine butter and lime peel; cover and refrigerate until ready to serve.

3. Preheat broiler. Spray nonstick baking sheet with nonstick cooking spray and arrange fillets on baking sheet. Broil until fish flakes easily when tested with a fork, about 2 minutes on each side.

4. To serve, on serving platter arrange salmon fillets; top each fillet with half of the lime butter and garnish with lemon and lime slices.

APPROXIMATE TOTAL TIME: 10 MINUTES (does not include marinating time)

MAKES 2 SERVINGS

Each serving provides: 3 Proteins; 25 Optional Calories
Per serving: 194 calories; 23 g protein; 10 g fat; 2 g carbohydrate; 19 mg calcium; 51 mg sodium; 70 mg cholesterol; dietary fiber data not available

Variation: Grilled Salmon with Lime Margarine—Substitute 1 tablespoon plus 1 teaspoon reduced-calorie margarine (tub) for the butter. In Serving Information add 1 Fat and omit Optional Calories.
Per serving: 201 calories; 23 g protein; 11 g fat; 2 g carbohydrate; 18 mg calcium; 130 mg sodium; 62 mg cholesterol; dietary fiber data not available

Salmon with Creamy Horseradish Sauce ▽ⓢ

¼ cup dry white table wine
2 tablespoons chopped onion
1 tablespoon lemon juice
1 teaspoon peppercorns
2 salmon steaks (5 ounces each)
2 tablespoons sour cream
2 teaspoons prepared horseradish
1 teaspoon *each* all-purpose flour
   and chopped fresh mint
⅛ teaspoon white pepper

1. In 10-inch nonstick skillet combine *½ cup water*, the wine, onion, lemon juice, and peppercorns; cover and cook over medium-high heat until mixture comes to a boil.

2. Reduce heat to medium-low; add salmon, cover, and simmer until salmon flakes easily when tested with a fork, 5 to 6 minutes (depending on thickness of salmon).

3. While salmon cooks, prepare horseradish mixture. In small mixing bowl combine sour cream, horseradish, flour, mint, and white pepper; stir to combine and set aside.

4. Transfer salmon to serving platter; keep warm.

5. Pour cooking liquid through sieve into bowl, discarding solids. Return to skillet and cook over medium-high heat until mixture comes to a boil; stir in horseradish mixture. Reduce heat to low and cook, stirring frequently, until mixture thickens, 2 to 3 minutes. Pour over salmon.

APPROXIMATE TOTAL TIME: 15 MINUTES

MAKES 2 SERVINGS

Each serving provides: 3 Proteins; 65 Optional Calories
Per serving: 267 calories; 29 g protein; 12 g fat; 4 g carbohydrate; 48 mg calcium; 79 mg sodium; 84 mg cholesterol; 0.5 g dietary fiber (this figure does not include horseradish; nutrition analysis not available)

Lite Sea Breeze

Cranberry Wheat Muffins
Oat-Raisin Pancakes with Sausage
Western Omelet

Mussels with
Pepper Vinaigrette
Clams Fra Diavolo
Corn with Basil Butter

Fresh Tomato-Basil Soup
Salmon Chowder
Puree of Green Bean Soup

Chicken Burgers
Orange-Poppy Cupcakes

Sole with Vegetable-Rice Stuffing ⱽ⃝F ⱽ⃝S

¼ cup *each* finely chopped
celery, finely chopped onion,
and shredded carrot
1 tablespoon plus 1 teaspoon
reduced-calorie margarine
(tub), divided
1 cup cooked regular long-grain
rice
¼ cup plain low-fat yogurt
1 tablespoon fresh grated lemon
peel
¼ teaspoon *each* thyme leaves
and paprika
2 lemon *or* grey sole fillets
(¼ pound each)
1 teaspoon all-purpose flour
½ cup bottled clam juice
1 tablespoon dry white table
wine

*If you are unable to purchase sole,
you can substitute flounder fillets in
this recipe.*

1. In 1-quart microwavable casserole combine celery, onion, carrot, and 2 teaspoons margarine; microwave on High (100%) for 2 minutes until celery is soft, stirring once halfway through cooking.

2. In small mixing bowl combine half of the vegetable mixture, the rice, yogurt, lemon peel, thyme, and paprika; mix well.

3. Onto center of each fillet arrange an equal amount of the vegetable-rice mixture; roll fillets to enclose filling. Arrange fillets on microwavable plate.

4. Microwave on High for 6 minutes, rotating plate ½ turn every 2 minutes, until fish flakes easily when tested with a fork. Set aside and keep warm.

5. In small microwavable mixing bowl melt remaining margarine on High for 30 seconds; stir in flour. Microwave on High for 30 seconds. Stir in clam juice, wine, and reserved vegetable mixture and microwave on High for 2 minutes, stirring once halfway through cooking, until hot.

6. To serve, spoon clam juice mixture onto serving platter; arrange fillets on serving platter.

APPROXIMATE TOTAL TIME: 30 MINUTES

MAKES 2 SERVINGS

Each serving provides: ¼ Milk; 1 Fat; 3 Proteins; ¾ Vegetable; 1 Bread; 20 Optional Calories
Per serving: 287 calories; 26 g protein; 6 g fat; 30 g carbohydrate; 111 mg calcium; 341 mg sodium; 56 mg cholesterol; 1 g dietary fiber

Fiesta Swordfish ▽C ▽S

2 teaspoons olive *or* vegetable oil
½ cup sliced red onion
½ medium mild chili pepper, seeded and minced
½ small jalapeño pepper, seeded and minced
1 small garlic clove, minced
4 large plum tomatoes, blanched, peeled, seeded, and chopped
¼ cup bottled clam juice
2 tablespoons *each* chopped cilantro (Chinese parsley) *or* Italian (flat-leaf) parsley and half-and-half (blend of milk and cream)
½ pound boneless swordfish steak
3 tablespoons lime juice (no sugar added)

1. Preheat broiler. In 9-inch nonstick skillet heat oil; add onion, chili pepper, jalapeño pepper, and garlic and cook over medium-high heat, stirring occasionally, until peppers are tender-crisp, about 1 minute.

2. Add tomatoes and clam juice and stir to combine; bring mixture to a boil. Reduce heat to low and let simmer until mixture is slightly reduced, about 3 minutes.

3. Remove skillet from heat and stir in cilantro and half-and-half. Return to low heat and cook until thoroughly heated. Set aside and keep warm.

4. Spray nonstick baking sheet with nonstick cooking spray and arrange swordfish on baking sheet. Broil for 2 minutes, basting with 1½ teaspoons lime juice. Turn swordfish over, baste with remaining lime juice, and broil until fish flakes easily when tested with a fork, about 2 minutes longer.

5. To serve, spoon tomato mixture onto serving platter; top with swordfish.

APPROXIMATE TOTAL TIME: 25 MINUTES

MAKES 2 SERVINGS

Each serving provides: 1 Fat; 3 Proteins; 2¾ Vegetables; 30 Optional Calories
Per serving: 242 calories; 25 g protein; 11 g fat; 11 g carbohydrate; 49 mg calcium; 187 mg sodium; 50 mg cholesterol; 2 g dietary fiber

Swordfish Kabobs ▽C ▽F

2 tablespoons reduced-sodium
   soy sauce
2 teaspoons minced pared
   gingerroot
1 garlic clove, minced
7 ounces boneless swordfish
   steak, cut into ¾-inch cubes
½ cup cubed yellow bell pepper
   (1-inch cubes)
½ cup cubed zucchini
6 cherry tomatoes
4 medium mushrooms
½ teaspoon Chinese sesame oil

*For a change of pace, grill kabobs
on the barbecue grill and serve with
parslied rice.*

1. In medium glass or stainless-steel bowl combine first 3 ingredients; add fish and stir to coat. Cover and refrigerate for at least 20 minutes or up to 2 hours.

2. Using a slotted spoon, remove fish from marinade, reserving marinade. Onto each of two 12-inch wooden skewers thread half of the fish cubes, bell pepper, zucchini, cherry tomatoes, and mushrooms, alternating ingredients.

3. Arrange kabobs on 12-inch microwavable serving platter. Using a pastry brush, brush kabobs with reserved marinade. Cover and microwave on High (100%) for 4 minutes, rotating platter halfway through cooking. Let stand for 1 minute to complete cooking. Brush kabobs evenly with sesame oil.

APPROXIMATE TOTAL TIME: 20 MINUTES (does not include marinating time)

MAKES 2 SERVINGS

Each serving provides: ¼ Fat; 2½ Proteins; 2 Vegetables
Per serving: 165 calories; 22 g protein; 5 g fat; 7 g carbohydrate; 20 mg calcium; 695 mg sodium; 39 mg cholesterol; 1 g dietary fiber

Italian-Style Tuna ⟨C⟩ ⟨S⟩

1 teaspoon olive oil
½ cup chopped onion
½ ounce pignolias (pine nuts)
1 anchovy fillet, rinsed and
   chopped
2 tablespoons dry white table
   wine
1 tablespoon *each* balsamic *or* red
   wine vinegar and rinsed
   drained capers
2 large plum tomatoes, blanched,
   peeled, seeded, and chopped
Dash *each* ground cinnamon and
   ground cloves
7 ounces boneless tuna steak
1 tablespoon chopped fresh
   Italian (flat-leaf) parsley

*This recipe uses tuna, but it's fresh
rather than canned.*

1. Preheat broiler. In 9-inch nonstick skillet heat oil; add onion, pignolias, and anchovy and cook over medium heat, stirring frequently, until onion is tender-crisp, about 3 minutes. Stir in wine and vinegar and bring mixture to a boil. Reduce heat to low; add capers, tomatoes, cinnamon, and cloves and stir to combine. Let simmer until flavors blend, about 5 minutes.

2. While tomato mixture is simmering broil tuna. Spray nonstick baking sheet with nonstick cooking spray and arrange tuna on baking sheet. Broil until fish flakes easily when tested with a fork, about 3 minutes on each side (depending on thickness of steak).

3. To serve, arrange tuna on serving platter; top with tomato mixture and sprinkle with parsley.

APPROXIMATE TOTAL TIME: 30 MINUTES

MAKES 2 SERVINGS

Each serving provides: 1 Fat; 3 Proteins; 1½ Vegetables; 15 Optional Calories
Per serving: 239 calories; 26 g protein; 11 g fat; 7 g carbohydrate; 25 mg calcium; 229 mg sodium; 39 mg cholesterol; 1 g dietary fiber (this figure does not include pignolias and capers; nutrition analyses not available)

Mexican Tuna Salad ⩒ ⩒

4 ounces drained canned tuna (packed in oil), flaked

½ medium tomato, finely chopped

¼ cup *each* finely chopped red onion and red *or* green bell pepper

2 tablespoons plus 2 teaspoons reduced-calorie mayonnaise

1 tablespoon *each* chopped cilantro (Chinese parsley) *or* Italian (flat-leaf) parsley and lime juice (no sugar added)

Serve this Mexican-style salad in a taco with shredded lettuce and diced tomato.

1. In small mixing bowl combine all ingredients, mixing well.

APPROXIMATE TOTAL TIME: 10 MINUTES

MAKES 4 SERVINGS

Each serving provides: 1½ Fats; 1 Protein; ½ Vegetable
Per serving: 92 calories; 9 g protein; 5 g fat; 3 g carbohydrate; 8 mg calcium; 157 mg sodium; 8 mg cholesterol; 0.5 g dietary fiber

Olive-Tuna Salad ▽ⓒ

4 ounces drained canned tuna
    (packed in oil), flaked
¼ cup *each* finely chopped onion
    and finely chopped rinsed
    drained pimiento
6 large pimiento-stuffed green
    olives, finely chopped
2 tablespoons reduced-calorie
    mayonnaise
1 tablespoon lemon juice

1. In small mixing bowl combine all ingredients, mixing well.

APPROXIMATE TOTAL TIME: 10 MINUTES

MAKES 4 SERVINGS

Each serving provides: 1½ Fats; 1 Protein; ¼ Vegetable
Per serving: 87 calories; 8 g protein; 5 g fat; 2 g carbohydrate; 11 mg calcium; 294 mg sodium; 7 mg cholesterol; 0.3 g dietary fiber (this figure does not include pimiento; nutrition analysis not available)

Oriental Tuna Salad ⌄C⌄

4 ounces drained canned tuna
(packed in oil), flaked
¼ cup *each* finely chopped
scallions (green onions), celery,
and drained canned bamboo
shoots
2 tablespoons plus 2 teaspoons
reduced-calorie mayonnaise
2 teaspoons reduced-sodium soy
sauce
1 teaspoon *each* grated pared
gingerroot and minced fresh
garlic

*This zippy variation of tuna salad
also makes a fabulous sandwich
filling.*

1. In small mixing bowl combine all ingredients, mixing well.

APPROXIMATE TOTAL TIME: 10 MINUTES

MAKES 4 SERVINGS

Each serving provides: 1½ Fats; 1 Protein; ¼ Vegetable
Per serving: 91 calories; 9 g protein; 5 g fat; 2 g carbohydrate; 13 mg calcium; 283 mg sodium; 8 mg cholesterol; 0.3 g dietary fiber (this figure does not include bamboo shoots; nutrition analysis not available)

Tuna-Rice Salad ▽C ▽F

1 tablespoon *each* sweet pickle
  relish and red wine vinegar
2 teaspoons vegetable oil
½ teaspoon Dijon-style mustard
1 cup cooked long-grain rice
2 ounces drained canned tuna
  (packed in water), flaked
¼ cup *each* diced green bell
  pepper, carrot, and cucumber
2 tablespoons diced drained
  pimiento

*This is a great way to use up leftover
cooked rice.*

1. In medium mixing bowl combine relish, vinegar, oil, and mustard, mixing well. Add remaining ingredients and toss to coat. Cover and refrigerate until flavors blend, at least 15 minutes.

APPROXIMATE TOTAL TIME: 15 MINUTES (does not include chilling time)

MAKES 2 SERVINGS

Each serving provides: 1 Fat; 1 Protein; ¾ Vegetable; 1 Bread; 15 Optional Calories
Per serving: 216 calories; 11 g protein; 5 g fat; 31 g carbohydrate; 22 mg calcium; 201 mg sodium; 12 mg cholesterol; 1 g dietary fiber (this figure does not include pimiento; nutrition analysis not available)

Pecan Trout

1 trout fillet (7 ounces)
1 tablespoon whole wheat *or* all-purpose flour
1 teaspoon *each* vegetable oil and margarine
½ ounce chopped pecans
¼ cup dry white table wine
1 tablespoon lemon juice
1 teaspoon chopped fresh parsley
½ teaspoon Worcestershire sauce

1. On sheet of wax paper dredge trout in flour, coating both sides.

2. In 10-inch nonstick skillet heat oil and margarine until margarine is melted; add trout and cook over medium heat until trout flakes easily when tested with a fork, 2 to 3 minutes on each side. Using a spatula, transfer trout to serving platter; keep warm.

3. To same skillet add pecans and cook over low heat, stirring frequently, until toasted, 1 to 2 minutes. Stir in remaining ingredients and cook until thoroughly heated, 1 to 2 minutes. Pour over trout.

APPROXIMATE TOTAL TIME: 15 MINUTES

MAKES 2 SERVINGS

Each serving provides: 1½ Fats; 3 Proteins; 40 Optional Calories
Per serving: 267 calories; 22 g protein; 16 g fat; 5 g carbohydrate; 52 mg calcium; 91 mg sodium; 58 mg cholesterol; 1 g dietary fiber

Poultry

Poultry continues to soar on the popularity charts because it's a source of low-fat protein for less money than most meats. These days turkey, as well as chicken, is available in easy-to-prepare parts, a boon for those who don't want to cope with a whole bird. Italian-style turkey sausage links become Skillet Sausages with Apple—an appetizing way to get in some of that fabled "apple a day." Our Creamy Chicken Fettuccine enables one chicken cutlet to stretch into two satisfying servings. For gourmet dining, try Braised Cornish Hen, prepared with a touch of dry sherry. You won't lay an egg with these dishes!

Chicken and Tomato Egg Drop Soup ▽C ▽F

2 cups tomato juice
¼ pound thinly sliced skinned and boned chicken breast
2 teaspoons reduced-sodium soy sauce
¼ cup *each* thawed frozen egg substitute and diagonally thinly sliced scallions (green onions)

Here's our variation of a familiar Chinese specialty.

1. In 1-quart microwavable casserole combine tomato juice, *1 cup water*, the chicken, and soy sauce and microwave on High (100%) for 4 minutes until chicken is no longer pink, stirring once halfway through cooking.

2. Remove casserole from oven and, stirring constantly, pour egg substitute into tomato juice mixture in a slow stream. Microwave on Medium (50%) for 1 minute. Stir in scallions.

APPROXIMATE TOTAL TIME: 10 MINUTES

MAKES 2 SERVINGS, ABOUT 1½ CUPS EACH

Each serving provides: 2 Proteins; 1¼ Vegetables
Per serving: 127 calories; 19 g protein; 1 g fat; 12 g carbohydrate; 50 mg calcium; 1,172 mg sodium; 33 mg cholesterol; 0.3 g dietary fiber

Hot and Spicy Chicken Soup ▽C ▽F

2 teaspoons vegetable oil
5 ounces thinly sliced chicken
  cutlets
½ cup *each* sliced mushrooms,
  onion, and Chinese chard (bok
  choy)
½ medium mild *or* hot chili
  pepper, seeded and thinly
  sliced
1 small garlic clove, minced
Dash Chinese five-spice powder
1 cup canned ready-to-serve low-
  sodium chicken broth
1 tablespoon *each* dry sherry and
  reduced-sodium soy sauce
1 cup drained canned *or* thawed
  frozen baby corn ears
½ cup *each* snow peas (Chinese
  pea pods), stem ends and
  strings removed; bean sprouts,
  and julienne-cut (matchstick
  pieces) red bell pepper
2 tablespoons thinly sliced
  scallion (green onion), green
  portion only

1. In 4-quart nonstick saucepan heat oil; add chicken and cook over high heat, stirring frequently, until browned, about 3 minutes.

2. Add mushrooms, onion, Chinese chard, chili pepper, garlic, and five-spice powder and cook, stirring frequently, until vegetables are tender-crisp, about 3 minutes.

3. Stir in broth, sherry, and soy sauce; bring mixture to a boil. Reduce heat to low; add remaining ingredients and stir to combine. Continue cooking until bell pepper is tender-crisp, about 2 minutes.

APPROXIMATE TOTAL TIME: 25 MINUTES

MAKES 2 SERVINGS, ABOUT 2½ CUPS EACH

Each serving provides: 1 Fat; 2 Proteins; 3¼ Vegetables; ½ Bread; 25 Optional Calories
Per serving: 255 calories; 25 g protein; 7 g fat; 22 g carbohydrate; 67 mg calcium; 410 mg sodium; 41 mg cholesterol; 6 g dietary fiber (this figure does not include Chinese chard; nutrition analysis not available)

Chicken Breasts Bonne Femme ⬦F⬦

2 chicken breasts (6 ounces
   each), skinned and cut into
   halves
1 tablespoon all-purpose flour
2 teaspoons olive *or* vegetable oil
1 cup *each* sliced onions and
   sliced shiitake *or* white
   mushrooms
¼ cup dry white table wine
6 ounces pared all-purpose
   potato, cut into quarters
1 packet instant chicken broth
   and seasoning mix
¼ teaspoon chopped fresh
   tarragon *or* ⅛ teaspoon
   tarragon leaves
⅛ teaspoon white pepper

*Our version of a classic French rec-
ipe is as fine as any you'll find in a
restaurant.*

1. On sheet of wax paper dredge chicken in flour, coating all sides.

2. In 3-quart nonstick saucepan heat oil; add chicken and cook over medium-high heat, turning occasionally, until browned on all sides, 3 to 4 minutes. Transfer chicken to plate and set aside.

3. In same saucepan combine onions and mushrooms and cook over medium-high heat, stirring frequently, until vegetables are softened, 1 to 2 minutes. Continuing to stir, add *1½ cups water* and the wine. Add remaining ingredients; return chicken to saucepan. Reduce heat to low, cover, and let simmer, stirring occasionally, until chicken and potato are tender, about 20 minutes.

APPROXIMATE TOTAL TIME: 35 MINUTES

MAKES 2 SERVINGS

Each serving provides: 1 Fat; 3 Proteins; 2 Vegetables;
1 Bread; 45 Optional Calories
Per serving: 307 calories; 31 g protein; 6 g fat; 27 g carbohydrate; 45 mg calcium; 578 mg sodium; 66 mg cholesterol; 3 g dietary fiber

Chicken Burgers

5 ounces skinned and boned chicken, sliced

⅓ cup plus 2 teaspoons plain dried bread crumbs, divided

2 tablespoons minced onion

1 tablespoon freshly squeezed lemon juice

1 teaspoon prepared horseradish

½ teaspoon Worcestershire sauce

⅛ teaspoon white pepper

2 teaspoons vegetable oil

2 small pitas (1 ounce each); each cut in half horizontally

2 lettuce leaves

4 tomato slices

1 tablespoon reduced-calorie Russian dressing (25 calories per tablespoon)

1. In food processor process chicken, using on-off motion, until chicken is finely ground. Transfer to medium mixing bowl; add ¼ cup bread crumbs, the onion, lemon juice, horseradish, Worcestershire sauce, and pepper and mix well until thoroughly combined.

2. Shape chicken mixture into 2 equal patties. On sheet of wax paper coat patties evenly with remaining bread crumbs.

3. In 10-inch nonstick skillet heat oil; add chicken patties and cook over medium heat until cooked through and lightly browned, 2 to 3 minutes on each side.

4. Onto bottom half of each pita arrange 1 lettuce leaf; top with 1 chicken patty, 2 tomato slices, and 1½ teaspoons dressing. Top each sandwich with remaining pita half.

APPROXIMATE TOTAL TIME: 20 MINUTES

MAKES 2 SERVINGS

Each serving provides: 1 Fat; 2 Proteins; 1 Vegetable; 2 Breads; 15 Optional Calories
Per serving: 310 calories; 21 g protein; 8 g fat; 37 g carbohydrate; 50 mg calcium; 463 mg sodium; 51 mg cholesterol; 2 g dietary fiber (this figure does not include horseradish; nutrition analysis not available)

Chicken Cordon Bleu

2 thin chicken cutlets (3 ounces each)
2 slices *each* turkey-ham and reduced-fat Swiss cheese (½ ounce each)
1 tablespoon plus 2 teaspoons Dijon-style mustard, divided
1 teaspoon honey
⅓ cup plus 2 teaspoons plain dried bread crumbs
2 teaspoons vegetable oil
½ cup canned ready-to-serve low-sodium chicken broth
2 teaspoons all-purpose flour
1 tablespoon sour cream

1. Preheat oven to 375°F. Top each chicken cutlet with 1 slice turkey-ham and 1 slice cheese; starting from the narrow end, roll each cutlet jelly-roll fashion. Secure with toothpicks.

2. In small mixing bowl combine 1 tablespoon mustard and the honey; spread half of the mixture evenly over each chicken roll.

3. On sheet of wax paper arrange bread crumbs; turn chicken rolls in bread crumbs, coating all sides and using all of the bread crumbs. Arrange chicken rolls on nonstick baking sheet and drizzle each with 1 teaspoon oil. Bake until chicken is cooked through, 20 to 25 minutes.

4. While chicken is baking prepare sauce. In small saucepan combine broth and flour, stirring to dissolve flour. Cook over medium-high heat, stirring frequently, until mixture thickens, 3 to 4 minutes. Reduce heat to low and stir in sour cream and remaining mustard; cook, stirring occasionally, 3 to 4 minutes longer *(do not boil)*.

5. To serve, remove toothpicks and cut each chicken roll crosswise into 4 equal slices. Onto each of 2 serving plates pour half of the sauce and top with 4 chicken roll slices.

APPROXIMATE TOTAL TIME: 40 MINUTES (includes baking time)

MAKES 2 SERVINGS

Each serving provides: 1 Fat; 3 Proteins; 1 Bread; 60 Optional Calories
Per serving: 329 calories; 31 g protein; 12 g fat; 22 g carbohydrate; 218 mg calcium; 750 mg sodium; 63 mg cholesterol; 1 g dietary fiber

Chicken in Flavored Vinegar ⬡

2 teaspoons olive *or* vegetable oil
2 chicken cutlets (¼ pound each)
1 cup sliced onions
½ cup sliced celery
1 small garlic clove, minced
3 tablespoons raspberry,
    balsamic, *or* red wine vinegar
1 tablespoon sour cream
1 teaspoon *each* country Dijon-
    style mustard and tomato paste
2 large plum tomatoes, blanched,
    peeled, seeded, and finely
    chopped
1 tablespoon finely chopped fresh
    Italian (flat-leaf) parsley

We recommend raspberry or bal-
samic vinegar for this unusual dish.

1. In 9-inch nonstick skillet heat oil; add chicken and cook over high heat until golden, 3 to 4 minutes on each side. Transfer to plate; set aside.

2. In same skillet combine onions, celery, and garlic and cook over medium-high heat, stirring occasionally, until celery is tender-crisp, about 3 minutes. Stir in vinegar, sour cream, mustard, and tomato paste; cook over medium-high heat, stirring constantly, until mixture thickens, 2 to 3 minutes.

3. Stir in plum tomatoes and bring mixture to a boil. Reduce heat to low and return chicken to skillet; cover and cook until chicken is heated through, 3 to 4 minutes. Sprinkle with parsley.

APPROXIMATE TOTAL TIME: 30 MINUTES

MAKES 2 SERVINGS

Each serving provides: 1 Fat; 3 Proteins; 2½ Vegetables; 20 Optional Calories
Per serving: 232 calories; 28 g protein; 8 g fat; 11 g carbohydrate; 60 mg calcium; 207 mg sodium; 69 mg cholesterol; 3 g dietary fiber

Chicken-in-the-Rye

2 tablespoons rye *or* all-purpose
  flour
½ teaspoon caraway seed,
  crushed
2 thin chicken cutlets (3 ounces
  each)
2 teaspoons vegetable oil
1 ounce diced fully cooked
  smoked ham
¼ cup chopped onion
1 teaspoon all-purpose flour
¼ cup canned ready-to-serve
  low-sodium chicken broth
½ teaspoon *each* Dijon-style
  mustard and chopped fresh dill
¼ cup plain low-fat yogurt
Garnish: dill sprigs

1. On sheet of wax paper combine rye flour and caraway seed. Dredge chicken in flour mixture, coating both sides, and set aside.

2. In 10-inch nonstick skillet heat oil; add chicken and cook over medium-high heat until cooked through, 3 to 4 minutes on each side. Remove from skillet; set aside and keep warm.

3. In same skillet combine ham and onion and cook over medium-high heat, stirring frequently, until onion is softened, 1 to 2 minutes. Sprinkle all-purpose flour over ham-onion mixture and stir quickly to combine; continuing to stir, add broth, mustard, and dill. Reduce heat to medium-low and cook, stirring frequently, until mixture thickens, 3 to 4 minutes. Stir in yogurt *(do not boil)*.

4. To serve, place chicken on serving platter, top with ham-onion sauce, and garnish with dill sprigs.

APPROXIMATE TOTAL TIME: 25 MINUTES

MAKES 2 SERVINGS

Each serving provides: ¼ Milk; 1 Fat; 2½ Proteins; ¼ Vegetable; 45 Optional Calories
Per serving: 214 calories; 25 g protein; 7 g fat; 10 g carbohydrate; 74 mg calcium; 290 mg sodium; 59 mg cholesterol; 1 g dietary fiber (this figure does not include caraway seed; nutrition analysis not available)

Chicken 'n' Biscuits

¼ cup *each* chopped onion and
   celery
3 tablespoons whipped cream
   cheese
1 teaspoon cornstarch
½ packet (about ½ teaspoon)
   instant chicken broth and
   seasoning mix
3 ounces cooked, skinned, and
   boned chicken, cut into cubes
½ cup *each* frozen whole-kernel
   corn and finely diced red *or*
   green bell pepper
Dash crushed red pepper
2 ready-to-bake refrigerated
   buttermilk flaky biscuits
   (1 ounce each); cut in half
   horizontally and baked
   according to package directions

*For variety, serve this creamy
chicken-vegetable mixture over rice
or noodles rather than biscuits.*

1. Spray 1-quart saucepan with nonstick cooking spray and heat; add onion and celery and cook over medium-high heat, stirring frequently, until onion is translucent, about 1 minute.

2. In small mixing bowl combine *½ cup water*, the cream cheese, cornstarch, and broth mix, stirring to dissolve cornstarch; add to onion-celery mixture. Reduce heat to medium and, using a wire whisk, cook, stirring, until mixture thickens slightly, 2 to 3 minutes.

3. Add remaining ingredients except biscuits to onion-celery mixture and cook, stirring frequently, until corn is heated through, about 5 minutes.

4. To serve, arrange biscuit halves on serving platter and top with chicken mixture.

APPROXIMATE TOTAL TIME: 25 MINUTES

MAKES 2 SERVINGS

Each serving provides: 1½ Proteins; 1 Vegetable; 1½ Breads; 60 Optional Calories
Per serving: 273 calories; 17 g protein; 12 g fat; 26 g carbohydrate; 30 mg calcium; 648 mg sodium; 52 mg cholesterol; 2 g dietary fiber (this figure does not include biscuits; nutrition analysis not available)

Chicken Pot Pie

2 teaspoons margarine
I cup *each* sliced mushrooms and
   broccoli florets
½ cup *each* diced onion and
   sliced carrot
¼ pound cooked, skinned, and
   boned chicken, cubed
I teaspoon all-purpose flour
½ cup canned ready-to-serve
   low-sodium chicken broth
I cup skim *or* nonfat milk
I egg white
⅓ cup plus 2 teaspoons
   buttermilk baking mix

*Use leftover cooked chicken in this
tasty pie.*

I. In 9-inch nonstick skillet melt margarine; add vegetables and sauté over medium heat until carrot is tender-crisp, 2 to 3 minutes. Add chicken and stir to combine.

2. Sprinkle flour over vegetable-chicken mixture and stir quickly to combine; cook, stirring constantly, for I minute. Continuing to stir, gradually add broth; bring mixture to a boil. Reduce heat to low and let simmer until mixture thickens, about 5 minutes.

3. Preheat oven to 350°F. In small mixing bowl add milk and egg white to baking mix and stir until thoroughly combined.

4. Spray 8-inch pie plate with nonstick cooking spray; spoon vegetable-chicken mixture into plate. Stir baking mix mixture and spread evenly over vegetable-chicken mixture. Bake until topping is golden brown, about 15 minutes.

APPROXIMATE TOTAL TIME: 35 MINUTES (includes baking time)

MAKES 2 SERVINGS

Each serving provides: ½ Milk; I Fat; 2 Proteins; 3 Vegetables; I Bread; 45 Optional Calories
Per serving: 346 calories; 28 g protein; 12 g fat; 32 g carbohydrate; 239 mg calcium; 487 mg sodium; 53 mg cholesterol; 2 g dietary fiber (this figure does not include broccoli florets; nutrition analysis not available)

Chicken Saté

¼ cup plain low-fat yogurt
1 teaspoon *each* minced fresh
   garlic and pared gingerroot
¼ teaspoon curry powder
5 ounces skinned and boned
   chicken breast, cut into twelve
   ¾-inch cubes
1 tablespoon peanut butter
1 teaspoon *each* cornstarch,
   lemon juice, and reduced-
   sodium soy sauce

1. In small mixing bowl combine yogurt, garlic, gingerroot, and curry powder; add chicken and turn to coat. Cover and refrigerate at least 30 minutes or overnight.

2. Onto each of six 6-inch wooden skewers arrange 2 chicken cubes, reserving marinade. Arrange skewers like spokes of a wheel on microwavable plate; cover and microwave on High (100%) for 2 minutes, rotating plate ½ turn halfway through cooking. Let stand 1 minute until chicken is cooked through.

3. In small microwavable mixing bowl combine reserved marinade, the remaining ingredients, and *1 teaspoon water*, stirring to dissolve cornstarch. Microwave on Medium-High (70%) for 1 minute, stirring once halfway through cooking.

4. To serve, arrange skewers on serving platter with bowl of sauce for dipping.

APPROXIMATE TOTAL TIME: 15 MINUTES (does not include marinating time)

MAKES 2 SERVINGS

Each serving provides: ¼ Milk; ½ Fat; 2½ Proteins; 5 Optional Calories
Per serving: 155 calories; 20 g protein; 5 g fat; 6 g carbohydrate; 68 mg calcium; 205 mg sodium; 43 mg cholesterol; 1 g dietary fiber

Chicken with Artichoke Hearts ▽Ⓢ

½ cup *each* julienne-cut
(matchstick pieces) red bell
pepper and thawed frozen
artichoke hearts

1 garlic clove, minced

1 teaspoon vegetable oil

2 tablespoons dry white table
wine

1 teaspoon cornstarch

¼ teaspoon Italian seasoning

7 ounces skinned and boned
chicken breast, cut into
¼-inch-thick strips

6 large pitted black olives, cut
into quarters

1 tablespoon rinsed drained
capers

1. Spray 1-quart microwavable casserole with non-stick cooking spray; add pepper, artichoke hearts, garlic, and oil and stir to coat. Cover and microwave on High (100%) for 1 minute.

2. In small mixing bowl combine wine, cornstarch, and Italian seasoning, stirring to dissolve cornstarch; stir into pepper-artichoke heart mixture. Add chicken, olives, and capers and stir to combine.

3. Cover and microwave on Medium-High (70%) for 4 minutes, stirring once halfway through cooking. Let stand 1 minute until chicken is cooked through.

APPROXIMATE TOTAL TIME: 20 MINUTES

MAKES 2 SERVINGS

Each serving provides: 1 Fat; 2½ Proteins; 1 Vegetable; 20 Optional Calories
Per serving: 192 calories; 24 g protein; 6 g fat; 7 g carbohydrate; 38 mg calcium; 391 mg sodium; 58 mg cholesterol; 2 g dietary fiber (this figure does not include capers; nutrition analysis not available)

Chicken with Herb-Caper Sauce ⬦Ⓢ

1 tablespoon chopped fresh
   rosemary *or* ½ teaspoon
   rosemary leaves
1 tablespoon lemon juice
2 teaspoons olive *or* vegetable
   oil, divided
1 small garlic clove, mashed
½ pound thin chicken cutlets
1 cup quartered small mushrooms
¼ cup *each* dry white table wine
   and canned ready-to-serve low-
   sodium chicken broth
1 tablespoon rinsed drained
   capers
⅛ teaspoon poultry seasoning

*This recipe requires a little time for
marinating, but the flavor it adds is
well worth it.*

1. In shallow glass or stainless-steel bowl combine rosemary, lemon juice, 1 teaspoon oil, and the garlic, stirring well; add chicken and turn to coat. Let stand at room temperature for 15 minutes.

2. Spray 9-inch nonstick skillet with nonstick cooking spray; add remaining oil and heat. Add chicken, reserving marinade, and cook over high heat until golden, 3 to 4 minutes on each side. Transfer to plate; set aside.

3. In same skillet cook mushrooms over medium-high heat until browned, about 4 minutes. Stir in remaining ingredients and reserved marinade and bring mixture to a boil. Reduce heat to low and return chicken to skillet; cook until chicken is heated through, 2 to 3 minutes.

APPROXIMATE TOTAL TIME: 20 MINUTES (does not include marinating time)

MAKES 2 SERVINGS

Each serving provides: 1 Fat; 3 Proteins; 1 Vegetable; 30 Optional Calories
Per serving: 202 calories; 27 g protein; 6 g fat; 3 g carbohydrate; 24 mg calcium; 195 mg sodium; 66 mg cholesterol; 0.5 g dietary fiber (this figure does not include capers; nutrition analysis not available)

Creamy Chicken Fettuccine

1 teaspoon vegetable oil
1 chicken cutlet (3 ounces)
½ cup sliced shiitake *or* white
   mushrooms
1 garlic clove, minced
1 teaspoon all-purpose flour
½ cup canned ready-to-serve
   low-sodium chicken broth
¼ cup evaporated skimmed milk
2 tablespoons whipped cream
   cheese
¾ ounce grated Parmesan cheese
⅛ teaspoon white pepper
1½ cups cooked fettuccine (hot)

1. In 10-inch nonstick skillet heat oil; add chicken and cook over medium-high heat until tender, 2 to 3 minutes on each side.

2. Remove chicken from skillet and cut into ½-inch cubes; set aside.

3. In same skillet combine mushrooms and garlic and cook over medium-high heat, stirring occasionally, for 1 minute. Sprinkle with flour and stir quickly to combine; continuing to stir, add chicken broth and milk. Reduce heat to low and let simmer, stirring frequently, until mixture thickens, 2 to 3 minutes. Stir in cheeses and pepper; return chicken to skillet and cook, stirring frequently, until chicken is heated through, 2 to 3 minutes.

4. To serve, on serving platter arrange fettuccine; top with chicken mixture.

APPROXIMATE TOTAL TIME: 25 MINUTES

MAKES 2 SERVINGS

Each serving provides: ¼ Milk; ½ Fat; 1½ Proteins; ½ Vegetable; 1½ Breads; 50 Optional Calories
Per serving: 342 calories; 23 g protein; 11 g fat; 35 g carbohydrate; 266 mg calcium; 314 mg sodium; 81 mg cholesterol; 3 g dietary fiber

Microwave Brunswick Stew ⏷F ⏷S

1 cup canned Italian tomatoes (reserve liquid), seeded and diced

¼ cup *each* chopped onion, dry white table wine, and canned ready-to-serve low-sodium chicken broth

1 tablespoon *each* all-purpose flour and Worcestershire sauce

1 small ear fresh *or* thawed frozen corn on the cob (5 inches long), cut into 4 equal pieces

½ cup *each* frozen okra, sliced, and frozen green lima beans

¾ pound chicken breasts, skinned and cut into halves

Corn on the cob makes an appearance in this satisfying stew.

1. In 3-quart microwavable casserole combine tomatoes with reserved liquid, onion, wine, broth, flour, and Worcestershire sauce, stirring to dissolve flour.

2. Add corn, okra, and lima beans; arrange chicken pieces over vegetables with meatier parts facing toward center of casserole.

3. Cover and microwave on High (100%) for 15 minutes, stirring once and rotating casserole ½ turn every 3 minutes.

APPROXIMATE TOTAL TIME: 25 MINUTES

MAKES 2 SERVINGS

Each serving provides: 3 Proteins; 1¾ Vegetables; 1 Bread; 45 Optional Calories
Per serving: 292 calories; 33 g protein; 3 g fat; 30 g carbohydrate; 104 mg calcium; 391 mg sodium; 66 mg cholesterol; 9 g dietary fiber

Oriental Chicken Salad with Peanuts ▽ⓒ

2 tablespoons reduced-sodium
  soy sauce
1 tablespoon creamy peanut
  butter
¼ teaspoon *each* minced pared
  gingerroot, minced garlic, and
  Chinese sesame oil
¾ teaspoon peanut oil
Dash ground red pepper
1 cup cooked thin spaghetti
3 ounces diced cooked chicken
½ cup rinsed drained bean
  sprouts
¼ cup sliced scallions (green
  onions)
½ ounce unsalted shelled roasted
  peanuts
1 cup shredded lettuce

Using leftover cooked chicken and cooked spaghetti will speed the preparation of this recipe.

1. In blender combine soy sauce, *1 tablespoon water*, the peanut butter, gingerroot, garlic, oils, and pepper and process until thoroughly combined. Set aside.

2. In medium mixing bowl combine remaining ingredients except lettuce; add soy sauce mixture and toss to coat.

3. On serving platter arrange lettuce; top with spaghetti mixture.

APPROXIMATE TOTAL TIME: 15 MINUTES

MAKES 2 SERVINGS

Each serving provides: 1½ Fats; 2½ Proteins; 1¾ Vegetables; 1 Bread
Per serving: 295 calories; 21 g protein; 14 g fat; 24 g carbohydrate; 48 mg calcium; 680 mg sodium; 38 mg cholesterol; 3 g dietary fiber

Variation: Oriental Chicken Salad—Omit peanuts from recipe. In Serving Information decrease Fat to 1 and Proteins to 2.
Per serving: 252 calories; 19 g protein; 10 g fat; 22 g carbohydrate; 48 mg calcium; 680 mg sodium; 38 mg cholesterol; 2 g dietary fiber

Pacific Chicken ⑤

2 teaspoons olive *or* vegetable oil
7 ounces thin chicken cutlets
½ cup *each* quartered mushrooms and drained canned pineapple chunks (no sugar added)
1 tablespoon dark rum
¼ cup canned ready-to-serve low-sodium chicken broth
½ cup sliced scallions (green onions)
½ ounce macadamia nuts, chopped

Macadamia nuts, rum, and pineapple combine to give this dish a tropical flavor.

1. In 9-inch nonstick skillet heat oil; add chicken and cook over high heat until golden, 3 to 4 minutes on each side. Transfer to plate and keep warm.

2. In same skillet cook mushrooms over medium-high heat, stirring frequently, until browned, about 2 minutes. Add pineapple and stir to combine; stir in rum.

3. Stir in broth and bring mixture to a boil. Reduce heat to low; return chicken to skillet and turn to coat with mushroom-pineapple mixture. Stir in scallions and nuts and cook until thoroughly heated.

APPROXIMATE TOTAL TIME: 20 MINUTES

MAKES 2 SERVINGS

Each serving provides: 1 Fat; 3 Proteins; 1 Vegetable; ½ Fruit; 45 Optional Calories
Per serving: 267 calories; 25 g protein; 11 g fat; 13 g carbohydrate; 40 mg calcium; 74 mg sodium; 58 mg cholesterol; 1 g dietary fiber (this figure does not include macadamia nuts; nutrition analysis not available)

Spicy Oriental Chicken ⟨F⟩

2 tablespoons reduced-sodium
    soy sauce
1 tablespoon *each* dry sherry and
    honey
1 small garlic clove, minced
1 teaspoon minced pared
    gingerroot
Dash *each* Chinese five-spice
    powder and crushed red pepper
½ pound thinly sliced skinned
    and boned chicken breasts
1½ teaspoons peanut *or*
    vegetable oil
½ cup *each* diagonally sliced
    scallions (green onions), red
    bell pepper strips, and
    diagonally thinly sliced carrot
½ teaspoon Chinese sesame oil
1 teaspoon sesame seed, toasted

*Marinating the chicken for a short
time in a mixture of seasonings im-
parts added flavor.*

1. In shallow glass or stainless-steel mixing bowl combine soy sauce, sherry, honey, garlic, gingerroot, five-spice powder, and crushed red pepper; add chicken and turn to coat. Let stand for 15 minutes.

2. In 9-inch nonstick skillet heat peanut oil; add chicken, reserving marinade, and cook over high heat, stirring occasionally, until golden, 3 to 4 minutes. Push chicken to side of skillet and add scallions, bell pepper, and carrot. Cover and cook until carrot is tender, about 2 minutes.

3. Stir in reserved marinade and Chinese sesame oil and bring mixture to a boil; cook, stirring constantly, until liquid evaporates, 1 to 2 minutes. Sprinkle with sesame seed.

APPROXIMATE TOTAL TIME: 25 MINUTES (does not include marinating time)

MAKES 2 SERVINGS

Each serving provides: 1 Fat; 3 Proteins; 1½ Vegetables; 45 Optional Calories
Per serving: 252 calories; 28 g protein; 7 g fat; 17 g carbohydrate; 44 mg calcium; 687 mg sodium; 66 mg cholesterol; 2 g dietary fiber (this figure does not include sesame seed; nutrition analysis not available)

Sweet and Savory Chicken Ⓕ Ⓢ

2 chicken cutlets (¼ pound each)
2 teaspoons all-purpose flour
1 tablespoon plus 1 teaspoon
  reduced-calorie margarine (tub)
1 cup *each* sliced mushrooms and
  sliced thoroughly washed leeks
  (white portion and some
  green)
1 small garlic clove, minced
4 large plum tomatoes, blanched,
  peeled, seeded, and chopped
2 tablespoons *each* balsamic *or*
  red wine vinegar and dry white
  table wine
1 tablespoon *each* chopped fresh
  Italian (flat-leaf) parsley and
  honey

1. On sheet of wax paper dredge chicken in flour.

2. In 9-inch nonstick skillet melt margarine; add chicken and cook over high heat until golden, 3 to 4 minutes on each side. Transfer to plate; set aside.

3. In same skillet combine mushrooms, leeks, and garlic and sauté over medium-high heat until leeks are tender-crisp, about 2 minutes. Stir in remaining ingredients and bring mixture to a boil.

4. Reduce heat to low and return chicken to skillet; cover and let simmer until chicken is heated through, about 3 minutes.

Many of our recipes are flavored with a small amount of wine. Make sure the wine you use in cooking is a wine that is good enough to drink.

APPROXIMATE TOTAL TIME: 30 MINUTES

MAKES 2 SERVINGS

Each serving provides: 1 Fat; 3 Proteins; 4 Vegetables; 55 Optional Calories
Per serving: 273 calories; 29 g protein; 6 g fat; 25 g carbohydrate; 58 mg calcium; 176 mg sodium; 66 mg cholesterol; 3 g dietary fiber

Franks and Beans Pizza ▽C̲

½ cup finely chopped onion
4 ounces (½ cup) canned baked
  beans (without meat)
1 large pita (2 ounces), toasted
3 ounces chicken frankfurters, cut
  into ½-inch-thick slices
¾ ounce reduced-fat Cheddar
  cheese, shredded

Pizza lovers will enjoy this recipe.

1. Preheat oven to 400°F. Spray small nonstick skillet with nonstick cooking spray and heat; add onion, cover, and cook over medium heat until translucent, about 2 minutes. Stir in beans; cover and cook until heated, about 3 minutes.

2. On baking sheet arrange pita; top with frankfurters and onion-bean mixture. Sprinkle with cheese. Bake until cheese is melted, 1 to 2 minutes.

3. To serve, cut into quarters.

APPROXIMATE TOTAL TIME: 15 MINUTES (includes baking time)

MAKES 2 SERVINGS

Each serving provides: 2 Proteins; ½ Vegetable; 1½ Breads; 25 Optional Calories
Per serving: 296 calories; 14 g protein; 11 g fat; 36 g carbohydrate; 177 mg calcium; 1,065 mg sodium; 50 mg cholesterol; 5 g dietary fiber

Braised Cornish Hen

1 Cornish hen (1 pound*), cut in half and skinned
1 tablespoon all-purpose flour
2 teaspoons olive *or* vegetable oil
1 cup *each* frozen pearl onions and sliced celery (1-inch pieces)
6 ounces baby carrots
¼ cup dry sherry
1 packet instant chicken broth and seasoning mix
2 teaspoons chopped fresh thyme *or* ½ teaspoon thyme leaves
⅛ teaspoon white pepper

1. On sheet of wax paper dredge hen halves in flour, coating all sides.

2. In 4-quart Dutch oven or saucepot heat oil; add hen halves and cook over medium-high heat until lightly browned, 2 to 3 minutes on each side. Transfer to plate and set aside.

3. In same pot combine onions, celery, and carrots and cook, over medium-high heat, stirring frequently, until onions are lightly browned, 2 to 3 minutes. Stir in *1 cup water*, the sherry, broth mix, and seasonings.

4. Return hen halves to pot. Reduce heat to low, partially cover, and let simmer, stirring occasionally, until hen halves are tender, 25 to 30 minutes.

* A 1-pound hen will yield about 6 ounces cooked poultry.

APPROXIMATE TOTAL TIME: 45 MINUTES

MAKES 2 SERVINGS

Each serving provides: 1 Fat; 3 Proteins; 4 Vegetables; 45 Optional Calories
Per serving: 347 calories; 28 g protein; 11 g fat; 26 g carbohydrate; 101 mg calcium; 663 mg sodium; 76 mg cholesterol; 4 g dietary fiber

Grilled Cornish Hen with Stuffing $\boxed{S}$

1 Cornish hen (about 1 pound*), cut in half
2 tablespoons lemon juice
1 tablespoon plus 1 teaspoon reduced-calorie margarine (tub), divided
1 small Golden Delicious apple (about ¼ pound), cored and chopped
½ cup *each* chopped celery and onion
1 small garlic clove, minced
½ teaspoon poultry seasoning
1 cup canned ready-to-serve low-sodium chicken broth, divided
6 small canned chestnuts (no sugar added), chopped
½ ounce seasoned croutons
2 teaspoons *each* all-purpose flour and honey

1. Preheat broiler. Spray rack in broiling pan with nonstick cooking spray; set hen halves on rack, skin-side down. Broil 6 to 8 inches from heat source, basting with lemon juice and turning once, about 8 minutes on each side, or until thickest portion of hen is pierced with a knife and juices run clear.

2. While hen halves are broiling, prepare stuffing. In 9-inch nonstick skillet melt 2 teaspoons margarine; add apple, celery, onion, garlic, and poultry seasoning and sauté over medium-high heat until apple is tender-crisp, 3 to 4 minutes. Stir in ½ cup broth and bring mixture to a boil. Add chestnuts and croutons and cook, stirring constantly, until liquid has evaporated, about 2 minutes. Transfer to serving platter and keep warm.

3. In same skillet melt remaining margarine; add flour and stir quickly to combine; cook, stirring constantly, for 1 minute. Stir in remaining broth and the honey and cook, stirring constantly, until mixture thickens, about 4 minutes.

4. To serve, remove and discard skin from hen. Arrange hen halves on serving platter; top with sauce and serve with stuffing.

* A 1-pound hen will yield about 6 ounces cooked poultry.

APPROXIMATE TOTAL TIME: 30 MINUTES

MAKES 2 SERVINGS

Each serving provides: 1 Fat; 3 Proteins; 1 Vegetable; 1 Bread; ½ Fruit; 50 Optional Calories
Per serving: 345 calories; 28 g protein; 13 g fat; 30 g carbohydrate; 59 mg calcium; 313 mg sodium; 76 mg cholesterol; 2 g dietary fiber (this figure does not include chestnuts; nutrition analysis not available)

Roast Duck with Cherry Relish ▽C ▽S

4 duck breasts (6 ounces each)
2 teaspoons olive *or* vegetable oil
1 cup *each* diced red bell peppers
  and red onions
1 tablespoon *each* granulated
  sugar and lemon juice
½ teaspoon cornstarch
48 large fresh *or* frozen pitted
  cherries (no sugar added)

---

*Duck breast is ready to serve in far
less time than it would take to prepare a whole duck, but it is just as
elegant.*

1. Preheat oven to 375°F. Spray rack in roasting pan with nonstick cooking spray. Arrange duck breasts, skin-side up, on rack and roast until skin is crisp and browned, about 20 minutes.

2. While duck breasts are roasting prepare relish. In 1-quart saucepan heat oil; add peppers and onions and cook over medium heat, stirring occasionally, until softened, 2 to 3 minutes.

3. In 1-cup liquid measure combine ½ *cup water*, the sugar, lemon juice, and cornstarch, stirring to dissolve cornstarch. Stir into pepper-onion mixture and cook, stirring constantly, until mixture thickens. Reduce heat to low; add cherries and let simmer until thoroughly heated, about 5 minutes.

4. To serve, remove and discard skin from duck. Serve duck breasts topped with relish.

APPROXIMATE TOTAL TIME: 30 MINUTES (includes baking time)

MAKES 4 SERVINGS

Each serving provides: ½ Fat; 3 Proteins; 1 Vegetable; 1 Fruit; 15 Optional Calories
Per serving: 198 calories; 12 g protein; 8 g fat; 21 g carbohydrate; 29 mg calcium; 30 mg sodium; 38 mg cholesterol; 2 g dietary fiber

Tex-Mex Turkey Cutlets

2 taco shells (1 ounce), made
   into crumbs
1 tablespoon uncooked yellow
   cornmeal
2 tablespoons low-fat buttermilk
   (1% milk fat)
1 teaspoon *each* chili powder and
   freshly squeezed lime juice
2 turkey cutlets (¼ pound each)
2 teaspoons vegetable oil
1 medium tomato, seeded and
   diced
½ cup mixed vegetable juice
2 tablespoons chopped scallion
   (green onion)
1 tablespoon seeded and minced
   mild chili pepper

1. On sheet of wax paper combine taco shell crumbs and cornmeal; set aside.

2. In small mixing bowl combine buttermilk, chili powder, and lime juice and stir to combine.

3. Dip turkey cutlets into buttermilk mixture and then dredge in cornmeal mixture, coating both sides and using all of the mixtures. Arrange cutlets on nonstick baking sheet; drizzle ½ teaspoon oil over each cutlet.

4. Broil 5 to 6 inches from heat source until lightly browned, 6 to 8 minutes. Turn cutlets over, drizzle each with ½ teaspoon oil, and continue broiling until cutlets are tender, about 5 minutes longer.

5. While cutlets are broiling prepare sauce. In small mixing bowl combine remaining ingredients.

6. To serve, transfer cutlets to serving platter and top with tomato mixture.

APPROXIMATE TOTAL TIME: 30 MINUTES

MAKES 2 SERVINGS

Each serving provides: 1 Fat; 3 Proteins; 1½ Vegetables; ¾ Bread; 5 Optional Calories
Per serving: 352 calories; 29 g protein; 12 g fat; 32 g carbohydrate; 51 mg calcium; 323 mg sodium; 71 mg cholesterol; 4 g dietary fiber

Turkey Cutlets Tonnato ⩔ᶠ ⩔ˢ

2 thin turkey cutlets (3 ounces each)
2 teaspoons dry white table wine
Dash salt
1 ounce drained canned tuna (packed in water)
1 tablespoon plus 1 teaspoon *each* reduced-calorie mayonnaise and plain low-fat yogurt
2 teaspoons rinsed drained capers, divided
1 teaspoon lemon juice
Dash pepper

Our version of this classic dish tops turkey with a sauce that includes canned tuna.

1. Spray 1-quart microwavable casserole with non-stick cooking spray. Arrange turkey cutlets in casserole; pour in wine and sprinkle with salt. Cover and microwave on Medium-High (70%) for 1½ minutes. Let stand 1 minute to complete cooking. Transfer turkey to serving platter; cover and refrigerate until chilled, about 30 minutes.

2. In blender combine tuna and *1 tablespoon water* and process until pureed, about 1 minute. Add mayonnaise, yogurt, 1 teaspoon capers, the lemon juice, and pepper and process until pureed, about 1 minute. Pour over turkey and garnish with remaining capers.

APPROXIMATE TOTAL TIME: 10 MINUTES (does not include chilling time)

MAKES 2 SERVINGS

Each serving provides: 1 Fat; 2½ Proteins; 10 Optional Calories
Per serving: 152 calories; 25 g protein; 4 g fat; 2 g carbohydrate; 31 mg calcium; 308 mg sodium, 63 mg cholesterol; dietary fiber data not available

Turkey Paprika

2 teaspoons vegetable oil
2 thin turkey cutlets (¼ pound each)
½ cup sliced mushrooms
¼ cup chopped onion
1 tablespoon all-purpose flour
½ cup canned ready-to-serve low-sodium chicken broth
¼ cup plain low-fat yogurt
1 teaspoon *each* paprika and chopped fresh parsley
⅛ teaspoon white pepper
1 cup cooked wide noodles (hot)

1. In 10-inch nonstick skillet heat oil; add turkey cutlets and cook over medium-high heat, until tender, 2 to 3 minutes on each side. Transfer to plate and set aside.

2. In same skillet combine mushrooms and onion and cook, stirring occasionally, until mushrooms are softened, 1 to 2 minutes. Sprinkle flour over vegetables and stir quickly to combine; continuing to stir, add broth. Cook over medium heat, stirring frequently, until mixture thickens, about 5 minutes.

3. In small mixing bowl combine yogurt, paprika, parsley, and pepper; stir in 1 tablespoon broth from vegetable mixture. Stir yogurt-broth mixture into skillet; return cutlets to skillet. Cook until cutlets are heated through, 2 to 3 minutes *(do not boil)*.

4. To serve, on serving platter arrange noodles; top with turkey mixture.

APPROXIMATE TOTAL TIME: 25 MINUTES

MAKES 2 SERVINGS

Each serving provides: ¼ Milk; 1 Fat; 3 Proteins; ¾ Vegetable; 1 Bread; 25 Optional Calories
Per serving: 324 calories; 33 g protein; 9 g fat; 27 g carbohydrate; 83 mg calcium; 113 mg sodium; 97 mg cholesterol; 2 g dietary fiber

Turkey with Orange Sauce ⌄Ⓕ ⌄Ⓢ

½ pound skinned and boned
  turkey breast, thinly sliced
1 tablespoon all-purpose flour
1 tablespoon plus 1 teaspoon
  reduced-calorie margarine (tub)
½ cup *each* red bell pepper strips
  and sliced thoroughly washed
  leeks (white portion only)
½ cup *each* canned ready-to-
  serve low-sodium chicken
  broth and skim *or* nonfat milk
2 tablespoons orange zest*
2 teaspoons chopped fresh
  rosemary *or* ¼ teaspoon
  rosemary leaves
Dash white pepper

1. On sheet of wax paper dredge turkey in flour, coating all sides and reserving any remaining flour.

2. In 9-inch nonstick skillet melt margarine; add turkey and cook over medium heat until golden, 5 to 6 minutes on each side. Transfer to plate and set aside.

3. In same skillet combine bell pepper and leeks and cook over medium heat until bell pepper is tender-crisp, about 3 minutes. Sprinkle any remaining flour over pepper-leek mixture and stir quickly to combine; cook, stirring constantly, for 1 minute.

4. Remove skillet from heat and, continuing to stir, add remaining ingredients; return turkey to skillet. Cover and let simmer over low heat until turkey is heated through and sauce has thickened, about 5 minutes.

* The zest of the orange is the peel without any of the pith (white membrane). To remove zest from orange, use a zester or vegetable peeler; wrap orange in plastic wrap and refrigerate for use at another time.

APPROXIMATE TOTAL TIME: 30 MINUTES

MAKES 2 SERVINGS

Each serving provides: ¼ Milk; 1 Fat; 3 Proteins; 1 Vegetable; 25 Optional Calories
Per serving: 235 calories; 30 g protein; 6 g fat; 13 g carbohydrate; 118 mg calcium; 207 mg sodium; 72 mg cholesterol; 1 g dietary fiber

Grilled Turkey Sandwich (C) (F)

4 slices reduced-calorie wheat *or* white bread (40 calories per slice)
2 teaspoons *each* Dijon-style mustard and pickle relish
2 ounces thinly sliced roast turkey breast
¾ ounce reduced-fat Cheddar *or* Swiss cheese, shredded
¼ cup *each* skim *or* nonfat milk and thawed frozen egg substitute
⅛ teaspoon *each* garlic powder and onion powder
Dash pepper

1. Onto each slice of bread spread ½ teaspoon mustard and ½ teaspoon relish; top each of 2 bread slices with half the turkey, half the cheese, and the remaining bread slices, mustard-relish side down.

2. Using a wire whisk, in shallow small mixing bowl beat together remaining ingredients. Spray 10-inch nonstick skillet with nonstick cooking spray and heat over medium-high heat. Dip each sandwich in milk mixture, coating both sides and using all of mixture. Add sandwiches to skillet and cook for 1 minute on each side. Reduce heat to medium and cook until bread is golden, about 3 minutes longer on each side.

3. To serve, cut each sandwich in half.

APPROXIMATE TOTAL TIME: 15 MINUTES

MAKES 2 SERVINGS

Each serving provides: 2 Proteins; 1 Bread; 20 Optional Calories
Per serving with Cheddar cheese: 199 calories; 20 g protein; 3 g fat; 23 g carbohydrate; 192 mg calcium; 540 mg sodium; 28 mg cholesterol; dietary fiber data not available
With Swiss cheese: 199 calories; 21 g protein; 3 g fat; 23 g carbohydrate; 227 mg calcium; 482 mg sodium; 28 mg cholesterol; dietary fiber data not available

Sausage and Macaroni Casserole

½ pound sweet Italian-style
  turkey sausage links, cut into
  ½-inch-thick pieces
2 teaspoons olive *or* vegetable oil
1½ cups canned stewed tomatoes
1 cup cooked elbow macaroni
1 teaspoon ketchup
½ teaspoon *each* Dijon-style
  mustard and Worcestershire
  sauce

1. In 1-quart microwavable casserole combine sausage and oil; microwave on High (100%) for 5 minutes, stirring once halfway through cooking. Add remaining ingredients and stir to combine; microwave on High for 5 minutes, stirring once halfway through cooking.

APPROXIMATE TOTAL TIME: 15 MINUTES

MAKES 2 SERVINGS

Each serving provides: 1 Fat; 3 Proteins; 1½ Vegetables; 1 Bread; 3 Optional Calories
Per serving: 385 calories; 24 g protein; 18 g fat; 33 g carbohydrate; 85 mg calcium; 1,149 mg sodium; 69 mg cholesterol; 1 g dietary fiber (this figure does not include stewed tomatoes; nutrition analysis not available)

Savory Sausage Puddings ▽

5 ounces turkey sausage links,
  cut into 1-inch pieces
½ cup skim *or* nonfat milk
¼ cup thawed frozen egg
  substitute
3 tablespoons all-purpose flour
1 teaspoon vegetable oil
¼ teaspoon *each* onion powder
  and garlic powder
Dash pepper

1. Spray 1-quart microwavable casserole with non-stick cooking spray and arrange sausage in casserole. Cover and microwave on High (100%) for 2 minutes.

2. In blender combine remaining ingredients and process until thoroughly combined, about 1 minute.

3. Spray two 10-ounce custard cups with nonstick cooking spray and spoon half of the sausage into each cup. Pour half of the milk mixture into each cup. Cover each cup and microwave on Medium-High (70%) for 3½ minutes, rotating cups ½ turn after 2 minutes. Let stand 1 minute to complete cooking.

APPROXIMATE TOTAL TIME: 15 MINUTES

MAKES 2 SERVINGS

Each serving provides: ¼ Milk; ½ Fat; 2½ Proteins; ½ Bread
Per serving: 231 calories; 19 g protein; 11 g fat; 13 g carbohydrate; 103 mg calcium; 473 mg sodium; 47 mg cholesterol; 0.3 g dietary fiber

Skillet Sausages with Apple

1 teaspoon margarine
½ pound Italian-style turkey
  sausage links
1 cup sliced onions
½ cup sliced celery
1 small Red Delicious apple
  (about ¼ pound), cored
  and sliced
2 teaspoons all-purpose flour
¾ cup canned ready-to-serve
  low-sodium chicken broth
½ cup apple juice (no sugar
  added)
⅛ teaspoon *each* crushed
  rosemary leaves and pepper

1. In 10-inch nonstick skillet melt margarine; add sausages and sauté over medium-high heat, turning occasionally, until browned on all sides, 4 to 5 minutes.

2. Add onions, celery, and apple and sauté until vegetables are softened, 1 to 2 minutes. Sprinkle with flour and stir quickly to combine; continuing to stir, add remaining ingredients. Reduce heat to low and let simmer, stirring occasionally, until apple is tender, 10 to 15 minutes.

APPROXIMATE TOTAL TIME: 30 MINUTES

MAKES 2 SERVINGS

Each serving provides: ½ Fat; 3 Proteins; 1½ Vegetables; 1 Fruit; 25 Optional Calories
Per serving: 322 calories; 21 g protein; 16 g fat; 25 g carbohydrate; 58 mg calcium; 653 mg sodium; 69 mg cholesterol; 3 g dietary fiber

California Chicken Salad ⬡

1 cup shredded lettuce

¼ pound cooked, skinned, and boned chicken, chilled and thinly sliced

½ small cantaloupe (about 1 pound), pared, seeded, and thinly sliced

¼ medium avocado (about 2 ounces), pared and thinly sliced

2 tablespoons *each* plain low-fat yogurt and mild chunky-style salsa

1 teaspoon *each* minced cilantro (Chinese parsley) *or* Italian (flat-leaf) parsley and lime juice (no sugar added)

Dash pepper

For a perfect summertime lunch, serve this salad with iced tea and warm rolls or biscuits.

1. Onto each of 2 individual plates arrange half of the lettuce; decoratively arrange half of the chicken, cantaloupe, and avocado over lettuce.

2. In small bowl combine remaining ingredients and stir to combine. Spoon over salad.

APPROXIMATE TOTAL TIME: 15 MINUTES

MAKES 2 SERVINGS

Each serving provides: 1 Fat; 2 Proteins; 1⅛ Vegetables; 1 Fruit; 10 Optional Calories
Per serving: 212 calories; 19 g protein; 9 g fat; 15 g carbohydrate; 70 mg calcium; 165 mg sodium; 51 mg cholesterol; 2 g dietary fiber

Chicken-Tahini Salad ⬢C ⬢S

3 ounces cooked, skinned, and
   boned chicken, chilled and cut
   into strips
½ cup *each* diagonally thinly
   sliced scallions (green onions)
   and chopped red bell pepper
¼ cup plain low-fat yogurt
2 tablespoons tahini (sesame
   paste), stirred until smooth
1 tablespoon finely chopped
   cilantro (Chinese parsley) *or*
   Italian (flat-leaf) parsley
2 teaspoons lime juice (no sugar
   added)
1 small garlic clove, minced
Dash *each* ground red pepper and
   ground cumin
8 lettuce leaves, torn into pieces

*This salad requires cooked, skinned,
and boned chicken that has had time
to chill. We suggest you cook it the
night before and refrigerate overnight.*

1. In small mixing bowl combine chicken, scallions, and bell pepper; set aside.

2. In small mixing bowl combine remaining ingredients except lettuce; pour over chicken mixture and toss to coat.

3. On serving platter arrange lettuce; top with chicken mixture.

APPROXIMATE TOTAL TIME: 10 MINUTES

MAKES 2 SERVINGS

Each serving provides: ¼ Milk; 1 Fat; 2½ Proteins; 2 Vegetables
Per serving: 209 calories; 17 g protein; 12 g fat; 10 g carbohydrate; 164 mg calcium; 80 mg sodium; 40 mg cholesterol; 3 g dietary fiber

"Fried" Chicken

⅓ cup plus 2 teaspoons low-fat
   buttermilk (1% milk fat)
1 pound 2 ounces chicken parts,
   skinned
1½ ounces cornflake crumbs
2 teaspoons sesame seed

*Cornflake crumbs provide the crispy
coating for the chicken in this recipe.
Prepare the crumbs by processing
the cereal in a blender or food processor or save time and purchase the
packaged crumbs.*

1. Preheat oven to 350°F. Pour buttermilk into shallow bowl; add chicken and turn to coat.

2. On paper plate combine cornflake crumbs and sesame seed; dredge chicken in crumb-seed mixture.

3. Arrange chicken on nonstick baking sheet and bake until chicken is browned and crispy, about 40 minutes.

APPROXIMATE TOTAL TIME: 50 MINUTES (includes baking time; does not include marinating time)

MAKES 2 SERVINGS

Each serving provides: 3 Proteins; 1 Bread; 40 Optional Calories
Per serving: 280 calories; 28 g protein; 8 g fat; 21 g carbohydrate; 96 mg calcium; 385 mg sodium; 78 mg cholesterol; 0.2 g dietary fiber (this figure does not include sesame seed; nutrition analysis not available)

Turkey, Bean, and Rice Salad ▽C

¼ pound ground turkey
2 teaspoons olive *or* vegetable oil
1 cup mild salsa
4 ounces rinsed drained canned black (turtle) beans
1 tablespoon lime juice (no sugar added)
1 cup cooked quick-cooking rice (hot)
2 cups torn lettuce leaves
¾ ounce reduced-fat Cheddar cheese, shredded

While this recipe is cooking in the microwave oven, have the rice cooking on the range.

1. In 1-quart microwavable casserole combine turkey and oil; microwave on High (100%) for 4 minutes, stirring once every 1½ minutes, until turkey is no longer pink. Stir in salsa, beans, and lime juice; microwave on Medium (50%) for 1 minute until thoroughly heated. Add rice and stir to combine.

2. To serve, on serving platter arrange lettuce; top with turkey mixture and sprinkle with cheese.

APPROXIMATE TOTAL TIME: 20 MINUTES

MAKES 2 SERVINGS

Each serving provides: 1 Fat; 2 Proteins; 3 Vegetables; 2 Breads
Per serving: 366 calories; 20 g protein; 13 g fat; 43 g carbohydrate; 182 mg calcium; 1,038 mg sodium (estimated); 46 mg cholesterol; 4 g dietary fiber

Turkey-Ham and Black-Eyed Pea Salad ⬇C

¼ pound turkey-ham, diced
4 ounces rinsed drained canned
   black-eyed peas
½ cup *each* diced onion, diced
   celery, and shredded carrot
½ medium tomato, chopped
2 tablespoons finely chopped
   Italian (flat-leaf) parsley
1 tablespoon *each* olive oil, red
   wine vinegar, and lemon juice
1 small garlic clove, minced
¼ teaspoon granulated sugar
4 drops hot sauce
8 lettuce leaves

*If you are trying to incorporate le-
gumes into your diet, this recipe of-
fers a tasty opportunity.*

1. In large mixing bowl combine turkey-ham, peas, onion, celery, carrot, tomato, and parsley.

2. In small mixing bowl combine remaining ingredients except lettuce; pour over turkey-ham mixture and toss to coat. Cover and refrigerate until ready to serve.

3. To serve, on serving platter arrange lettuce leaves; toss turkey-ham mixture and spoon onto lettuce leaves.

APPROXIMATE TOTAL TIME: 15 MINUTES (does not include chilling time)

MAKES 2 SERVINGS

Each serving provides: 1½ Fats; 2 Proteins; 3 Vegetables; 1 Bread; 3 Optional Calories
Per serving: 245 calories; 17 g protein; 10 g fat; 23 g carbohydrate; 86 mg calcium; 799 mg sodium (estimated); 0 mg cholesterol; 8 g dietary fiber

Meats

The good word about meats is *leaner*, thanks to improved methods of breeding and feeding livestock. Retail butchers are trimming more fat, and packaged ground meats are often labeled with the percent of fat content. (For the leanest products, select those that read "10% or less fat.") Our recipes take advantage of this health-conscious trend in exotic ways such as Thai-Marinated Steak. Citrus-rich orange juice delicately flavors Orange Veal Marsala and vitamin-packed vegetables add new appeal to favorite foods, as in Lamb with Pepper and Olives. Isn't it great to welcome these meats aboard the nutrition bandwagon?

Beef 'n' Barley Stew ▽F

1 tablespoon tomato paste
1 packet instant beef broth and
  seasoning mix
1½ ounces uncooked medium
  pearl barley
1 cup *each* frozen pearl onions
  and sliced carrots (1-inch
  pieces)
½ cup green beans, cut in half
1 tablespoon all-purpose flour
6 ounces cubed cooked top round
  steak (1-inch pieces)
¼ teaspoon *each* rosemary leaves
  and pepper

Leftover steak can be used as the basis for this flavorful stew.

1. In shallow 1-quart microwavable casserole combine *1 cup water*, the tomato paste, and broth mix, stirring to dissolve tomato paste. Add barley and stir to combine; cover and microwave on High (100%) for 10 minutes, stirring every 2½ minutes.

2. Add onions, carrots, and green beans to barley mixture. Cover and microwave on High for 5 minutes, stirring once and rotating casserole ½ turn halfway through cooking.

3. In 1-cup liquid measure combine ¼ *cup water* and the flour, stirring to dissolve flour. Stir into barley-vegetable mixture. Cover and microwave on High for 5 minutes, until carrots are tender.

4. Add beef, rosemary, and pepper to barley-vegetable mixture and stir to combine. Cover and microwave on High for 2 minutes, until beef is heated through.

APPROXIMATE TOTAL TIME: 30 MINUTES

MAKES 2 SERVINGS

Each serving provides: 3 Proteins; 2½ Vegetables; 1 Bread; 25 Optional Calories
Per serving: 333 calories; 33 g protein; 6 g fat; 37 g carbohydrate; 75 mg calcium; 614 mg sodium; 71 mg cholesterol; 5 g dietary fiber

Beef 'n' Mushrooms on a Roll

2 teaspoons margarine
¾ cup chopped mushrooms
¼ cup diced onion
1 teaspoon all-purpose flour
¼ pound broiled lean ground beef
¼ cup *each* low-fat milk (1% milk fat) and canned ready-to-serve low-sodium chicken broth
2 teaspoons chopped fresh parsley
1 teaspoon Worcestershire sauce
1 whole wheat *or* white hamburger roll (2 ounces), split in half and toasted

This tasty meat mixture can be served over cooked rice, noodles, or with a baked potato.

1. In 10-inch nonstick skillet melt margarine; add mushrooms and onion and sauté over medium-high heat, until onion is softened, about 1 minute. Sprinkle with flour and stir quickly to combine; continuing to stir, cook 1 minute longer.

2. Add remaining ingredients except hamburger roll to mushroom-onion mixture and stir to combine. Reduce heat to medium and cook until mixture thickens slightly, about 3 minutes.

3. To serve, onto each half of roll spoon half of the beef-mushroom mixture.

APPROXIMATE TOTAL TIME: 15 MINUTES

MAKES 2 SERVINGS

Each serving provides: 1 Fat; 2 Proteins; 1 Vegetable; 1 Bread; 25 Optional Calories
Per serving: 295 calories; 19 g protein; 16 g fat; 19 g carbohydrate; 81 mg calcium; 289 mg sodium; 51 mg cholesterol; 3 g dietary fiber

California Burgers

5 ounces ground beef sirloin
1 slice (¾ ounce) reduced-fat
  Monterey Jack cheese,
  cut in half
2 kaiser rolls (1 ounce each);
  each cut in half horizontally
  and lightly toasted
2 lettuce leaves
2 tablespoons ketchup
4 tomato slices
4 slices avocado (½ ounce each),
  pared
¼ cup alfalfa sprouts
1 medium pickle, cut in half

*For that great outdoor flavor, cook
burgers on the barbecue grill.*

1. Preheat broiler. Shape sirloin into 2 equal patties and arrange on rack in broiling pan; broil 5 inches from heat source until medium-rare, 2 to 3 minutes on each side, or until done to taste.

2. Top each burger with half of the cheese and broil until cheese melts, about 1 minute.

3. Onto bottom half of each roll arrange 1 lettuce leaf and 1 burger; then top each with 1 tablespoon ketchup, 2 tomato slices, 2 avocado slices, 2 tablespoons sprouts, and remaining half of roll. Serve each burger with pickle half.

APPROXIMATE TOTAL TIME: 20 MINUTES

MAKES 2 SERVINGS

Each serving provides: 1 Fat; 2½ Proteins; 2⅛ Vegetables; 1 Bread; 15 Optional Calories
Per serving: 303 calories; 24 g protein; 11 g fat; 26 g carbohydrate; 135 mg calcium; 884 mg sodium; 59 mg cholesterol; 2 g dietary fiber

Philly Burgers ▽F

5 ounces ground beef sirloin
2 slices reduced-fat Cheddar
  cheese (½ ounce each)
1 teaspoon margarine
½ cup *each* sliced onion and
  green *or* red bell pepper
2 tablespoons sliced pepperoncini
  peppers (pickled hot peppers)
2 sandwich rolls (2 ounces each);
  each cut in half horizontally

1. Preheat broiler. Shape sirloin into 2 equal patties and arrange on rack in broiling pan; broil 5 inches from heat source until medium-rare, 2 to 3 minutes on each side, or until done to taste.

2. Top each burger with 1 slice of cheese and broil until cheese melts, about 1 minute.

3. While burgers are broiling prepare topping. In 9-inch nonstick skillet melt margarine; add onion and peppers and sauté until lightly browned, 2 to 3 minutes. Stir in ¼ *cup water* and continue cooking until water has evaporated, 1 to 2 minutes.

4. Onto bottom half of each roll arrange 1 burger; top each with half of the onion-pepper mixture and remaining half of roll.

APPROXIMATE TOTAL TIME: 20 MINUTES

MAKES 2 SERVINGS

Each serving provides: ½ Fat; 2½ Proteins; 1⅛ Vegetables; 2 Breads; 10 Optional Calories
Per serving: 379 calories; 27 g protein; 12 g fat; 39 g carbohydrate; 170 mg calcium; 628 mg sodium; 62 mg cholesterol; 2 g dietary fiber

Meatballs with Stewed Tomatoes

5 ounces ground beef

¼ cup *each* part-skim ricotta cheese and thawed frozen egg substitute

1 tablespoon *each* plain dried bread crumbs and chopped fresh basil

2 teaspoons grated Parmesan cheese

1 teaspoon chopped shallot *or* onion

2 cups canned stewed tomatoes

1. Preheat oven to 425°F. In medium mixing bowl thoroughly combine all ingredients except tomatoes. Shape mixture into 6 equal balls. Spray rack set on 8 × 8 × 2-inch baking pan with nonstick cooking spray and arrange meatballs on rack. Bake, turning once, until cooked through, about 20 minutes.

2. In 1-quart saucepan bring tomatoes to a boil. Reduce heat to low and, using the back of a fork, press tomatoes against side of pan, breaking into smaller pieces. Add meatballs to tomatoes and simmer until flavors blend, about 10 minutes.

APPROXIMATE TOTAL TIME: 40 MINUTES (includes baking time)

MAKES 2 SERVINGS

Each serving provides: 3 Proteins; 2 Vegetables; 25 Optional Calories
Per serving: 289 calories; 24 g protein; 13 g fat; 22 g carbohydrate; 221 mg calcium; 820 mg sodium; 69 mg cholesterol; 0.1 g dietary fiber (this figure does not include stewed tomatoes; nutrition analysis not available)

London Broil with Mixed Vegetables ⑤

15 ounces boneless top round
   steak
¼ cup balsamic *or* red wine
   vinegar
1 tablespoon plus 1 teaspoon
   olive *or* vegetable oil
1 cup *each* sliced onions *or*
   shallots, red bell pepper strips,
   and sliced mushrooms
1 small garlic clove, minced
1 package (9 ounces) thawed
   frozen artichoke hearts, cut
   into halves
½ cup canned ready-to-serve
   low-sodium chicken broth
2 tablespoons dry red table wine
1 teaspoon cornstarch
1 tablespoon *each* chopped fresh
   mint and fresh basil *or* ½
   teaspoon basil leaves

*Marinate the steak while preparing
the remainder of this recipe, or marinate the steak overnight in the
refrigerator.*

1. In glass or stainless-steel bowl combine steak and vinegar, turning to coat; set aside.

2. In 10-inch nonstick skillet heat oil; add onions, pepper, mushrooms, and garlic and cook over medium-high heat, stirring occasionally, until pepper is tender-crisp, 3 to 4 minutes. Add artichokes and stir to combine. Reduce heat to medium, cover, and cook for about 5 minutes.

3. In 1-cup liquid measure combine broth, wine, and cornstarch, stirring to dissolve cornstarch; stir into skillet. Cook over low heat, stirring constantly, until mixture thickens slightly. Remove steak from marinade and set aside. Stir marinade, mint, and basil into vegetable mixture and cook, stirring constantly, until mixture comes to a boil, about 2 minutes. Set aside and keep warm.

4. Preheat broiler. Spray rack in broiling pan with nonstick cooking spray; arrange steak on rack and broil until browned and done to taste, 6 to 8 minutes on each side.

5. To serve, thinly slice steak diagonally across the grain and arrange on serving platter; top with vegetable mixture.

APPROXIMATE TOTAL TIME: 30 MINUTES (does not include marinating time)

MAKES 4 SERVINGS

Each serving provides: 1 Fat, 3 Proteins; 2½ Vegetables; 30 Optional Calories
Per serving: 273 calories; 30 g protein; 11 g fat; 12 g carbohydrate; 36 mg calcium; 91 mg sodium; 71 mg cholesterol; 4 g dietary fiber

Steak with Madeira-Mushroom Sauce ⬇ⓢ

½ pound boneless sirloin steak *or*
  boneless top round steak
2 teaspoons olive *or* vegetable oil
½ cup *each* sliced white
  mushrooms and shiitake
  mushrooms
2 teaspoons all-purpose flour
½ cup canned ready-to-serve
  low-sodium beef broth
¼ cup dry Madeira wine
Dash pepper

1. Preheat broiler. Arrange steak on rack in broiling pan and broil 5 to 6 inches from heat source, until medium-rare, 3 to 4 minutes on each side, or until done to taste.

2. In 10-inch nonstick skillet heat oil; add mushrooms and cook over medium-high heat, stirring frequently, until lightly browned, 1 to 2 minutes. Sprinkle with flour and stir quickly to combine. Continuing to stir, add remaining ingredients; cook, stirring frequently, until mixture thickens, 3 to 4 minutes.

3. To serve, thinly slice steak diagonally across the grain and arrange on serving platter; top with mushroom mixture.

APPROXIMATE TOTAL TIME: 20 MINUTES

MAKES 2 SERVINGS

Each serving provides: 1 Fat; 3 Proteins; 1 Vegetable; 45 Optional Calories
Per serving: 288 calories; 27 protein; 13 g fat; 8 g carbohydrate; 14 mg calcium; 61 mg sodium; 76 mg cholesterol; 1 g dietary fiber

Steak with Sauerbraten Sauce ⩔ⓢ

½ **pound boneless sirloin steak** *or*
boneless top round steak
1 **teaspoon olive** *or* **vegetable oil**
2 **tablespoons finely chopped
onion**
¾ **cup canned ready-to-serve
low-sodium beef broth**
2 **tablespoons red wine vinegar**
⅛ **teaspoon ground nutmeg**
3 **whole cloves**
3 **gingersnap cookies (½ ounce),
finely crushed**

*Weather permitting, broil the steak
on an outdoor grill.*

1. Preheat broiler. On rack in broiling pan arrange steak and broil 5 to 6 inches from heat source until medium-rare, 4 to 5 minutes on each side, or until done to taste.

2. While steak is broiling prepare sauce. In 10-inch nonstick skillet heat oil; add onion and cook over medium-high heat, stirring frequently, until lightly browned, 1 to 2 minutes.

3. Add remaining ingredients except gingersnaps and cook until liquid is slightly reduced, 2 to 3 minutes. Remove and discard cloves. Add gingersnaps and stir to combine; cook 1 minute longer.

4. To serve, thinly slice steak diagonally across the grain and arrange on serving platter; top with gingersnap mixture.

APPROXIMATE TOTAL TIME: 20 MINUTES

MAKES 2 SERVINGS

Each serving provides: ½ Fat; 3 Proteins; ⅛ Vegetable; 55 Optional Calories
Per serving: 243 calories; 26 g protein; 11 g fat; 8 g carbohydrate; 18 mg calcium; 99 mg sodium; 78 mg cholesterol; 0.2 g dietary fiber (this figure does not include gingersnap cookies; nutrition analysis not available)

Thai-Marinated Steak

1 medium mild chili pepper, seeded and finely chopped

¼ cup *each* finely chopped scallions (green onions), finely chopped fresh cilantro (Chinese parsley) *or* Italian (flat-leaf) parsley, and reduced-sodium soy sauce

2 tablespoons freshly squeezed lime juice

2 garlic cloves, finely chopped

1 pound boneless sirloin steak *or* boneless top round steak

Garnish: 4 *each* lime slices, cut into halves, and cilantro (Chinese parsley) sprigs

Delicious when prepared on the barbecue grill.

1. In small mixing bowl combine all ingredients except steak and garnish and mix well.

2. In glass or stainless-steel mixing bowl arrange steak; add pepper mixture and turn to coat. Cover with plastic wrap and refrigerate overnight or at least 1 hour.

3. Preheat broiler. Transfer steak to rack in broiling pan, reserving marinade. Broil 5 to 6 inches from heat source, basting with marinade mixture until medium-rare, 3 to 4 minutes on each side, or until done to taste.

4. Thinly slice steak diagonally across the grain and arrange on plate; garnish each portion with a lime slice and cilantro sprig.

APPROXIMATE TOTAL TIME: 15 MINUTES (does not include marinating time)

MAKES 4 SERVINGS

Each serving provides: 3 Proteins; ¼ Vegetable
Per serving: 199 calories; 27 g protein; 8 g fat; 4 g carbohydrate; 22 mg calcium; 658 mg sodium; 76 mg cholesterol; 0.2 g dietary fiber

Lamb Chops with Fennel ▽Ⓢ

2 rib *or* loin lamb chops
  (5 ounces each)
1½ teaspoons vegetable oil
1 cup *each* chopped onions and
  thinly sliced fennel
1 small garlic clove, minced
4 large plum tomatoes, blanched,
  peeled, seeded, and chopped
5 small Gaeta, Calamata, *or* black
  olives, pitted and finely
  chopped
1 tablespoon chopped Italian
  (flat-leaf) parsley
1 teaspoon Italian seasoning
Dash pepper

*The licorice taste of fennel adds a
unique flavor to this hearty dish.*

1. Preheat broiler. Spray rack in broiling pan with nonstick cooking spray; arrange chops on rack and broil 6 inches from heat source, until browned and done to taste, 4 to 5 minutes on each side.

2. While chops are broiling prepare fennel mixture. In 9-inch nonstick skillet heat oil; add onions, fennel, and garlic and cook over medium-high heat until fennel is tender-crisp, 3 to 4 minutes. Stir in remaining ingredients and bring to a boil. Reduce heat to low, cover, and let simmer until flavors blend, about 4 minutes.

3. To serve, on serving platter arrange fennel mixture; top with lamp chops.

APPROXIMATE TOTAL TIME: 30 MINUTES

MAKES 2 SERVINGS

Each serving provides: 1 Fat; 3 Proteins; 4 Vegetables
Per serving: 305 calories; 26 g protein; 16 g fat; 13 g carbohydrate; 80 mg calcium; 203 mg sodium; 77 mg cholesterol; 3 g dietary fiber

Lamb Chops with Vegetable Chutney ⬦Ⓢ

1 teaspoon vegetable oil
½ cup *each* diced green bell
    pepper and onion
1½ teaspoons minced pared
    gingerroot
1 garlic clove, minced
4 large plum tomatoes, blanched,
    peeled, seeded, and chopped
2 tablespoons apple cider vinegar
1½ teaspoons firmly packed light
    or dark brown sugar
¼ teaspoon grated lemon peel
Dash *each* ground cinnamon,
    ground cloves, and powdered
    mustard
2 rib *or* loin lamb chops
    (5 ounces each)

1. In small saucepan heat oil; add pepper, onion, gingerroot, and garlic and cook over medium heat until pepper is tender, about 3 minutes.

2. Stir in remaining ingredients except lamb chops and bring to a boil. Reduce heat to low and let simmer, stirring occasionally, until liquid evaporates, about 15 minutes.

3. While vegetable-chutney mixture simmers broil lamb chops. Preheat broiler. Spray rack in broiling pan with nonstick cooking spray; arrange chops on rack and broil 6 inches from heat source, until browned and done to taste, 4 to 5 minutes on each side.

4. To serve, arrange chops on serving platter and top with vegetable-chutney mixture.

APPROXIMATE TOTAL TIME: 30 MINUTES

MAKES 2 SERVINGS

Each serving provides: ½ Fat; 3 Proteins; 3 Vegetables; 15 Optional Calories
Per serving: 278 calories; 25 g protein; 14 g fat; 14 g carbohydrate; 41 mg calcium; 84 mg sodium; 77 mg cholesterol; 2 g dietary fiber

Lamb with Pepper and Olives ⟨s⟩

1 medium yellow *or* red bell
  pepper
2 loin lamb chops (5 ounces
  each)
1 teaspoon olive *or* vegetable oil
1 garlic clove, minced
6 large Calamata *or* black olives,
  pitted and cut into halves
2 tablespoons dry sherry
1 tablespoon balsamic *or* red
  wine vinegar
¼ teaspoon rosemary leaves,
  crushed

1. Preheat broiler. On baking sheet lined with heavy-duty foil broil pepper 3 inches from heat source, turning frequently, until charred on all sides; let stand until cool enough to handle, 15 to 20 minutes.

2. Peel pepper; remove and discard stem ends and seeds. Cut pepper into thin strips and set aside.

3. On rack in broiling pan arrange lamb chops and broil 6 inches from heat source, until medium-rare, 3 to 4 minutes on each side, or until done to taste.

4. While lamb is broiling prepare pepper-olive mixture. In 9-inch nonstick skillet heat oil; add garlic and cook over medium-high heat until softened. Add pepper strips, olives, *2 tablespoons water*, the sherry, vinegar, and rosemary and stir to combine. Reduce heat to low and let simmer until reduced by half, about 5 minutes.

5. To serve, on serving platter arrange lamb chops and top with pepper-olive mixture.

APPROXIMATE TOTAL TIME: 35 MINUTES

MAKES 2 SERVINGS

Each serving provides: 1 Fat; 3 Proteins; 1 Vegetable; 15 Optional Calories
Per serving: 262 calories; 26 g protein; 13 g fat; 5 g carbohydrate; 37 mg calcium; 166 mg sodium; 81 mg cholesterol; 1 g dietary fiber

German-Style Pork Patties ⬦S⬦

½ pound ground pork

⅓ cup plus 2 teaspoons plain dried bread crumbs, divided

¼ cup *each* rinsed and drained sauerkraut,* applesauce (no sugar added), and chopped onion

1 teaspoon caraway seed, crushed

½ cup canned ready-to-serve low-sodium chicken broth

1½ teaspoons Dijon-style mustard

1 teaspoon *each* cornstarch, prepared horseradish, and honey

1. Preheat broiler. In medium mixing bowl combine pork, all but 2 tablespoons of the bread crumbs, the sauerkraut, applesauce, onion, and caraway seed, mixing well. Shape mixture into 4 equal patties and arrange on rack in broiling pan.

2. Sprinkle 1 tablespoon of the remaining bread crumbs evenly over patties. Broil 5 inches from heat source, until patties are lightly browned, about 5 minutes.

3. Turn patties over; sprinkle with remaining bread crumbs. Broil until patties are cooked through, about 5 minutes longer.

4. While patties are broiling prepare sauce. In small saucepan combine remaining ingredients, stirring to dissolve cornstarch. Cook over medium heat, stirring frequently, until mixture thickens, 3 to 5 minutes.

5. To serve, on serving platter arrange patties and top with horseradish-honey mixture.

* Use the sauerkraut that is packaged in plastic bags and stored in the refrigerator section of the supermarket; it is usually crisper and less salty than the canned.

APPROXIMATE TOTAL TIME: 25 MINUTES

MAKES 2 SERVINGS

Each serving provides: 3 Proteins; ½ Vegetable; 1 Bread; ¼ Fruit; 35 Optional Calories

Per serving: 346 calories; 24 g protein; 16 g fat; 25 g carbohydrate; 47 mg calcium; 397 mg sodium; 84 mg cholesterol; 2 g dietary fiber (this figure does not include caraway seed and horseradish; nutrition analyses not available)

Pork Chops in Wine Sauce ▽ⓢ

2 pork loin chops (5 ounces each)
2 teaspoons olive *or* vegetable oil
1 cup *each* chopped onions and
    quartered mushrooms
½ cup chopped red bell pepper
1 small garlic clove, minced
¼ cup dry white table wine
½ teaspoon powdered mustard
1 tablespoon rinsed drained
    capers
1 teaspoon Italian seasoning
2 large plum tomatoes, blanched,
    peeled, seeded, and finely
    chopped

1. Preheat broiler. Arrange chops on rack and broil 6 inches from heat source, until browned and done to taste, 5 minutes on each side.

2. While chops are broiling prepare sauce. In 9-inch nonstick skillet heat oil; add onions, mushrooms, pepper, and garlic and cook over medium-high heat, stirring frequently, until pepper is tender-crisp, about 3 minutes.

3. In 1-cup liquid measure combine wine and mustard, stirring to combine; stir into skillet. Add capers and Italian seasoning; cook, stirring constantly, until mixture comes to a boil.

4. Reduce heat to low; stir in tomatoes. Add pork chops to skillet and turn to coat. Cover and let simmer until flavors blend, about 5 minutes.

APPROXIMATE TOTAL TIME: 30 MINUTES

MAKES 2 SERVINGS

Each serving provides: 1 Fat; 3 Proteins; 3½ Vegetables; 25 Optional Calories
Per serving: 315 calories; 30 g protein; 14 g fat; 12 g carbohydrate; 37 mg calcium; 194 mg sodium; 83 mg cholesterol; 3 g dietary fiber (this figure does not include capers; nutrition analysis not available)

Buttery Braised Scallops
Spinach Salad with Oysters
Grilled Salmon with Lime Butter

Thai Two-Noodle Stir-Fry
Spicy Country Pasta and Cheese
Pasta with Broccoli
Mushroom Risotto

Spring Peas and Carrots
Chicken-in-the-Rye
Lemon-Raspberry Cloud

Spicy Oven-"Fried"
Potato Wedges
Bean Burritos
Two-Bean Chili
Savory Corn Fritters

Cherry-Vanilla "Ice Cream" Soda
Mocha Pudding Pie

Pork Chops with Raisin-Pignolia Sauce ⬇Ⓢ

2 boneless pork loin chops
   (¼ pound each)
1 teaspoon olive *or* vegetable oil
½ ounce pignolias (pine nuts)
¼ cup sliced shallots *or* chopped
   onion
1 teaspoon all-purpose flour
½ cup canned ready-to-serve
   low-sodium chicken broth
2 tablespoons dry vermouth
¼ cup golden raisins
1 teaspoon chopped fresh
   rosemary *or* ¼ teaspoon
   rosemary leaves

1. Preheat broiler. Spray rack in broiling pan with nonstick cooking spray; arrange chops on rack and broil 6 inches from heat source, until browned and done to taste, 4 to 5 minutes on each side.

2. While chops are broiling prepare sauce. In 9-inch nonstick skillet heat oil; add pignolias and shallots and cook over medium heat, stirring constantly, until pignolias are golden brown, about 2 minutes. Sprinkle with flour and stir quickly to combine; continuing to stir, cook 1 minute longer. Stir in broth and vermouth and bring mixture to a boil. Reduce heat to low; stir in raisins and rosemary and let simmer until flavors blend, 3 to 4 minutes.

3. To serve, arrange chops on serving platter and top with sauce.

APPROXIMATE TOTAL TIME: 25 MINUTES

MAKES 2 SERVINGS

Each serving provides: 1 Fat; 3 Proteins; ¼ Vegetable; 1 Fruit; 30 Optional Calories
Per serving: 358 calories; 31 g protein; 15 g fat; 22 g carbohydrate; 26 mg calcium; 86 mg sodium; 83 mg cholesterol; 1 g dietary fiber (this figure does not include pignolias; nutrition analysis not available)

Roast Pork with Raisin-Onion Sauce ⱱF ⱱS

½ pound pork tenderloin
½ teaspoon cracked pepper
1 teaspoon vegetable oil
¼ cup sliced onion
2 teaspoons all-purpose flour
½ cup canned ready-to-serve
  low-sodium chicken broth
¼ cup *each* dark raisins and port
  wine

1. Preheat oven to 425°F. Rub all sides of pork with pepper and set on rack in roasting pan. Roast until pork is cooked through, 15 to 18 minutes.

2. While pork is roasting prepare raisin-onion mixture. In 6-inch nonstick skillet heat oil; add onion and cook over medium-high heat, stirring frequently, until softened, 1 to 2 minutes. Sprinkle with flour and stir quickly to combine; continuing to stir, add chicken broth, raisins, and wine.

3. Reduce heat to medium-low and cook, stirring occasionally, until mixture thickens, 8 to 10 minutes.

4. To serve, slice pork diagonally and arrange on serving platter; top with raisin-onion mixture.

APPROXIMATE TOTAL TIME: 30 MINUTES

MAKES 2 SERVINGS

Each serving provides: ½ Fat; 3 Proteins; ¼ Vegetable; 1 Fruit; 70 Optional Calories
Per serving: 287 calories; 26 g protein; 7 g fat; 22 g carbohydrate; 27 mg calcium; 76 mg sodium; 79 mg cholesterol; 1 g dietary fiber

Orange Veal Marsala ⟨F⟩ ⟨S⟩

½ pound veal scallops *or* thin
   veal cutlets
1 tablespoon plus 1 teaspoon all-
   purpose flour
1 teaspoon *each* margarine and
   olive oil
½ cup orange juice (no sugar
   added)
1 small orange (about 6 ounces),
   peeled and sectioned
¼ cup dry Marsala wine
1 tablespoon chopped fresh
   parsley
Dash pepper

*If veal cutlets do not fit into your
budget, chicken cutlets will work as
well in this recipe.*

1. On sheet of wax paper dredge veal in flour, coating both sides.

2. In 10-inch nonstick skillet heat margarine and oil until margarine is melted; add veal and cook over medium-high heat, until lightly browned, 4 to 5 minutes on each side. Transfer to plate and set aside.

3. In same skillet combine remaining ingredients and cook over high heat, until thoroughly heated, 3 to 5 minutes, scraping particles from bottom of pan.

4. Return veal to skillet and turn to coat with orange mixture; cook until veal is heated through, 1 to 2 minutes.

APPROXIMATE TOTAL TIME: 25 MINUTES

MAKES 2 SERVINGS

Each serving provides: 1 Fat; 3 Proteins; 1 Fruit; 45 Optional Calories
Per serving: 281 calories; 26 g protein; 6 g fat; 22 g carbohydrate; 45 mg calcium; 99 mg sodium; 89 mg cholesterol; 2 g dietary fiber

Veal Scaloppine with Sun-Dried Tomatoes ⋁F ⋁S

1 tablespoon plus 1½ teaspoons
   all-purpose flour
1 teaspoon Italian seasoning
½ pound veal scallops *or* thin
   veal cutlets, pounded to
   ⅛-inch thickness
2 teaspoons reduced-calorie
   margarine (tub)
1 teaspoon olive oil
2 small garlic cloves, minced
2 tablespoons dry white table
   wine
4 large plum tomatoes, blanched,
   peeled, seeded, and finely
   chopped
8 sun-dried tomato halves (not
   packed in oil), plumped,
   drained, and thinly sliced
1 tablespoon *each* chopped fresh
   basil and Italian (flat-leaf)
   parsley
1 teaspoon grated lemon peel

1. On sheet of wax paper combine flour and Italian seasoning; dredge veal in flour mixture, coating both sides.

2. In 10-inch nonstick skillet heat margarine and oil until margarine is melted; add veal and cook over medium-high heat until cooked through and lightly browned, about 2 minutes on each side. Transfer veal to serving platter and keep warm.

3. To same skillet add garlic and cook over medium heat until golden brown; stir in wine and bring to a boil. Stir in remaining ingredients and return to a boil. Reduce heat to low and let simmer until flavors blend, about 5 minutes. Spoon over veal.

APPROXIMATE TOTAL TIME: 25 MINUTES

MAKES 2 SERVINGS

Each serving provides: 1 Fat; 3 Proteins; 4 Vegetables; ¼ Bread; 15 Optional Calories
Per serving: 250 calories; 27 g protein; 7 g fat; 18 g carbohydrate; 46 mg calcium; 145 mg sodium; 89 mg cholesterol; 4 g dietary fiber

Variation: Veal Scaloppine with Tomatoes—Omit sun-dried tomatoes. In Serving Information decrease Vegetables to 2.
Per serving: 217 calories; 26 g protein; 7 g fat; 11 g carbohydrate; 34 mg calcium; 131 mg sodium; 89 mg cholesterol; 2 g dietary fiber

Marinated Veal Chops with Sage ⬡

¼ cup dry white table wine
1 tablespoon balsamic *or* red wine vinegar
2 garlic cloves, minced
4 to 5 fresh sage leaves, chopped
2 veal loin chops (5 ounces each)
2 teaspoons *each* olive *or* vegetable oil and all-purpose flour

1. In shallow glass or stainless-steel mixing bowl combine first 4 ingredients, mixing well; add veal and turn to coat. Cover with plastic wrap and refrigerate overnight or at least 30 minutes.

2. In 10-inch nonstick skillet heat oil; transfer chops to skillet, reserving marinade. Cook over medium heat until medium, or until done to taste, 3 to 4 minutes on each side. Transfer chops to plate and set aside.

3. Add flour to reserved marinade, stirring to dissolve flour. To same skillet add marinade-flour mixture and cook over high heat, stirring frequently, until mixture thickens, 2 to 3 minutes. Return chops to skillet, turn to coat with mixture, and cook until heated through, about 1 minute.

4. To serve, on serving platter arrange chops and top with sauce.

APPROXIMATE TOTAL TIME: 20 MINUTES (does not include marinating time)

MAKES 2 SERVINGS

Each serving provides: 1 Fat; 3 Proteins; 35 Optional Calories
Per serving: 224 calories; 23 g protein; 10 g fat; 4 g carbohydrate; 29 mg calcium; 84 mg sodium; 90 mg cholesterol; 0.1 g dietary fiber

Stuffed Veal Chops

3 tablespoons plain dried bread
  crumbs
5 small Calamata *or* black olives,
  pitted and chopped
2 sun-dried tomato halves (not
  packed in oil), finely chopped
1 tablespoon *each* chopped fresh
  parsley and grated Parmesan
  cheese
1½ teaspoons olive oil
1 small garlic clove, minced
2 veal loin *or* rib chops
  (5 ounces each)

1. In small mixing bowl combine all ingredients except veal; mix well until thoroughly combined. Set aside.

2. Preheat broiler. Using a sharp knife, cut along thick edge of each chop, making a pocket. Fill pocket of each chop with half of the bread crumb mixture.

3. Arrange chops on rack in broiling pan and broil 5 to 6 inches from heat source, until cooked through, 4 to 5 minutes on each side.

APPROXIMATE TOTAL TIME: 25 MINUTES

MAKES 2 SERVINGS

Each serving provides: 1 Fat; 3 Proteins; ½ Vegetable; ½ Bread; 15 Optional Calories
Per serving: 251 calories; 25 g protein; 12 g fat; 10 g carbohydrate; 79 mg calcium; 260 mg sodium; 93 mg cholesterol; 1 g dietary fiber

Veal Chops with Swiss Chard ⟨S⟩

1 tablespoon plus 1½ teaspoons
  all-purpose flour
1 teaspoon Italian seasoning
2 veal top loin *or* loin chops
  (5 ounces each)
2 teaspoons reduced-calorie
  margarine (tub)
1 teaspoon olive *or* vegetable oil
½ cup *each* sliced onion and red
  bell pepper strips
1 small garlic clove, minced
4 cups thoroughly washed and
  drained Swiss chard,* shredded
2 tablespoons dry white table
  wine *or* dry vermouth

1. On sheet of wax paper combine flour and Italian seasoning; dredge chops in flour mixture, coating both sides.

2. In 10-inch nonstick skillet combine margarine and oil and heat until margarine is melted; add chops and cook over medium-high heat until done to taste, 2 to 3 minutes on each side. Transfer to serving platter; keep warm.

3. In same skillet combine onion, pepper, and garlic and cook over medium-high heat until tender-crisp, about 3 minutes. Reduce heat to low; add Swiss chard, cover, and cook until wilted, 3 to 4 minutes. Stir in wine and cook, stirring occasionally, for 2 minutes. Spoon Swiss chard mixture over chops.

* Four cups fresh Swiss chard yield about 1 cup cooked Swiss chard.

APPROXIMATE TOTAL TIME: 30 MINUTES

MAKES 2 SERVINGS

Each serving provides: 1 Fat; 3 Proteins; 2 Vegetables; ¼ Bread; 15 Optional Calories
Per serving with wine: 255 calories; 25 g protein; 11 g fat; 13 g carbohydrate; 70 mg calcium; 286 mg sodium; 90 mg cholesterol; 1 g dietary fiber (this figure does not include Swiss chard; nutrition analysis not available)
With vermouth: 260 calories; 25 g protein; 11 g fat; 13 g carbohydrate; 70 mg calcium; 286 mg sodium; 90 mg cholesterol; 1 g dietary fiber (this figure does not include Swiss chard; nutrition analysis not available)

Legumes

What a lot you get for your money with legumes! Low in both cost and fat, legumes (dry beans, lentils, and peas) are high in nutritional pluses such as B vitamins, potassium, and iron, as well as being a good source of protein and dietary fiber. Legumes are also convenient to stock up on, since they're available both canned and dried. The canned varieties make for easy dishes like Cuban Black Bean Salad, which takes a mere 15 minutes to prepare, or our economically meatless Two-Bean Chili. For an attention-getting combination, we've combined bulgur with chick-peas in Tabouleh with Chick-Peas. As a bonus, legumes are often interchangeable, so by varying the ingredients you get more mileage from the recipes.

Bean and Barley Soup ⧩C ⧩F

1½ ounces uncooked medium pearl barley

3 packets instant vegetable broth and seasoning mix

8 ounces rinsed drained canned pinto *or* pink beans

½ cup *each* diced onion, diced celery, diced carrot, and canned Italian tomatoes (reserve liquid), seeded and chopped

1 garlic clove, minced

1 tablespoon chopped fresh parsley

⅛ teaspoon *each* white pepper and thyme leaves

1. In 3-quart microwavable casserole combine *1 quart water*, the barley, and broth mix. Cover and microwave on High (100%) for 10 minutes, rotating casserole ½ turn halfway through cooking.

2. Add beans, onion, celery, carrot, tomatoes with reserved liquid, and garlic and stir to combine. Cover and microwave on High for 15 minutes, rotating casserole ½ turn halfway through cooking. Let soup stand 3 to 5 minutes, until barley is tender.

3. Stir in remaining ingredients.

APPROXIMATE TOTAL TIME: 40 MINUTES

MAKES 4 SERVINGS, ABOUT 1¼ CUPS EACH

Each serving provides: 1 Protein; 1 Vegetable; ½ Bread; 10 Optional Calories
Per serving: 133 calories; 7 g protein; 0.5 g fat; 26 g carbohydrate; 51 mg calcium; 834 mg sodium (estimated); 0 mg cholesterol; 5 g dietary fiber

Ranch Bean Soup with Sour Cream ∇C ∇F

1 teaspoon vegetable oil
¼ cup *each* chopped onion,
  chopped green bell pepper, and
  diced carrot
1 cup spicy mixed vegetable juice
6 ounces rinsed drained canned
  pink beans
½ cup drained canned Italian
  tomatoes
2 tablespoons *each* barbecue
  sauce and sour cream
2 corn tortillas (6-inch diameter
  each), lightly toasted, each cut
  into 6 wedges

1. In 3-quart nonstick saucepan heat oil; add onion, pepper, and carrot and cook over medium-high heat, stirring frequently, until onion is tender, 1 to 2 minutes.

2. Add *1 cup water*, the juice, beans, tomatoes, and barbecue sauce and stir to combine. Reduce heat to low and let simmer, stirring occasionally, until carrot is tender, 15 to 20 minutes.

3. To serve, ladle soup into 2 soup bowls and top each with 1 tablespoon sour cream; serve each portion with 6 tortilla wedges.

APPROXIMATE TOTAL TIME: 30 MINUTES

MAKES 2 SERVINGS, ABOUT 1½ CUPS EACH

Each serving provides: ½ Fat; 1½ Proteins; 1¾ Vegetables; 1 Bread; 50 Optional Calories
Per serving: 277 calories; 10 g protein; 7 g fat; 45 g carbohydrate; 134 mg calcium; 979 mg sodium (estimated); 6 mg cholesterol; 6 g dietary fiber

Variation: Ranch Bean Soup—Omit sour cream from recipe. In Serving Information decrease Optional Calories to 15.
Per serving: 246 calories; 10 g protein; 4 g fat; 44 g carbohydrate; 118 mg calcium; 972 mg sodium (estimated); 0 mg cholesterol; 6 g dietary fiber

Tuscan White Bean Soup (C) (F)

½ cup chopped onion
2 teaspoons olive oil
2 garlic cloves, minced
3 tablespoons all-purpose flour
12 ounces rinsed drained canned white kidney (cannellini) beans
3 packets instant vegetable broth and seasoning mix
2 large plum tomatoes, blanched, peeled, seeded, and chopped
2 teaspoons *each* chopped fresh parsley and rosemary *or* ½ teaspoon rosemary leaves
⅛ teaspoon white pepper

The Italian province of Tuscany lends its name to this classic dish.

1. In 3-quart microwavable casserole combine onion, oil, and garlic and stir to coat; microwave on High (100%) for 1 minute, stirring once halfway through cooking.

2. In medium mixing bowl combine *1 quart water* and the flour, stirring to dissolve flour; stir into onion mixture. Add beans and broth mix and stir to combine. Microwave on High for 10 minutes, stirring once halfway through cooking, until mixture thickens.

3. Using half of bean mixture, pour 1 cup into blender and process until pureed. Transfer pureed mixture to 1-quart bowl and repeat procedure with remaining bean mixture, 1 cup at a time. Pour pureed mixture back into casserole. Add tomatoes and stir to combine. Microwave on High for 5 minutes, until flavors blend.

4. Stir in remaining ingredients.

APPROXIMATE TOTAL TIME: 30 MINUTES

MAKES 4 SERVINGS, ABOUT 1¼ CUPS EACH

Each serving provides: ½ Fat; 1½ Proteins; ¾ Vegetable; ¼ Bread; 10 Optional Calories
Per serving: 158 calories; 9 g protein; 3 g fat; 26 g carbohydrate; 54 mg calcium; 869 mg sodium (estimated); 0 mg cholesterol; 4 g dietary fiber

Italian Chick-Pea Soup ⬇C ⬇F

½ cup *each* chopped onion, diced
   celery, and diced carrot
1 teaspoon olive *or* vegetable oil
1 large garlic clove, minced
1 cup *each* canned Italian
   tomatoes (reserve liquid),
   seeded and diced, and canned
   ready-to-serve low-sodium
   chicken broth
8 ounces rinsed drained canned
   chick-peas
1 tablespoon grated Parmesan
   cheese
1 tablespoon *each* chopped fresh
   parsley and chopped fresh basil
   or ½ teaspoon basil leaves
Dash pepper

1. In 3-quart microwavable casserole combine onion, celery, carrot, oil, and garlic and stir to coat. Microwave on High (100%) for 3 minutes, stirring once halfway through cooking, until onion is softened.

2. Add *1 cup water*, the tomatoes with reserved liquid, broth, and chick-peas to onion mixture and stir to combine; cover and microwave on High for 15 minutes, until carrot is tender.

3. Stir in remaining ingredients.

APPROXIMATE TOTAL TIME: 30 MINUTES

MAKES 2 SERVINGS, ABOUT 2 CUPS EACH

Each serving provides: ½ Fat; 2 Proteins; 2½ Vegetables;
35 Optional Calories
Per serving: 243 calories; 12 g protein; 7 g fat; 37 g carbohydrate; 148 mg calcium; 696 mg sodium (estimated);
2 mg cholesterol; 5 g dietary fiber

Bean Burritos

4 flour tortillas (6-inch diameter
    each)
1 teaspoon olive *or* vegetable oil
½ cup *each* finely chopped onion
    and green bell pepper
1 small garlic clove, minced
8 ounces rinsed drained canned
    pink *or* pinto beans
½ cup canned Italian tomatoes
    (reserve liquid), chopped
½ teaspoon finely chopped
    cilantro (Chinese parsley) *or*
    Italian (flat-leaf) parsley
Dash *each* chili powder and
    ground cumin
½ cup mild salsa

*Here is a Mexican specialty that you
can easily prepare at home.*

1. Preheat oven to 375°F. Wrap each tortilla in foil and bake for 10 minutes.

2. In 9-inch nonstick skillet heat oil; add onion, pepper, and garlic and cook over medium-high heat, stirring occasionally, until vegetables are softened, about 2 minutes. Add beans, tomatoes with reserved liquid, cilantro, and seasonings and stir to combine. Reduce heat to low and cook, stirring occasionally, until moisture has evaporated, 3 to 4 minutes.

3. Remove tortillas from oven. Unwrap 1 tortilla and spread ¼ of bean mixture across tortilla; fold sides of tortilla over filling. Fold bottom of tortilla up over filling and roll to enclose filling. Place seam side down on serving plate. Repeat procedure using remaining bean mixture and tortillas, making 3 more burritos.

4. To serve, arrange burritos on serving platter and top with salsa.

APPROXIMATE TOTAL TIME: 25 MINUTES (includes baking time)

MAKES 2 SERVINGS, 2 BURRITOS EACH

Each serving provides: ½ Fat; 2 Proteins; 2 Vegetables; 2 Breads
Per serving: 338 calories; 13 g protein; 7 g fat; 59 g carbohydrate; 156 mg calcium; 1,124 mg sodium (estimated); 0 mg cholesterol; 8 g dietary fiber

Black Bean and Rice Bake � ⌣F⌣

2 cups cooked long-grain rice
8 ounces rinsed drained canned
  black (turtle) beans
1½ ounces reduced-fat Monterey
  Jack cheese, shredded
½ cup thawed frozen egg
  substitute
¼ cup *each* finely chopped red
  bell pepper and onion
1 tablespoon minced fresh
  cilantro (Chinese parsley) *or*
  Italian (flat-leaf) parsley
1 small garlic clove, minced
½ cup mild salsa

Rice and beans are a nutritious and delicious combination. This recipe provides a great opportunity for using up leftover rice.

1. Preheat oven to 350°F. In large mixing bowl combine all ingredients except salsa, mixing well. Spray 8 x 8 x 2-inch baking dish with nonstick cooking spray and spread bean-rice mixture in dish. Bake for 20 minutes (until golden and a knife, inserted in center, comes out dry).

2. To serve, cut into 4 equal portions and top each with ¼ of the salsa.

APPROXIMATE TOTAL TIME: 30 MINUTES (includes baking time)

MAKES 4 SERVINGS

Each serving provides: 2 Proteins; ½ Vegetable; 1 Bread
Per serving: 253 calories; 12 g protein; 2 g fat; 44 g carbohydrate; 142 mg calcium; 481 mg sodium (estimated); 8 mg cholesterol; 3 g dietary fiber

Serving Suggestion: Top each portion with 2 tablespoons plain low-fat yogurt. In Serving Information add ¼ Milk.
Per serving: 257 calories; 13 g protein; 3 g fat; 45 g carbohydrate; 155 mg calcium; 486 mg sodium (estimated); 8 mg cholesterol; 3 g dietary fiber

Haitian Black Beans ⧖C⧗ ⧖F⧗

2 tablespoons *each* **chopped onion, chopped seeded tomato, and chopped green bell pepper**
1½ teaspoons chopped seeded mild chili pepper
½ teaspoon olive oil
4 ounces rinsed drained canned black (turtle) beans, divided
½ ounce diced boiled ham
Dash pepper
1 cup cooked long-grain rice (hot)

1. In shallow 1-quart microwavable casserole combine onion, tomato, bell pepper, chili pepper, and oil and stir to coat. Microwave on High (100%) for 1 minute, until onion is softened.

2. Using a fork, mash 2 ounces beans. Add mashed and whole beans, *⅓ cup water*, the ham, and pepper to onion mixture and stir to combine. Cover and microwave on High for 7 minutes, stirring once every 2 minutes, until flavors blend.

3. Serve over rice.

APPROXIMATE TOTAL TIME: 20 MINUTES

MAKES 2 SERVINGS

Each serving provides: ¼ Fat; 1¼ Proteins; ½ Vegetable; 1 Bread
Per serving: 204 calories; 8 g protein; 2 g fat; 38 g carbohydrate; 38 mg calcium; 278 mg sodium (estimated); 4 mg cholesterol; 3 g dietary fiber

Cannellini with Pasta and Vegetables ▽ᶜ ▽ᶠ ▽ˢ

2 teaspoons olive oil
½ cup *each* sliced red onion and
 red bell pepper (¼-inch wide
 strips)
1 cup cooked penne *or* ziti
 macaroni
8 ounces rinsed drained canned
 white kidney (cannellini) beans
1 tablespoon chopped fresh basil
 or ½ teaspoon basil leaves
½ teaspoon oregano leaves

While preparing the onion and bell
pepper for this recipe you might
want to slice more than you need
and add it to a salad or sandwich.

1. In 9-inch nonstick skillet heat oil; add onion and pepper and cook over medium-high heat until tender-crisp, about 3 minutes.

2. Reduce heat to low; add remaining ingredients and stir to combine. Cook, stirring frequently, until thoroughly heated, about 5 minutes.

APPROXIMATE TOTAL TIME: 20 MINUTES

MAKES 2 SERVINGS

Each serving provides: 1 Fat; 2 Proteins; 1 Vegetable; 1 Bread
Per serving: 287 calories; 13 g protein; 6 g fat; 47 g carbohydrate; 84 mg calcium; 392 mg sodium (estimated); 0 mg cholesterol; 6 g dietary fiber

Maple Baked Beans ⛛C ⛛F

1 ounce diced fully-cooked smoked ham
¼ cup chopped onion
1 tablespoon maple syrup
2 teaspoons margarine, melted
1 teaspoon dark molasses
½ teaspoon powdered mustard
6 ounces rinsed drained canned small white beans

The microwave oven bakes these flavorful beans in minutes.

1. In 2-cup microwavable casserole combine all ingredients except beans; mix well. Add beans and stir to combine. Cover and microwave on High (100%) for 5 minutes, rotating casserole ½ turn halfway through cooking, until heated through.

APPROXIMATE TOTAL TIME: 10 MINUTES

MAKES 2 SERVINGS

Each serving provides: 1 Fat; ½ Protein; ¼ Vegetable; 1½ Breads; 40 Optional Calories
Per serving: 189 calories; 9 g protein; 5 g fat; 28 g carbohydrate; 91 mg calcium; 540 mg sodium (estimated); 7 mg cholesterol; 3 g dietary fiber

Two-Bean Chili

2 teaspoons vegetable oil
½ cup *each* diced onion and
   green bell pepper
1 small garlic clove, minced
1 tablespoon all-purpose flour
1 cup canned Italian tomatoes
   (reserve liquid), seeded
   and diced
3 ounces *each* rinsed drained
   canned pink beans and rinsed
   drained canned black (turtle)
   beans
1 tablespoon chili powder
½ packet (about ½ teaspoon)
   instant vegetable broth and
   seasoning mix
Dash pepper
¾ ounce reduced-fat Monterey
   Jack *or* Cheddar cheese,
   shredded

1. In 3-quart nonstick saucepan heat oil; add onion, bell pepper, and garlic and cook over medium-high heat, stirring frequently, until onion is softened, 1 to 2 minutes.

2. Sprinkle flour over vegetables and stir quickly to combine; cook, stirring constantly, for 1 minute. Continuing to stir, add *2 cups water*, the tomatoes with reserved liquid, beans, chili powder, broth mix, and pepper.

3. Reduce heat to low, cover, and cook until mixture thickens, 15 to 20 minutes.

4. To serve, into each of 2 serving bowls spoon half of the chili; top each with half of the cheese.

APPROXIMATE TOTAL TIME: 30 MINUTES

MAKES 2 SERVINGS, ABOUT 1½ CUPS EACH

Each serving provides: 1 Fat; 2 Proteins; 2 Vegetables; 20 Optional Calories
Per serving with Monterey Jack cheese: 241 calories; 12 g protein; 8 g fat; 33 g carbohydrate; 185 mg calcium; 781 mg sodium (estimated); 8 mg cholesterol; 7 g dietary fiber
With Cheddar cheese: 245 calories; 12 g protein; 8 g fat; 33 g carbohydrate; 185 mg calcium; 788 mg sodium (estimated); 8 mg cholesterol; 7 g dietary fiber

Chick-Peas, Pasta, and Broccoli

2 tablespoons golden raisins
½ cup sliced onion
½ ounce pignolias (pine nuts)
2 teaspoons reduced-calorie margarine (tub)
1 small garlic clove, minced
1 tablespoon tomato paste
2 cups broccoli florets
1 cup cooked pasta twists
4 ounces rinsed drained canned chick-peas

1. In small mixing bowl combine raisins and ¼ *cup water*; set aside.

2. In 3-quart microwavable casserole combine onion, pignolias, margarine, and garlic; cover and microwave on High (100%) for 2 minutes.

3. Add tomato paste to raisin-water mixture and stir to combine; stir into onion mixture. Add broccoli florets and stir to combine. Cover and microwave on High for 5 minutes, stirring once halfway through cooking.

4. Add pasta and chick-peas and stir to combine. Cover and microwave on High for 3 minutes, until thoroughly heated.

APPROXIMATE TOTAL TIME: 20 MINUTES

MAKES 2 SERVINGS

Each serving provides: 1 Fat; 1½ Proteins; 2½ Vegetables; 1 Bread; ½ Fruit; 5 Optional Calories
Per serving: 305 calories; 14 g protein; 8 g fat; 51 g carbohydrate; 102 mg calcium; 333 mg sodium (estimated); 0 mg cholesterol; 4 g dietary fiber (this figure does not include pignolias and broccoli florets; nutrition analyses not available)

Braised Chestnuts and Lentils ⬇C ⬇F

2 teaspoons olive *or* vegetable oil
1 cup sliced mushrooms
¼ cup *each* sliced shallots *or*
  onion and diced red bell pepper
2 garlic cloves, minced
6 ounces rinsed drained canned
  lentils
6 small bottled chestnuts (packed
  without sugar),* chopped
2 tablespoons dry red table wine
½ packet (about ½ teaspoon)
  instant vegetable broth and
  seasoning mix

1. In 10-inch nonstick skillet heat oil; add mushrooms, shallots, pepper, and garlic and cook over medium-high heat, stirring frequently, until mushrooms are softened, 1 to 2 minutes.

2. Add lentils, chestnuts, *½ cup water*, the wine, and broth mix and stir to combine. Reduce heat to low and let simmer, stirring occasionally, until liquid is reduced by half, 4 to 5 minutes.

* Shelled roasted chestnuts may be substituted for the bottled chestnuts.

APPROXIMATE TOTAL TIME: 20 MINUTES

MAKES 2 SERVINGS

Each serving provides: 1 Fat; 1½ Proteins; 1½ Vegetables; ½ Bread; 15 Optional Calories
Per serving: 193 calories; 10 g protein; 5 g fat; 26 g carbohydrate; 36 mg calcium; 487 mg sodium (estimated); 0 mg cholesterol; 4 g dietary fiber (this figure does not include chestnuts; nutrition analysis not available)

Lentils and Spinach ▽C ▽F

¼ cup chopped onion
2 garlic cloves, minced
1 teaspoon vegetable oil
½ cup thawed frozen chopped
  spinach
4 ounces rinsed drained canned
  lentils
1 teaspoon cornstarch, dissolved
  in ½ cup water
1 packet instant vegetable broth
  and seasoning mix

1. In shallow 1-quart microwavable casserole combine onion, garlic, and oil and stir to coat; microwave on High (100%) for 1 minute.

2. Add remaining ingredients to onion mixture and stir to combine. Cover and microwave on High for 4 minutes, stirring once halfway through cooking, until mixture thickens.

APPROXIMATE TOTAL TIME: 10 MINUTES

MAKES 2 SERVINGS

Each serving provides: ½ Fat; ¾ Vegetable; 1 Bread; 10 Optional Calories
Per serving: 117 calories; 8 g protein; 3 g fat; 17 g carbohydrate; 75 mg calcium; 620 mg sodium (estimated); 0 mg cholesterol; 4 g dietary fiber

Lentils 'n' Barley Sauté ▽C ▽F

1 teaspoon vegetable oil
1 cup sliced mushrooms
¼ cup *each* finely chopped carrot and scallions (green onions)
1 packet instant chicken broth and seasoning mix
¼ teaspoon *each* pepper and thyme leaves
1 cup cooked medium pearl barley
4 ounces rinsed drained canned lentils

1. In 10-inch nonstick skillet heat oil; add mushrooms, carrot, and scallions and cook over medium-high heat, stirring frequently, until mushrooms are softened, 1 to 2 minutes.

2. Add *¾ cup water*, the broth mix, pepper, and thyme to mushroom mixture, stirring to dissolve broth mix. Reduce heat to low, cover, and cook until carrot is tender, 4 to 5 minutes.

3. Stir in barley and lentils and cook, uncovered, stirring occasionally, until liquid is absorbed, 2 to 3 minutes.

APPROXIMATE TOTAL TIME: 20 MINUTES

MAKES 2 SERVINGS

Each serving provides: ½ Fat; 1 Protein; 1½ Vegetables; 1 Bread; 5 Optional Calories
Per serving: 208 calories; 10 g protein; 3 g fat; 37 g carbohydrate; 33 mg calcium; 696 mg sodium (estimated); 0 mg cholesterol; 7 g dietary fiber

Lentil 'n' Macaroni Casserole ▽C ▽F

½ cup chopped onion
1 garlic clove, minced
1 teaspoon vegetable oil
6 ounces rinsed drained canned
  lentils
1 cup cooked elbow *or* small shell
  macaroni
½ cup tomato sauce
1 tablespoon chopped fresh
  Italian (flat-leaf) parsley
¼ teaspoon oregano leaves
Dash ground red pepper

1. In 1-quart microwavable casserole combine onion, garlic, and oil and stir to coat. Cover and microwave on Medium (50%) for 2 minutes, stirring once halfway through cooking, until onion is translucent.

2. Add remaining ingredients to onion-garlic mixture and stir to combine. Cover and microwave on High (100%) for 3 minutes, stirring once halfway through cooking, until thoroughly heated.

APPROXIMATE TOTAL TIME: 15 MINUTES

MAKES 2 SERVINGS

Each serving provides: ½ Fat; 1½ Proteins; 1 Vegetable; 1 Bread
Per serving: 226 calories; 11 g Protein; 3 g fat; 40 g carbohydrate; 42 mg calcium; 659 mg sodium (estimated); 0 mg cholesterol; 5 g dietary fiber

Creole Black-Eyed Peas ▽C ▽F

2 teaspoons olive *or* vegetable oil
½ cup finely chopped onion
¼ cup *each* finely chopped carrot, celery, and red *or* green bell pepper
½ cup canned crushed tomatoes
1 bay leaf
¼ teaspoon powdered mustard
⅛ teaspoon *each* ground red pepper, ground ginger, and ground cumin
8 ounces rinsed drained canned black-eyed peas
1½ teaspoons finely chopped fresh Italian (flat-leaf) parsley

1. In 9-inch nonstick skillet heat oil; add onion, carrot, celery, and bell pepper and cook over medium-high heat, stirring occasionally, until tender-crisp, about 5 minutes.

2. Add tomatoes, bay leaf, mustard, pepper, ginger, and cumin to vegetable mixture; stir to combine and bring to a boil. Reduce heat to low; stir in peas and let simmer until peas are heated through, about 3 minutes. Remove and discard bay leaf. Sprinkle with parsley.

APPROXIMATE TOTAL TIME: 25 MINUTES

MAKES 2 SERVINGS

Each serving provides: 1 Fat; 2 Proteins; 1¾ Vegetables
Per serving: 208 calories; 10 g protein; 5 g fat; 31 g carbohydrate; 84 mg calcium; 504 mg sodium (estimated); 0 mg cholesterol; 12 g dietary fiber

Caponata with Chick-Peas ▽ⓒ

2 teaspoons olive *or* vegetable oil
1 cup *each* cubed pared eggplant,
  diced red *or* yellow bell
  peppers, diced onions, diced
  celery, diced zucchini, and
  quartered mushrooms
½ ounce pignolias (pine nuts)
1 small garlic clove, minced
1 cup canned Italian tomatoes
  (reserve liquid), chopped
8 ounces rinsed drained canned
  chick-peas
3 *each* large pitted black and
  pimiento-stuffed green olives,
  sliced
1 tablespoon rinsed drained
  capers
¾ ounce mozzarella cheese,
  shredded

*Pack this flavorful salad to take to
the office for lunch. Include 1 small
pita and a fruit and you're all set.*

1. In 10-inch nonstick skillet heat oil; add eggplant, peppers, onions, celery, zucchini, mushrooms, pignolias, and garlic and cook over medium-high heat, stirring frequently, until lightly browned, about 2 minutes.

2. Reduce heat to medium, cover, and cook until eggplant is tender, about 5 minutes. Add tomatoes with reserved liquid, chick-peas, olives, and capers and stir to combine. Cover and let simmer until thoroughly heated, about 8 minutes.

3. Transfer to serving bowl, cover, and refrigerate until chilled, about 1 hour. To serve, toss salad again and sprinkle with cheese.

APPROXIMATE TOTAL TIME: 30 MINUTES (does not include chilling time)

MAKES 4 SERVINGS

Each serving provides: 1 Fat; 1½ Proteins; 3½ Vegetables
Per serving: 183 calories; 8 g protein; 8 g fat; 23 g carbohydrate; 105 mg calcium; 491 mg sodium (estimated); 4 mg cholesterol; 4 g dietary fiber (this figure does not include pignolias and capers; nutrition analyses not available)

Tofu, Tomato, and Onion Salad �ᵛС ⱽS

6 ounces firm-style tofu, thinly
   sliced
1 medium tomato, thinly sliced
½ cup thinly sliced red onion
¼ cup fresh basil
1 tablespoon *each* olive oil and
   balsamic *or* red wine vinegar
1 teaspoon Italian seasoning

*Tofu, also known as bean curd, is
available in the produce or refrigerator section of your supermarket.
Fresh tofu is packed in water in
small plastic containers. Once the
package is opened, change the water
daily.*

1. On serving platter decoratively arrange tofu, tomato, onion, and basil, overlapping edges slightly.

2. In small bowl combine remaining ingredients and
drizzle evenly over salad.

APPROXIMATE TOTAL TIME: 10 MINUTES

MAKES 2 SERVINGS

Each serving provides: 1½ Fats; 1½ Proteins; 1½
Vegetables
Per serving: 218 calories; 15 g protein; 14 g fat; 12 g
carbohydrate; 236 mg calcium; 27 mg sodium; 0 mg cholesterol; 1 g dietary fiber (this figure does not include tofu;
nutrition analysis not available)

Cajun Tofu ▽_C

2 teaspoons vegetable oil
½ cup *each* diced onion and
   celery
1 garlic clove, minced
½ cup *each* diced green bell
   pepper, diced yellow squash,
   and tomato sauce
¼ cup dry red table wine
1 teaspoon Cajun seasoning
2 tablespoons Worcestershire
   sauce
1 teaspoon cornstarch
½ pound firm-style tofu, cut into
   1-inch cubes

1. In 10-inch nonstick skillet heat oil; add onion, celery, and garlic and cook over medium-high heat, stirring occasionally, until onion begins to soften, about 1 minute. Add pepper and squash and cook until tender-crisp, about 2 minutes.

2. Add tomato sauce, wine, and Cajun seasoning to vegetable mixture and stir to combine.

3. In small bowl combine Worcestershire sauce and cornstarch, stirring to dissolve cornstarch; stir into vegetable mixture. Add tofu and stir to combine; cook, stirring occasionally, until mixture thickens, about 3 minutes.

APPROXIMATE TOTAL TIME: 20 MINUTES

MAKES 2 SERVINGS

Each serving provides: 1 Fat; 2 Proteins; 2½ Vegetables; 30 Optional Calories
Per serving: 303 calories; 21 g protein; 15 g fat; 22 g carbohydrate; 275 mg calcium; 1,003 mg sodium; 0 mg cholesterol; 3 g dietary fiber (this figure does not include tofu; nutrition analysis not available)

Hot and Spicy Tofu with Pasta ⟨C⟩

1¾ teaspoons peanut *or* vegetable oil
½ cup *each* red bell pepper strips and sliced onion *or* scallions (green onions)
1 small garlic clove, minced
½ cup canned ready-to-serve low-sodium chicken broth
2 tablespoons reduced-sodium soy sauce
1 tablespoon dry sherry
1 teaspoon cornstarch
¼ teaspoon hot chili oil
½ pound firm-style tofu, cut into 1-inch cubes
1 cup cooked Japanese buckwheat pasta (soba) *or* thin egg noodles (hot)
1 tablespoon finely chopped cilantro (Chinese parsley) *or* Italian (flat-leaf) parsley

We recommend you prepare this dish using Japanese buckwheat pasta, known as soba. Look for it in your supermarket or in an Oriental specialty store. Thin egg noodles can be used as an alternative.

1. In 9-inch nonstick skillet heat peanut oil; add pepper, onion, and garlic and cook over medium-high heat, stirring occasionally, until tender-crisp, about 3 minutes.

2. In 1-cup liquid measure combine broth, soy sauce, sherry, cornstarch, and chili oil, stirring to dissolve cornstarch. Stir into vegetable mixture and cook, stirring constantly, until mixture comes to a boil. Reduce heat to low; add tofu, stir to combine, and cook until heated through, about 2 minutes.

3. To serve, on serving platter arrange pasta, top with vegetable-tofu mixture, and sprinkle with cilantro.

APPROXIMATE TOTAL TIME: 20 MINUTES

MAKES 2 SERVINGS

Each serving provides: 1 Fat; 2 Proteins; 1 Vegetable; 1 Bread; 20 Optional Calories
Per serving with pasta: 331 calories; 23 g protein; 15 g fat; 29 g carbohydrate; 258 mg calcium; 800 mg sodium; 0 mg cholesterol; 1 g dietary fiber (this figure does not include tofu and pasta; nutrition analyses not available)
With noodles: 366 calories; 24 g protein; 16 g fat; 33 g carbohydrate; 260 mg calcium; 637 mg sodium; 26 mg cholesterol; 3 g dietary fiber (this figure does not include tofu; nutrition analysis not available)

Tofu with Hoisin Sauce

½ cup *each* red bell pepper strips
    and sliced celery
1½ teaspoons vegetable oil
1 teaspoon minced pared
    gingerroot
1 small garlic clove, minced
2 tablespoons dry sherry
2 teaspoons hoisin sauce
1 teaspoon reduced-sodium soy
    sauce
½ teaspoon Chinese sesame oil
½ pound firm-style tofu, cut into
    cubes
½ cup sliced scallions (green
    onions), green portion only

1. In 1-quart microwavable casserole combine pepper, celery, oil, gingerroot, and garlic and stir to coat. Microwave on High (100%) for 2 minutes, stirring once halfway through cooking.

2. Add sherry, hoisin sauce, soy sauce, and sesame oil and stir to combine; microwave on High for 1 minute.

3. Add tofu and microwave on High for 1 minute; sprinkle with scallions.

APPROXIMATE TOTAL TIME: 15 MINUTES

MAKES 2 SERVINGS

Each serving provides: 1 Fat; 2 Proteins; 1½ Vegetables; 25 Optional Calories
Per serving: 256 calories; 19 g protein; 15 g fat; 13 g carbohydrate; 265 mg calcium; 316 mg sodium; 0 mg cholesterol; 1 g dietary fiber (this figure does not include tofu; nutrition analysis not available)

Bean and Tuna Salad ▽C ▽F

1¾ cups broccoli florets
¼ cup thinly sliced red bell
  pepper
4 ounces rinsed drained canned
  black (turtle) beans
1 ounce drained canned tuna
  (packed in water)
1 tablespoon red wine vinegar
2 teaspoons olive *or* vegetable oil
1 teaspoon *each* lemon juice and
  Dijon-style mustard

1. Fill bottom portion of microwavable steamer with *½ cup water*. Set steamer insert in place and fill with broccoli florets and pepper; cover and microwave on High (100%) for 4 minutes. Let stand 1 minute until vegetables are tender-crisp.

2. Transfer vegetables to 1-quart microwavable casserole; add beans and tuna and stir to combine. Cover and microwave on High for 1 minute.

3. Using a wire whisk, in small mixing bowl combine *1 tablespoon water*, the vinegar, oil, lemon juice, and mustard and beat until well combined; pour over vegetable-bean mixture.

APPROXIMATE TOTAL TIME: 15 MINUTES

MAKES 2 SERVINGS

Each serving provides: 1 Fat; 1½ Proteins; 2 Vegetables
Per serving: 165 calories; 12 g protein; 5 g fat; 20 g carbohydrate; 75 mg calcium; 344 mg sodium (estimated); 6 mg cholesterol; 3 g dietary fiber (this figure does not include broccoli florets; nutrition analysis not available)

Cuban Black Bean Salad ⌄C⌄ ⌄F⌄

¼ cup orange juice (no sugar added)

2 tablespoons freshly squeezed lime juice

1 tablespoon *each* chopped fresh cilantro (Chinese parsley) *or* Italian (flat-leaf) parsley and red wine vinegar

1 teaspoon olive oil

¼ teaspoon granulated sugar

Dash pepper

6 ounces rinsed drained canned black (turtle) beans

½ cup cooked long-grain rice

¼ cup diagonally sliced scallions (green onions)

5 small pimiento-stuffed green olives, sliced

2 tablespoons chopped rinsed and drained pimiento

4 green leaf lettuce leaves

½ cup chicory (curly endive)

¼ medium avocado (about 2 ounces), pared and thinly sliced

1 small orange (about 6 ounces), peeled and sliced

Garnish: cilantro (Chinese parsley) *or* Italian (flat-leaf) parsley sprig

1. In 1-cup liquid measure combine orange juice, lime juice, cilantro, vinegar, oil, sugar, and pepper and stir to combine. Set aside.

2. In medium mixing bowl combine beans, rice, scallions, olives, and pimiento.

3. Around edge of serving platter arrange lettuce and chicory; spoon bean mixture onto center of platter and decoratively arrange avocado and orange slices around bean mixture. Pour dressing over entire salad. Garnish with cilantro sprig.

APPROXIMATE TOTAL TIME: 15 MINUTES

MAKES 2 SERVINGS

Each serving provides: 1¾ Fats; 1½ Proteins; 1¼ Vegetables; ½ Bread; ¾ Fruit; 3 Optional Calories
Per serving: 293 calories; 10 g protein; 7 g fat; 50 g carbohydrate; 143 mg calcium; 489 mg sodium (estimated); 0 mg cholesterol; 7 g dietary fiber (this figure does not include pimiento; nutrition analysis not available)

Greek-Style Chick-Pea Salad � C ⟆ ⟆

1 tablespoon *each* chopped fresh
  dill, red wine vinegar, and
  freshly squeezed lemon juice
2 teaspoons olive oil
Dash white pepper
1 cup cooked long-grain rice,
  chilled
4 ounces rinsed drained canned
  chick-peas
¼ cup *each* seeded and diced
  tomato, diced green bell
  pepper, sliced scallions (green
  onions), and diced cucumber
2 tablespoons sliced radishes
8 lettuce leaves
¾ ounce feta cheese, cut into
  ¼-inch cubes

*This recipe provides a great way to
use leftover rice.*

1. In medium mixing bowl combine dill, *1 tablespoon
water*, the vinegar, lemon juice, oil, and pepper, stirring well.

2. Add remaining ingredients except lettuce and feta
cheese to dill mixture, tossing to coat.

3. Line serving bowl with lettuce; top with chick-pea
mixture and feta cheese.

APPROXIMATE TOTAL TIME: 20 MINUTES

MAKES 2 SERVINGS

Each serving provides: 1 Fat; 1½ Proteins; 2⅛ Vegetables;
1 Bread
Per serving: 272 calories; 8 g protein; 8 g fat; 42 g carbohydrate; 125 mg calcium; 322 mg sodium (estimated);
9 mg cholesterol; 3 g dietary fiber

Tabouleh with Chick-Peas ⒸⒻ

3 ounces uncooked bulgur
  (cracked wheat)
2 tablespoons freshly squeezed
  lemon juice
1 tablespoon chopped fresh mint
2 teaspoons olive oil
1 garlic clove, minced
½ cup pared and diced cucumber
4 ounces rinsed drained canned
  chick-peas
2 small plum tomatoes, diced
¼ cup sliced scallions (green
  onions)
Dash pepper
8 lettuce leaves

1. In medium mixing bowl pour *1½ cups water* over bulgur and let stand until bulgur is slightly softened, about 20 minutes. Pour bulgur through fine sieve, discarding cooking liquid; set aside.

2. In medium mixing bowl combine lemon juice, *2 tablespoons water*, the mint, oil, and garlic, stirring to combine. Add bulgur and remaining ingredients, except lettuce, and stir to coat.

3. Line serving bowl with lettuce and top with bulgur mixture. Cover and refrigerate until flavors blend, at least 15 minutes.

APPROXIMATE TOTAL TIME: 30 MINUTES (does not include chilling time)

MAKES 2 SERVINGS

Each serving provides: 1 Fat; 1 Protein; 2¼ Vegetables; 1½ Breads
Per serving: 288 calories; 9 g protein; 6 g fat; 51 g carbohydrate; 75 mg calcium; 205 mg sodium (estimated); 0 mg cholesterol; 10 g dietary fiber

Tofu and Vegetable Salad ▽C ▽S

1 medium tomato, blanched, peeled, and seeded
1 tablespoon rice vinegar
1½ teaspoons peanut *or* vegetable oil
1 teaspoon *each* reduced-sodium soy sauce and honey
½ teaspoon Chinese sesame oil
6 ounces firm-style tofu, cut into cubes
1 cup *each* sliced seeded pared cucumbers and julienne-cut (matchstick pieces) carrots
½ cup *each* julienne-cut (matchstick pieces) red bell pepper, sliced mushrooms, sliced scallions (green onions), and bean sprouts

Tofu takes on the flavor of the food around it. Combined with soy sauce, honey, Chinese sesame oil, and fresh vegetables, it becomes a tasty treat.

1. In blender combine tomato, vinegar, peanut oil, soy sauce, honey, and Chinese sesame oil and process until smooth.

2. In large mixing bowl combine remaining ingredients; add tomato mixture and toss to coat.

3. Cover and refrigerate until chilled, at least 30 minutes, or overnight. Toss again before serving.

APPROXIMATE TOTAL TIME: 15 MINUTES (does not include chilling time)

MAKES 2 SERVINGS

Each serving provides: 1 Fat; 1½ Proteins; 5 Vegetables; 10 Optional Calories
Per serving: 246 calories; 17 g protein; 12 g fat; 23 g carbohydrate; 227 mg calcium; 146 mg sodium; 0 mg cholesterol; 4 g dietary fiber (this figure does not include tofu; nutrition analysis not available)

Spicy Bean Patties

6 ounces rinsed drained canned white (cannellini) beans
1 cup cooked brown rice
¼ cup thawed frozen egg substitute
3 tablespoons plain dried bread crumbs
¼ teaspoon Mexican seasoning
Dash *each* ground red pepper and salt
¼ cup *each* diced red bell pepper and finely chopped scallions (green onions)
1 tablespoon finely chopped green chili pepper
1 small garlic clove, minced
2 teaspoons olive *or* vegetable oil

1. Preheat oven to 400°F. Using a fork, in medium mixing bowl mash beans; add rice, egg substitute, bread crumbs, Mexican seasoning, ground red pepper, and salt and stir to thoroughly combine; set aside.

2. Spray small nonstick skillet with nonstick cooking spray and heat; add bell pepper, scallions, chili pepper, and garlic and cook over medium heat, stirring frequently, until softened, about 1 minute. Add to bean mixture and stir to combine.

3. Shape bean mixture into 4 equal patties. Spray nonstick baking sheet with nonstick cooking spray and arrange patties on baking sheet. Brush each patty with ¼ teaspoon oil and bake for 15 minutes. Carefully turn each patty over and brush each with ¼ teaspoon oil. Bake 5 minutes longer.

APPROXIMATE TOTAL TIME: 30 MINUTES (includes baking time)

MAKES 2 SERVINGS, 2 PATTIES EACH

Each serving provides: 1 Fat; 2 Proteins; ½ Vegetable; 1½ Breads
Per serving: 302 calories; 13 g protein; 6 g fat; 49 g carbohydrate; 83 mg calcium; 540 mg sodium (estimated); 0.5 mg cholesterol; 6 g dietary fiber

Side Dishes

Nutrition won't get sidetracked when you serve our unusual side dishes, with complex carbohydrates playing a major role for those who want to lower their cholesterol and increase their intake of dietary fiber. Our dishes feature pasta and rice and, for a change of pace, barley, cornmeal, and couscous. Vegetables brighten meals in a colorful Confetti Sweet and Sour Slaw or turn into such sophisticated fare as Parmesan Broccoli in Wine. Pasta, once a dietary "no-no," is featured in such delightful dishes as Greek Pasta Salad and Parmesan Pasta Provençal. And roam the culinary globe with such nutrient-laden treats as Greek Eggplant Salad and Tropical Squash Rings prepared with rum. (Who says healthy eating can't be happy eating??)

Asparagus Vinaigrette

18 asparagus spears
¼ cup canned ready-to-serve low-sodium chicken broth
2 tablespoons raspberry *or* rice vinegar
2 teaspoons olive oil
½ teaspoon grated orange peel
⅛ teaspoon pepper

This recipe is also delicious when served chilled. Simply refrigerate for 30 minutes or as long as overnight.

1. In 1-quart shallow microwavable casserole arrange asparagus spears; add broth. Cover and microwave on High (100%) for 2½ minutes, rotating casserole ½ turn after 1 minute.

2. Add remaining ingredients; cover and microwave on High for 30 seconds, until asparagus spears are tender-crisp.

APPROXIMATE TOTAL TIME: 10 MINUTES

MAKES 2 SERVINGS

Each serving provides: 1 Fat; 1½ Vegetables; 5 Optional Calories

Per serving: 76 calories; 4 g protein; 5 g fat; 6 g carbohydrate; 31 mg calcium; 12 mg sodium; 0 mg cholesterol; 1 g dietary fiber

Parmesan Broccoli in Wine ▽C

½ cup sliced onion
1½ teaspoons walnut *or* olive oil
1 small garlic clove, minced
2 cups broccoli florets
1 tablespoon *each* finely chopped Italian (flat-leaf) parsley and dry red table wine
3 large Calamata olives, pitted and chopped
2 teaspoons grated Parmesan cheese

1. In 1-quart microwavable casserole combine first 3 ingredients and stir to coat; microwave on High (100%) for 2 minutes.

2. Add broccoli and stir to combine; cover and microwave on High for 5 minutes, stirring once halfway through cooking.

3. Add remaining ingredients except cheese; stir to combine. Microwave, uncovered, on Medium (50%) for 1 minute, stirring once halfway through cooking.

4. Let stand for 1 minute for flavors to blend. Sprinkle with cheese.

APPROXIMATE TOTAL TIME: 15 MINUTES

MAKES 2 SERVINGS

Each serving provides: 1 Fat; 2½ Vegetables; 15 Optional Calories
Per serving: 113 calories; 6 g protein; 6 g fat; 11 g carbohydrate; 97 mg calcium; 205 mg sodium; 1 mg cholesterol; 1 g dietary fiber (this figure does not include broccoli florets; nutrition analysis not available)

Variation: Broccoli in Wine—Omit Parmesan cheese from recipe. In Serving Information decrease Optional Calories to 5.
Per serving: 105 calories; 5 g protein; 5 g fat; 11 g carbohydrate; 74 mg calcium; 174 mg sodium; 0 mg cholesterol; 1 g dietary fiber (this figure does not include broccoli florets; nutrition analysis not available)

Brussels Sprouts and Pasta Vinaigrette $\triangledown^{C}$ $\triangledown^{F}$ $\triangledown^{S}$

2 teaspoons olive *or* vegetable oil
½ cup *each* sliced mushrooms,
   sliced onion, and red bell
   pepper strips
1 small garlic clove, minced
2 cups brussels sprouts, trimmed,
   cooked, and cut into quarters
1 cup cooked spiral macaroni
1 slice crisp bacon, crumbled
1 tablespoon *each* chopped fresh
   parsley and balsamic *or* red
   wine vinegar
Dash pepper

*Don't overcook the brussels sprouts
or they will taste bitter.*

1. In 10-inch nonstick skillet heat oil; add mushrooms, onion, bell pepper, and garlic and cook over medium heat until bell pepper is tender-crisp, about 3 minutes.

2. Add remaining ingredients and stir to combine; cook, stirring occasionally, until heated through, about 1 minute.

APPROXIMATE TOTAL TIME: 30 MINUTES

MAKES 2 SERVINGS

Each serving provides: 1 Fat; 3½ Vegetables; 1 Bread; 20 Optional Calories
Per serving: 201 calories; 7 g protein; 7 g fat; 30 g carbohydrate; 60 mg calcium; 76 mg sodium; 3 mg cholesterol; 8 g dietary fiber

Sweet and Sour Red Cabbage with Bacon ⊽ ⊽

¼ cup chopped onion
1 teaspoon *each* olive *or*
  vegetable oil and margarine
1 tablespoon apple cider vinegar
2 teaspoons firmly packed dark
  brown sugar
3 cups shredded red cabbage
1 slice crisp bacon, crumbled
⅛ teaspoon pepper
Dash ground cloves

*It takes no time at all to crisp the
bacon in your microwave oven.*

1. In 3-quart microwavable casserole combine onion, oil, and margarine and stir to coat; microwave on High (100%) for 1 minute, until onion is translucent.

2. Add ¼ *cup water*, the vinegar, and sugar, stirring to dissolve sugar; add cabbage and stir to combine. Cover and microwave on High for 4 minutes, stirring every 2 minutes, until cabbage is tender-crisp.

3. Top cabbage mixture with bacon; cover and microwave on High for 1 minute. Add pepper and cloves and stir to combine.

APPROXIMATE TOTAL TIME: 20 MINUTES

MAKES 2 SERVINGS

Each serving provides: 1 Fat; 3¼ Vegetables; 40 Optional Calories
Per serving: 109 calories; 3 g protein; 6 g fat; 13 g carbohydrate; 65 mg calcium; 86 mg sodium; 3 mg cholesterol; 2 g dietary fiber

Variation: Sweet and Sour Red Cabbage—Omit bacon from recipe. In Serving Information decrease Optional Calories to 20.
Per serving: 91 calories; 2 g protein; 4 g fat; 13 g carbohydrate; 65 mg calcium; 36 mg sodium; 0 mg cholesterol; 2 g dietary fiber

Sweet and Sour Sauerkraut ▽C

1 cup chopped onions
1 teaspoon vegetable oil
1 cup rinsed drained sauerkraut*
¼ cup unfermented apple cider
½ teaspoon caraway seed

This pungent side dish is a wonderful accompaniment to pork or chicken.

1. In 1-quart microwavable casserole combine onions and oil and stir to coat; microwave on High (100%) for 2 minutes, stirring once halfway through cooking.

2. Add remaining ingredients and stir to combine. Microwave on Medium (50%) for 5 minutes, until flavors blend.

* Use the sauerkraut that is packaged in plastic bags and stored in the refrigerator section of the supermarket; it is usually crisper and less salty than the canned.

APPROXIMATE TOTAL TIME: 15 MINUTES

MAKES 2 SERVINGS

Each serving provides: ½ Fat; 2 Vegetables; ¼ Fruit; 5 Optional Calories
Per serving: 75 calories; 2 g protein; 3 g fat; 12 g carbohydrate; 38 mg calcium; 274 mg sodium; 0 mg cholesterol; 3 g dietary fiber (this figure does not include caraway seed; nutrition analysis not available)

Parmesan Braised Citrus Fennel ⧗ ⧗

½ cup canned ready-to-serve
  low-sodium chicken broth
2 tablespoons lemon juice
2 teaspoons grated lemon peel
1 teaspoon *each* grated orange
  peel and chopped fresh parsley
1 garlic clove, minced
⅛ teaspoon pepper
3 cups thinly sliced fennel
2 teaspoons grated Parmesan
  cheese

1. In 10-inch nonstick skillet combine broth, lemon juice, lemon peel, orange peel, parsley, garlic, and pepper; cover and bring to a boil.

2. Add fennel and reduce heat to medium; cover and cook, stirring frequently, until fennel is tender-crisp, 3 to 4 minutes.

3. Transfer fennel mixture to serving bowl and sprinkle with cheese.

APPROXIMATE TOTAL TIME: 15 MINUTES

MAKES 2 SERVINGS

Each serving provides: 3 Vegetables; 20 Optional Calories
Per serving: 51 calories; 3 g protein; 1 g fat; 7 g carbohydrate; 112 mg calcium; 210 mg sodium; 1 mg cholesterol; 2 g dietary fiber

Variation: Braised Citrus Fennel—Omit Parmesan cheese from recipe. In Serving Information decrease Optional Calories to 10.
Per serving: 43 calories; 3 g protein; 1 g fat; 7 g carbohydrate; 89 mg calcium; 179 mg sodium; 0 mg cholesterol; 2 g dietary fiber

Creamy Dijon Green Beans ▽C

2 teaspoons *each* reduced-calorie
   margarine (tub) and all-
   purpose flour
½ cup low-fat milk (1% milk fat)
2 tablespoons sour cream
2 teaspoons Dijon-style mustard
⅛ teaspoon white pepper
3 cups cooked green beans (hot)

1. In 1-quart saucepan melt margarine over medium-high heat; add flour and stir quickly to combine. Continuing to stir, gradually add milk. Reduce heat to low and cook, stirring frequently, until mixture thickens, 3 to 4 minutes. Stir in remaining ingredients except green beans.

2. In serving bowl arrange green beans; add sour cream mixture and stir to coat.

APPROXIMATE TOTAL TIME: 15 MINUTES

MAKES 2 SERVINGS

Each serving provides: ¼ Milk; ½ Fat; 3 Vegetables; 50 Optional Calories
Per serving: 154 calories; 6 g protein; 7 g fat; 21 g carbohydrate; 178 mg calcium; 234 mg sodium; 9 mg cholesterol; 3 g dietary fiber

Oven-"Fried" Onion Rings ⊽ⓒ ⊽ⓢ

**2 cups thinly sliced onions
(separated into rings)
2 teaspoons vegetable oil
¾ ounce (5 tablespoons)
cornflake crumbs**

*Crunchy onion rings without deep-
fat frying.*

1. Preheat oven to 450°F. In medium mixing bowl combine onions and oil; stir to thoroughly coat. Add cornflake crumbs and toss to coat.

2. Spray nonstick baking sheet with nonstick cooking spray and spread onion mixture on sheet. Bake, turning frequently, until onion rings are crisp and browned, about 20 minutes.

**APPROXIMATE TOTAL TIME: 30 MINUTES
(includes baking time)**

MAKES 2 SERVINGS

Each serving provides: 1 Fat; 2 Vegetables; ½ Bread
Per serving: 136 calories; 3 g protein; 5 g fat; 21 g carbohydrate; 40 mg calcium; 135 mg sodium; 0 mg cholesterol; 3 g dietary fiber

Braised Vegetable Medley ▽C ▽F ▽S

¼ cup dry white table wine
2 tablespoons *each* lemon juice
 and balsamic *or* red wine
 vinegar
2 garlic cloves
¼ teaspoon *each* mustard seed
 and fennel seed
1 teaspoon chopped fresh parsley
1 cup *each* sliced carrots and
 zucchini (1-inch-thick pieces),
 and quartered mushrooms
½ cup frozen pearl onions

1. In 10-inch nonstick skillet combine ¼ *cup water*, the wine, lemon juice, vinegar, garlic, mustard seed, fennel seed, and parsley; cover and cook over high heat until mixture comes to a boil. Boil for 2 minutes, until flavors blend.

2. Set sieve over small mixing bowl and pour wine mixture through sieve, reserving liquid and discarding solids. Return wine mixture to skillet.

3. Bring wine mixture to a boil; add carrots. Reduce heat to medium-low, cover, and cook until tender-crisp, 5 to 7 minutes. Add remaining ingredients, cover, and cook until vegetables are fork-tender, about 5 minutes.

APPROXIMATE TOTAL TIME: 25 MINUTES

MAKES 2 SERVINGS

Each serving provides: 3½ Vegetables; 25 Optional Calories
Per serving: 91 calories; 3 g protein; 1 g fat; 16 g carbohydrate; 59 mg calcium; 33 mg sodium; 0 mg cholesterol; 3 g dietary fiber

Barley Casserole

2 teaspoons sweet margarine
½ cup *each* diced onion and
   sliced shiitake *or* white
   mushrooms
1 small garlic clove, minced
2¼ ounces uncooked pearl barley
½ teaspoon Italian seasoning
Dash salt

1. In 1-quart microwavable casserole melt margarine on High (100%) for 30 seconds. Add onion, mushrooms, and garlic and stir to combine. Cover and microwave on High for 2 minutes, stirring once halfway through cooking, until onion is softened.

2. Add *1½ cups water* and remaining ingredients. Cover and microwave on High for 25 minutes, until barley is tender and liquid is almost completely absorbed.

3. Let stand, covered, for 2 minutes, until all liquid is absorbed.

APPROXIMATE TOTAL TIME: 35 MINUTES

MAKES 2 SERVINGS

Each serving provides: 1 Fat; 1 Vegetable; 1½ Breads
Per serving: 167 calories; 4 g protein; 4 g fat; 29 g carbohydrate; 23 mg calcium; 75 mg sodium; 0 mg cholesterol; 6 g dietary fiber

Bacon-Flavored "Fried" Corn ⱱ(C) ⱱ(S)

¼ cup *each* diced red bell pepper
  and onion
2 teaspoons reduced-calorie
  margarine (tub)
1 cup thawed frozen whole-
  kernel corn
1 slice crisp bacon, crumbled
1 tablespoon half-and-half (blend
  of milk and cream)
¼ teaspoon granulated sugar
Dash pepper

1. In 1-quart microwavable casserole combine bell pepper, onion, and margarine; microwave on High (100%) for 2 minutes, stirring once halfway through cooking.

2. Add remaining ingredients except pepper and stir to combine; microwave on High for 4 minutes, stirring once halfway through cooking.

3. Add pepper and stir.

APPROXIMATE TOTAL TIME: 10 MINUTES

MAKES 2 SERVINGS

Each serving provides: ½ Fat; ½ Vegetable; 1 Bread; 35 Optional Calories
Per serving: 129 calories; 4 g protein; 5 g fat; 20 g carbohydrate; 18 mg calcium; 97 mg sodium; 5 mg cholesterol; 2 g dietary fiber

Variation: "Fried" Corn—Omit bacon. In Serving Information decrease Optional Calories to 15.
Per serving: 111 calories; 3 g protein; 4 g fat; 20 g carbohydrate; 17 mg calcium; 46 mg sodium; 3 mg cholesterol; 2 g dietary fiber

Chinese Corn and Peppers ▽C ▽F ▽S

½ cup *each* red bell pepper strips, green bell pepper strips, sliced onion, and quartered small mushrooms
¾ teaspoon vegetable oil
1 small garlic clove, minced
1 cup frozen *or* drained canned whole baby corn ears
1 tablespoon dry sherry
1½ teaspoons *each* rice vinegar and reduced-sodium soy sauce
¼ teaspoon *each* cornstarch and Chinese sesame oil

1. In 1-quart microwavable casserole combine peppers, onion, mushrooms, oil, and garlic; stir to coat. Cover and microwave on High (100%) for 4 minutes, stirring once halfway through cooking.

2. Add corn and stir to combine; cover and microwave on High for 1 minute.

3. In small bowl combine *1 tablespoon water* and the remaining ingredients, stirring to dissolve cornstarch. Add to vegetable mixture and stir to combine.

4. Microwave, uncovered, on High for 2 minutes, stirring once halfway through cooking.

APPROXIMATE TOTAL TIME: 15 MINUTES

MAKES 2 SERVINGS

Each serving provides: ½ Fat; 2 Vegetables; ½ Bread; 10 Optional Calories
Per serving: 116 calories; 5 g protein; 3 g fat; 16 g carbohydrate; 17 mg calcium; 174 mg sodium; 0 mg cholesterol; 5 g dietary fiber

Corn with Basil Butter

2 ears corn on the cob (each 10 inches long), with husks attached
1 tablespoon plus 1 teaspoon reduced-calorie margarine (tub)
1 tablespoon whipped butter, softened
¼ teaspoon grated orange peel
1 tablespoon chopped fresh basil

1. Set corn on floor of microwave oven and microwave on High (100%) for 5 minutes, turning corn over halfway through cooking, until corn is tender.

2. Using a fork, in small mixing bowl combine margarine, butter, and orange peel, mixing well; stir in basil.

3. To serve, pull back corn husks and remove corn silk. Brush each ear with half of the butter mixture.

APPROXIMATE TOTAL TIME: 10 MINUTES

MAKES 2 SERVINGS

Each serving provides: 1 Fat; 2 Breads; 25 Optional Calories
Per serving: 193 calories; 5 g protein; 9 g fat; 30 g carbohydrate; 16 mg calcium; 133 mg sodium; 8 mg cholesterol; 5 g dietary fiber

Corn with Chive "Cream" ▽c ▽s

2 small ears corn on the cob
(each 5 inches long)
1 tablespoon plus 1 teaspoon
reduced-calorie margarine
(tub), melted
1 tablespoon *each* chopped fresh
chives *or* chopped chives and
sour cream
⅛ teaspoon pepper

1. In 1-quart shallow microwavable casserole arrange corn; add *¼ cup water*. Cover and microwave on High (100%) for 5 minutes, rotating casserole ½ turn halfway through cooking, until corn is tender.

2. In small mixing bowl combine remaining ingredients; stir to combine.

3. Remove corn from casserole, discarding cooking liquid. Serve each ear of corn with half of the chive mixture.

APPROXIMATE TOTAL TIME: 10 MINUTES

MAKES 2 SERVINGS

Each serving provides: 1 Fat; 1 Bread; 15 Optional Calories
Per serving: 116 calories; 3 g protein; 6 g fat; 15 g carbohydrate; 12 mg calcium; 95 mg sodium; 3 mg cholesterol; 3 g dietary fiber

Savory Corn Fritters

1/3 cup plus 2 teaspoons all-
purpose flour
1/4 teaspoon double-acting baking
powder
1 egg
1/2 cup *each* thawed frozen
whole-kernel corn and canned
cream-style corn
2 tablespoons finely chopped red
bell pepper
2 teaspoons vegetable oil, divided
1/2 medium red bell pepper, cut
into rings
2 jalapeño peppers

1. On sheet of wax paper sift together flour and baking powder; set aside.

2. Using a fork, in small mixing bowl beat egg; stir in corns and chopped red bell pepper. Add flour mixture and stir until thoroughly combined.

3. In 10-inch nonstick skillet heat 1 teaspoon oil; using half of the batter, drop batter by tablespoonfuls into skillet, forming 4 fritters. Cook over medium heat until bottoms are lightly browned, 2 to 3 minutes; using pancake turner, turn fritters over and cook until other sides are browned, 2 to 3 minutes longer.

4. Transfer fritters to serving platter; keep warm. Repeat procedure with remaining oil and batter, making 4 more fritters. Garnish platter with red bell pepper rings and jalapeño peppers.

APPROXIMATE TOTAL TIME: 20 MINUTES

MAKES 4 SERVINGS, 2 FRITTERS EACH

Each serving provides: 1/2 Fat; 1/4 Protein; 1/4 Vegetable;
1 Bread
Per serving: 126 calories; 4 g protein; 4 g fat; 20 g carbohydrate; 23 mg calcium; 134 mg sodium; 53 mg cholesterol; 1 g dietary fiber

Polenta Toasts

3 ounces uncooked instant
   polenta (quick-cooking yellow
   cornmeal)
3 ounces reduced-fat Cheddar
   cheese, shredded

*Serve Polenta Toasts with salsa for
dipping.*

1. Preheat oven to 450°F. In 1-quart saucepan bring *3 cups water* to a full boil; stir in polenta and cook, stirring constantly, for 5 minutes.

2. Spray 15 × 10½ × 1-inch jelly-roll pan with nonstick cooking spray and spread polenta evenly in prepared pan; sprinkle with cheese. Bake until cheese is melted, about 20 minutes.

3. Let cool slightly. Cut polenta into 24 equal strips; transfer to wire rack and let cool.

APPROXIMATE TOTAL TIME: 30 MINUTES (includes baking time; does not include cooling time)

MAKES 4 SERVINGS, 6 TOASTS EACH

Each serving provides: 1 Protein; 1 Bread
Per serving: 145 calories; 8 g protein; 4 g fat; 17 g carbohydrate; 189 mg calcium; 151 mg sodium; 15 mg cholesterol; 1 g dietary fiber

Southwestern Polenta �C⃝ F⃝

1 teaspoon vegetable oil
¼ cup *each* chopped onion and
 diced red bell pepper
1 tablespoon seeded and finely
 diced jalapeño pepper
1 garlic clove, minced
⅛ teaspoon salt
2¼ ounces uncooked instant
 polenta (quick-cooking yellow
 cornmeal)
¾ ounce reduced-fat Monterey
 Jack *or* Cheddar cheese,
 shredded
1 teaspoon margarine
¼ cup mild salsa

*Jalapeño pepper and salsa add spice
to the mild flavor of polenta.*

1. In 1½-quart nonstick saucepan heat oil; add onion, peppers, and garlic and cook over medium-high heat, stirring occasionally, until onion is softened, about 2 minutes.

2. Increase heat to high; add *1½ cups water* and the salt and bring mixture to a boil. Stirring constantly, add polenta in a thin steady stream; stir in cheese and margarine.

3. Reduce heat to medium and cook, stirring constantly, until mixture thickens, about 4 minutes.

4. Spray 7-inch pie plate with nonstick cooking spray; transfer polenta to pie plate. Let cool for 5 minutes.

5. To serve, top with salsa.

APPROXIMATE TOTAL TIME: 20 MINUTES

MAKES 2 SERVINGS

Each serving provides: 1 Fat; ½ Protein; ¾ Vegetable; 1½ Breads
Per serving with Monterey Jack cheese: 206 calories; 6 g protein; 7 g fat; 30 g carbohydrate; 106 mg calcium; 410 mg sodium; 8 mg cholesterol; 2 g dietary fiber
With Cheddar cheese: 210 calories; 6 g protein; 7 g fat; 30 g carbohydrate; 106 mg calcium; 418 mg sodium; 8 mg cholesterol; 2 g dietary fiber

Spicy Cornmeal Biscuits ▽Ⓒ

½ cup plus 1 tablespoon all-
purpose flour
1½ ounces uncooked yellow
cornmeal
2 ounces reduced-fat Cheddar
cheese, shredded
½ teaspoon *each* baking soda and
seeded and finely chopped
jalapeño pepper
¾ cup low-fat buttermilk
(1% milk fat)
2 tablespoons plus 2 teaspoons
reduced-calorie margarine
(tub), melted

1. Preheat oven to 450°F. In medium mixing bowl combine flour, cornmeal, cheese, baking soda, and pepper; set aside.

2. In small mixing bowl combine buttermilk and margarine; pour into flour mixture and stir to combine (mixture will be sticky).

3. Onto nonstick baking sheet drop batter by tablespoonfuls, making 8 biscuits. Bake in middle of center oven rack until biscuits are golden brown, about 15 minutes. Transfer to wire rack and let cool.

APPROXIMATE TOTAL TIME: 25 MINUTES (includes baking time)

MAKES 4 SERVINGS, 2 BISCUITS EACH

Each serving provides: 1 Fat; ½ Protein; 1¼ Breads; 30 Optional Calories
Per serving: 200 calories; 8 g protein; 7 g fat; 24 g carbohydrate; 182 mg calcium; 331 mg sodium; 12 mg cholesterol; 1 g dietary fiber

Southwestern Succotash ⊽ᶜ ⊽ᶠ ⊽ˢ

2 teaspoons reduced-calorie
   margarine (tub)
½ cup *each* julienne-cut
   (matchstick pieces) red bell
   pepper and diced zucchini
¼ cup finely chopped onion
½ medium mild chili pepper,
   seeded and minced
½ small garlic clove, minced
2 large plum tomatoes, blanched,
   peeled, seeded, and finely
   chopped
¾ cup drained canned whole
   yellow hominy
¼ cup *each* frozen green lima
   beans and canned ready-to-
   serve low-sodium chicken
   broth
Dash pepper

*This version of succotash combines
lima beans with hominy rather than
corn kernels. Hominy is hulled dried
corn kernels. Canned hominy has
been reconstituted and cooked prior
to canning.*

1. In 9-inch nonstick skillet melt margarine; add bell pepper, zucchini, onion, chili pepper, and garlic and sauté over medium-high heat until tender-crisp, 2 to 3 minutes.

2. Add remaining ingredients and stir to combine; bring to a boil. Continue cooking, stirring frequently, until mixture is reduced by half, 6 to 8 minutes.

APPROXIMATE TOTAL TIME: 20 MINUTES

MAKES 2 SERVINGS

Each serving provides: ½ Fat; 2½ Vegetables; 1 Bread; 5 Optional Calories
Per serving: 117 calories; 4 g protein; 3 g fat; 20 g carbohydrate; 29 mg calcium; 191 mg sodium; 0 mg cholesterol; 6 g dietary fiber

Tex-Mex Posole ▽C

1 cup drained canned whole
   yellow hominy
¼ cup evaporated skimmed milk
2 tablespoons sour cream
1 teaspoon *each* margarine and
   olive *or* vegetable oil
¼ cup *each* chopped onion and
   green bell pepper
1 tablespoon crushed dried chili
   pepper
1 garlic clove, minced
½ cup canned Italian tomatoes
   (reserve liquid), seeded and
   diced
¾ ounce reduced-fat Monterey
   Jack cheese, shredded

*In the Southwest, posole is another
word for hominy.*

1. In food processor combine hominy, milk, and sour cream and process, using on-off motion, until hominy is coarsely chopped; set aside.

2. In 9-inch nonstick skillet heat margarine and oil until margarine is melted; add onion, peppers, and garlic and sauté over medium-high heat until vegetables are softened, 1 to 2 minutes.

3. Add tomatoes with reserved liquid to onion-pepper mixture and stir to combine. Reduce heat to low and cook, stirring frequently, until flavors blend, 5 to 7 minutes.

4. Stir hominy mixture into tomato mixture and cook until heated through, about 5 minutes. Stir in cheese.

APPROXIMATE TOTAL TIME: 25 MINUTES

MAKES 2 SERVINGS

Each serving provides: ¼ Milk; 1 Fat; ½ Protein; 1 Vegetable; 1 Bread; 35 Optional Calories
Per serving: 219 calories; 9 g protein; 10 g fat; 25 g carbohydrate; 236 mg calcium; 555 mg sodium; 15 mg cholesterol; 4 g dietary fiber

Curried Couscous Pilaf ▽C ▽F ▽S

3 ounces uncooked couscous (dry precooked semolina)

1 tablespoon plus 1 teaspoon olive *or* vegetable oil

½ cup *each* shredded carrot, diced red *or* yellow bell pepper, and sliced scallions (green onions)

⅓ cup plus 2 teaspoons golden raisins

½ cup apple juice (no sugar added)

½ medium tomato, diced

1 teaspoon curry powder

1. In 1-quart saucepan bring 1½ cups *water* to a full boil. Remove from heat and stir in couscous. Cover and let stand, stirring occasionally, until water is absorbed, about 5 minutes.

2. In 9-inch nonstick skillet heat oil; add carrot, pepper, and scallions and cook over medium heat, stirring occasionally, until carrot is tender, about 2 minutes. Stir in raisins and apple juice and bring mixture to a boil. Reduce heat to low; stir in tomato and curry powder and let simmer until flavors blend, about 2 minutes. Stir in couscous.

APPROXIMATE TOTAL TIME: 20 MINUTES

MAKES 4 SERVINGS

Each serving provides: 1 Fat; 1 Vegetable; 1 Bread; 1 Fruit
Per serving: 184 calories; 4 g protein; 5 g fat; 34 g carbohydrate; 25 mg calcium; 13 mg sodium; 0 mg cholesterol; 2 g dietary fiber (this figure does not include couscous; nutrition analysis not available)

Hungarian Noodles ▽F̄

⅓ cup low-fat cottage cheese
   (2% milk fat)
¼ cup evaporated skimmed milk
2 tablespoons sour cream
1 teaspoon paprika
Dash white pepper
2 teaspoons margarine
¼ cup chopped onion
1 garlic clove, minced
1 tablespoon *each* Worcestershire
   sauce and all-purpose flour
1½ cups cooked medium noodles
   (hot)

1. In blender combine first 5 ingredients and process until smooth, scraping down sides of container as necessary; set aside.

2. In 1-quart nonstick saucepan melt margarine; add onion and garlic and sauté over medium-high heat until onion is softened, 1 to 2 minutes. Stir in Worcestershire sauce.

3. Sprinkle flour over onion mixture and stir quickly to combine; stir in cottage cheese mixture. Cook, stirring frequently, until mixture thickens, 4 to 5 minutes. Add noodles and stir to combine.

APPROXIMATE TOTAL TIME: 20 MINUTES

MAKES 2 SERVINGS

Each serving provides: ¼ Milk; 1 Fat; ½ Protein; ¼ Vegetable; 1½ Breads; 50 Optional Calories
Per serving: 275 calories; 13 g protein; 9 g fat; 35 g carbohydrate; 154 mg calcium; 326 mg sodium; 39 mg cholesterol; 1 g dietary fiber

Lemon-Poppy Seed Noodles ▽Ⓢ

1 tablespoon *each* whipped
    butter and freshly squeezed
    lemon juice
1 teaspoon *each* poppy seed and
    margarine
½ teaspoon grated lemon peel
⅛ teaspoon white pepper
1 cup cooked noodles (hot)

*A little butter adds a lot of flavor to
this simple side dish.*

1. In small nonstick saucepan combine all ingredients except noodles; cook over high heat until butter and margarine are melted, about 1 minute. Add noodles and stir to coat with butter mixture.

APPROXIMATE TOTAL TIME: 15 MINUTES

MAKES 2 SERVINGS

Each serving provides: ½ Fat; 1 Bread; 35 Optional Calories
Per serving: 135 calories; 3 g protein; 6 g fat; 16 g carbohydrate; 31 mg calcium; 53 mg sodium; 28 mg cholesterol; 1 g dietary fiber (this figure does not include poppy seed; nutrition analysis not available)

Thai Two-Noodle Stir-Fry ▽C ▽F

2 cups boiling water
1 ounce uncooked rice sticks (rice noodles)*
¼ cup canned ready-to-serve low-sodium chicken broth
1 tablespoon *each* firmly packed dark brown sugar, reduced-sodium soy sauce, and freshly squeezed lime juice
1¾ teaspoons peanut oil
¼ teaspoon chili oil
¼ cup *each* thinly sliced red bell pepper and scallions (green onions)
1 teaspoon crushed dried chili pepper
1 garlic clove, minced
1 cup *each* cooked thin noodles and bean sprouts

This recipe calls for rice sticks, a type of Chinese rice noodle. Look for it in the Oriental section of your supermarket.

1. In medium mixing bowl pour water over rice sticks and let stand for 10 minutes. Drain, discarding water, and set aside.

2. In 1-cup liquid measure combine broth, sugar, soy sauce, and lime juice, stirring to dissolve sugar; set aside.

3. In 10-inch nonstick skillet heat oils; add bell pepper, scallions, chili pepper, and garlic and cook over high heat, stirring frequently, until scallions are lightly browned, 1 to 2 minutes. Stir in broth mixture; add rice sticks, noodles, and sprouts and stir to combine. Cook, stirring frequently, until liquid is reduced by half, 3 to 5 minutes.

* One ounce uncooked rice sticks yields about ½ cup cooked.

APPROXIMATE TOTAL TIME: 30 MINUTES

MAKES 2 SERVINGS

Each serving provides: 1 Fat; 1½ Vegetables; 1½ Breads; 35 Optional Calories
Per serving: 240 calories; 6 g protein; 6 g fat; 41 g carbohydrate; 33 mg calcium; 316 mg sodium; 20 mg cholesterol; 2 g dietary fiber

Cuban Black Bean Salad

Microwave Brunswick Stew
Italian Seafood Stew
Beef 'n' Barley Stew
Oriental Hot Pot

Tropical Oatmeal Cookies
Spicy Deviled Eggs
Bibb and Grapefruit Salad
"Fried" Chicken

Blueberry-Oat Bran Loaf
Quick Rugalach (Raisin Crescents)
Iced Apple Turnovers

California Burgers
Thai Marinated Steak
Swordfish Kabobs

Parmesan Pasta Provençal ▽C ▽F

**1 cup *each* diced eggplant and
zucchini**
2 teaspoons olive oil
1 large garlic clove, minced
**2½ cups canned Italian tomatoes,
divided**
**1 tablespoon chopped fresh basil
or ½ teaspoon basil leaves**
**1½ cups cooked orecchiette pasta
(saucer-shaped pasta) *or* small
shell macaroni (hot)**
**1 tablespoon grated Parmesan
cheese**

*To speed preparation, cook the
pasta on the range while the vegetables cook in the microwave oven.*

1. In 3-quart microwavable casserole combine
eggplant, zucchini, oil, and garlic and stir to coat.
Microwave on High (100%) for 2 minutes, until
softened.

2. In blender process 1½ cups tomatoes until
smooth. Set sieve over eggplant mixture and press
processed tomatoes through sieve into casserole, discarding solids.

3. Seed and dice remaining tomatoes; add to eggplant
mixture and stir to combine. Add ¼ *cup water* and
stir to combine.

4. Cover and microwave on High for 12 minutes,
stirring once every 4 minutes, until mixture thickens.
Stir in basil.

5. To serve, in serving bowl arrange pasta; top with
eggplant mixture and sprinkle with cheese.

APPROXIMATE TOTAL TIME: 25 MINUTES

MAKES 2 SERVINGS

Each serving provides: 1 Fat; 4½ Vegetables; 1½ Breads;
15 Optional Calories
Per serving: 253 calories; 9 g protein; 7 g fat; 42 g carbohydrate; 157 mg calcium; 540 mg sodium; 2 mg cholesterol; 4 g dietary fiber

*Variation: Pasta Provençal—*Omit Parmesan cheese from
recipe. In Serving Information omit Optional Calories.
Per serving: 241 calories; 8 g protein; 6 g fat; 42 g carbohydrate; 123 mg calcium; 494 mg sodium; 0 mg cholesterol; 4 g dietary fiber

Parmesan Pasta with Broccoli Rabe ▽C ▽F ▽S

2 teaspoons olive oil
½ cup *each* diced red bell pepper,
   yellow bell pepper, and onion
1 small garlic clove, minced
4 cups thoroughly washed and
   trimmed broccoli rabe, chopped
1½ cups cooked elbow *or* small
   shell macaroni (hot)
2 teaspoons grated Parmesan
   cheese
Dash pepper

*Prepare the pasta for this dish while
the broccoli rabe is cooking.*

1. In 10-inch nonstick skillet heat oil; add bell peppers, onion, and garlic and cook over medium heat, stirring occasionally, until tender-crisp, about 2 minutes.

2. Add broccoli rabe and stir to combine. Reduce heat to low, partially cover, and cook until tender, about 10 minutes.

3. Add macaroni and stir to combine. Sprinkle with cheese and pepper.

APPROXIMATE TOTAL TIME: 25 MINUTES

MAKES 2 SERVINGS

Each serving provides: 1 Fat; 5½ Vegetables; 1½ Breads; 10 Optional Calories
Per serving: 229 calories; 10 g protein; 6 g fat; 37 g carbohydrate; 144 mg calcium; 103 mg sodium; 1 mg cholesterol; 7 g dietary fiber

Variation: Pasta with Broccoli Rabe—Omit Parmesan cheese. In Serving Information omit Optional Calories.
Per serving: 221 calories; 9 g protein; 6 g fat; 37 g carbohydrate; 121 mg calcium; 72 mg sodium; 0 mg cholesterol; 7 g dietary fiber

Pasta and Vegetable Toss � ⟁ ⟁ ⟁

2 teaspoons olive *or* vegetable oil
1 cup *each* sliced onions,
    shredded zucchini, and
    shredded carrots
1 small garlic clove, minced
1½ cups cooked spiral macaroni
1 tablespoon chopped fresh
    Italian (flat-leaf) parsley
2 teaspoons balsamic *or* red wine
    vinegar

*For an Italian-style topping sprinkle
with grated Parmesan cheese before
serving.*

1. In 9-inch nonstick skillet heat oil; add onions, zucchini, carrots, and garlic and cook over medium heat, stirring occasionally, until onions are tender, about 5 minutes.

2. Add macaroni to skillet and stir to combine. Add parsley and vinegar and stir to combine. Reduce heat to low; cook, stirring frequently, until thoroughly heated, about 1 minute.

APPROXIMATE TOTAL TIME: 30 MINUTES

MAKES 2 SERVINGS

Each serving provides: 1 Fat; 3 Vegetables; 1½ Breads
Per serving: 219 calories; 6 g protein; 5 g fat; 38 g carbohydrate; 57 mg calcium; 25 mg sodium; 0 mg cholesterol; 5 g dietary fiber

Pasta-Stuffed Artichokes ⟨C⟩

2 artichokes (½ pound each)
½ lemon
2 teaspoons olive *or* vegetable
   oil, divided
½ cup sliced shiitake *or* white
   mushrooms
1 small garlic clove, minced
1 cup cooked thin spaghetti (hot)
¾ ounce grated Parmesan cheese
   (reserve 2 teaspoons)
1½ teaspoons *each* chopped fresh
   Italian (flat-leaf) parsley and
   balsamic *or* red wine vinegar
½ teaspoon grated lemon peel
Garnish: lemon wedges

1. Using large stainless-steel knife, cut off stem of each artichoke flush with base so that artichokes will stand upright; snap off any small or discolored leaves, at base. Using scissors, remove barbed tips of leaves, cutting about ½ inch off tip of each leaf.

2. In 2-quart saucepan add artichokes and lemon to *1 quart water*. Bring water to a full boil and cook until artichokes are tender, about 20 minutes. Drain and let cool.

3. While artichokes are cooking prepare filling. In 9-inch nonstick skillet heat 1 teaspoon oil; add mushrooms and garlic and cook over medium-high heat, stirring frequently, until mushrooms are tender, about 3 minutes. Add spaghetti, cheese, parsley, vinegar, remaining oil, and the lemon peel and stir to combine.

4. Using a spoon or fork, remove and discard center chokes from artichokes. Fill center of each artichoke with ½ of the spaghetti-mushroom mixture; sprinkle each with 1 teaspoon reserved cheese. Garnish with lemon wedges.

APPROXIMATE TOTAL TIME: 45 MINUTES

MAKES 2 SERVINGS, 1 ARTICHOKE EACH

Each serving provides: 1 Fat; ½ Protein; 1½ Vegetables; 1 Bread
Per serving: 240 calories; 11 g protein; 8 g fat; 32 g carbohydrate; 199 mg calcium; 273 mg sodium; 8 mg cholesterol; 6 g dietary fiber

Pasta with Broccoli ▽C ▽S

2 teaspoons olive oil
½ ounce pignolias (pine nuts)
2 garlic cloves, minced
1 cup broccoli florets
½ cup canned ready-to-serve
   low-sodium chicken broth
2 tablespoons dried currants
1½ cups cooked orecchiette
   (saucer-shaped pasta) *or* small
   shell macaroni (hot)

If you prefer, dark raisins may be used in place of currants in this recipe.

1. In 10-inch nonstick skillet heat oil; add pignolias and garlic and cook over medium-high heat, stirring frequently, until pignolias are lightly browned, 1 to 2 minutes.

2. Add broccoli, broth, and currants. Reduce heat to medium-low, cover, and cook until broccoli is tender, 4 to 5 minutes. Add pasta and stir to combine.

APPROXIMATE TOTAL TIME: 25 MINUTES

MAKES 2 SERVINGS

Each serving provides: 1½ Fats; ½ Protein; 1 Vegetable; 1½ Breads; ½ Fruit; 10 Optional Calories
Per serving: 251 calories; 9 g protein; 9 g fat; 37 g carbohydrate; 51 mg calcium; 31 mg sodium; 0 mg cholesterol; 1 g dietary fiber (this figure does not include pignolias and broccoli florets; nutrition analyses not available)

Pasta with Double Tomato Sauce ⬇C ⬇F ⬇S

2 teaspoons olive *or* vegetable oil
½ cup finely chopped onion
1 small garlic clove, minced
6 large plum tomatoes, blanched,
    peeled, seeded, and chopped
6 sun-dried tomato halves (not
    packed in oil), chopped
½ cup low-fat milk (1% milk fat)
1 tablespoon chopped fresh
    Italian (flat-leaf) parsley
1½ cups cooked penne *or* ziti
    macaroni (hot)

*While preparing the tomato sauce,
you can also be cooking the pasta.*

1. In 9-inch nonstick skillet heat oil; add onion and garlic and cook over medium heat until softened, about 2 minutes. Stir in plum tomatoes and sun-dried tomatoes.

2. Reduce heat to low and gradually stir in milk; stir in parsley. Cook, stirring occasionally, for 5 minutes.

3. Add pasta to tomato mixture and stir to combine.

APPROXIMATE TOTAL TIME: 30 MINUTES

MAKES 2 SERVINGS

Each serving provides: ¼ Milk; 1 Fat; 5 Vegetables; 1½ Breads; 5 Optional Calories
Per serving: 251 calories; 9 g protein; 6 g fat; 43 g carbohydrate; 117 mg calcium; 56 mg sodium; 2 mg cholesterol; 6 g dietary fiber

Variation: Pasta with Tomato Sauce—Omit sun-dried tomatoes. In Serving Information decrease Vegetables to 3½.
Per serving: 226 calories; 7 g protein; 6 g fat; 37 g carbohydrate; 108 mg calcium; 45 mg sodium; 2 mg cholesterol; 4 g dietary fiber

Pasta with Swiss Chard and Cheese ⌄C⌄ ⌄F⌄ ⌄S⌄

2 teaspoons olive *or* vegetable oil
1 tablespoon chopped onion
2 small garlic cloves, minced
1 cup thoroughly washed and
   drained Swiss chard,* chopped
Dash *each* black pepper and
   crushed red pepper
¼ cup canned ready-to-serve
   low-sodium chicken broth
1½ cups cooked spaghetti *or*
   linguine (hot)
2 teaspoons grated Parmesan *or*
   Romano cheese

1. In 10-inch nonstick skillet heat oil; add onion and garlic and cook over medium-high heat, stirring frequently, until onion is translucent, about 1 minute. Add Swiss chard, black pepper, and red pepper. Reduce heat to medium and cook, stirring frequently, for 2 minutes.

2. Add broth and reduce heat to low; let simmer until Swiss chard is tender-crisp, about 8 minutes.

3. Add spaghetti and toss to combine. Sprinkle with cheese.

* One cup fresh Swiss chard yields about ¼ cup cooked Swiss chard.

APPROXIMATE TOTAL TIME: 20 MINUTES

MAKES 2 SERVINGS

Each serving provides: 1 Fat; ¼ Vegetable; 1½ Breads; 15 Optional Calories
Per serving with Parmesan cheese: 208 calories; 6 g protein; 6 g fat; 32 g carbohydrate; 45 mg calcium; 78 mg sodium; 1 mg cholesterol; 2 g dietary fiber (this figure does not include Swiss chard; nutrition analysis not available)
With Romano cheese: 207 calories; 6 g protein; 6 g fat; 32 g carbohydrate; 40 mg calcium; 67 mg sodium; 2 mg cholesterol; 2 g dietary fiber (this figure does not include Swiss chard; nutrition analysis not available)

Variation: Pasta with Swiss Chard—Omit cheese. In Serving Information decrease Optional Calories to 5.
Per serving: 200 calories; 6 g protein; 5 g fat; 32 g carbohydrate; 22 mg calcium; 47 mg sodium; 0 mg cholesterol; 2 g dietary fiber (this figure does not include Swiss chard; nutrition analysis not available)

Sicilian Pasta with Peas ▽C ▽F

¼ cup chopped onion
1 teaspoon olive oil
1 garlic clove, minced
2 cups canned Italian tomatoes, pureed
½ cup frozen tiny peas
1 cup cooked rotelle (spiral macaroni), hot
¼ cup part-skim ricotta cheese
1 tablespoon grated Parmesan cheese

1. In shallow 1-quart microwavable casserole combine first 3 ingredients, stirring to coat; microwave on High (100%) for 1 minute.

2. Set sieve over casserole and pour pureed tomatoes through sieve into casserole, discarding solids. Add peas and stir to combine. Cover with wax paper and microwave on High for 10 minutes, stirring once every 3 minutes.

3. To serve, in serving bowl combine pasta and half of the tomato mixture and stir to combine. Top with remaining tomato mixture, the ricotta cheese, and Parmesan cheese.

APPROXIMATE TOTAL TIME: 25 MINUTES

MAKES 2 SERVINGS

Each serving provides: ½ Fat; ½ Protein; 2¼ Vegetables; 1½ Breads; 15 Optional Calories
Per serving: 240 calories; 12 g protein; 6 g fat; 35 g carbohydrate; 202 mg calcium; 541 mg sodium; 12 mg cholesterol; 4 g dietary fiber

Spicy Country Pasta and Cheese ▽c ▽F

2 tablespoons chopped onion
2 garlic cloves, minced
1 teaspoon olive oil
1 cup shiitake *or* white
  mushrooms, sliced
1 cup canned Italian tomatoes
  (reserve liquid), seeded and
  chopped
5 small pitted black cured olives,
  cut into halves
⅛ teaspoon crushed red pepper
2 cups cooked penne *or* ziti
  macaroni (hot)
2 teaspoons grated Parmesan
  cheese
Garnish: fresh basil leaves

1. In 3-quart microwavable casserole combine onion, garlic, and oil and stir to coat. Microwave on High (100%) for 1 minute. Add mushrooms and tomatoes with reserved liquid and stir to combine. Cover and microwave on High for 7 minutes, stirring once every 3 minutes.

2. Add olives and pepper and stir until thoroughly combined.

3. To serve, in serving bowl arrange pasta; top with mushroom-tomato mixture and toss to combine. Sprinkle with Parmesan cheese and garnish with basil.

APPROXIMATE TOTAL TIME: 25 MINUTES

MAKES 2 SERVINGS

Each serving provides: ¾ Fat; 2⅛ Vegetables; 2 Breads; 10 Optional Calories
Per serving: 275 calories; 10 g protein; 5 g fat; 49 g carbohydrate; 81 mg calcium; 300 mg sodium; 1 mg cholesterol; 4 g dietary fiber

Variation: Spicy Country Pasta—Omit Parmesan cheese. In Serving Information omit Optional Calories.
Per serving: 267 calories; 9 g protein; 4 g fat; 49 g carbohydrate; 58 mg calcium; 269 mg sodium; 0 mg cholesterol; 4 g dietary fiber

Greek Pasta Salad ⟨c⟩

1½ teaspoons olive oil
2 garlic cloves, cut into halves
1½ cups cooked thin spaghetti
12 cherry tomatoes, cut into
  halves
10 small pitted black *or* Calamata
  olives, cut into halves
¾ ounce feta cheese, crumbled,
  divided
1 tablespoon chopped fresh mint
¼ teaspoon grated lemon peel
⅛ teaspoon pepper
Garnish: mint sprig

1. In small saucepan heat oil; add garlic and cook over medium heat, until lightly browned, 1 to 2 minutes. Remove and discard garlic, reserving oil.

2. In medium mixing bowl combine spaghetti, tomatoes, olives, ½ ounce feta cheese, the mint, lemon peel, and pepper; add heated oil and toss to coat.

3. To serve, transfer spaghetti mixture to serving bowl and sprinkle with remaining feta cheese; garnish with mint sprig.

APPROXIMATE TOTAL TIME: 20 MINUTES

MAKES 2 SERVINGS

Each serving provides: 1¼ Fats; ½ Protein; 1 Vegetable; 1½ Breads
Per serving: 221 calories; 6 g protein; 9 g fat; 29 g carbohydrate; 89 mg calcium; 241 mg sodium; 9 mg cholesterol; 2 g dietary fiber

Pasta Salad with Broccoli ⊽C⊽ ⊽F⊽

2 tablespoons plain low-fat
   yogurt
1 tablespoon plus 1 teaspoon
   reduced-calorie mayonnaise
1 tablespoon pickle relish
2 teaspoons red wine vinegar
1 teaspoon finely chopped shallot
   or onion
1 cup cooked shell macaroni,
   chilled
½ cup broccoli florets, blanched
2 ounces rinsed drained canned
   chick-peas
¼ cup *each* diced tomato and red
   or green bell pepper

Prepare the pasta for this dish ahead
so it will have time to chill.

1. Using a wire whisk, in medium mixing bowl blend together first 5 ingredients; add remaining ingredients and toss to coat.

2. Cover and refrigerate until ready to serve.

APPROXIMATE TOTAL TIME: 20 MINUTES

MAKES 2 SERVINGS

Each serving provides: 1 Fat; ½ Protein; 1 Vegetable; 1 Bread; 25 Optional Calories
Per serving: 178 calories; 7 g protein; 4 g fat; 30 g carbohydrate; 60 mg calcium; 247 mg sodium (estimated); 4 mg cholesterol; 2 g dietary fiber (this figure does not include broccoli florets; nutrition analysis not available)

Spring Peas and Carrots ⑂ⓕⓢ

2 cups sugar snap peas *or* snow
    peas (Chinese pea pods), stem
    ends and strings removed
1 cup thinly sliced carrots
½ cup apple juice (no sugar
    added)
2 teaspoons reduced-calorie
    margarine (tub)
Garnish: mint sprigs

*This brightly colored side dish goes
from the microwave oven to the dinner table in no time.*

1. In 1-quart microwavable casserole combine first 3 ingredients. Cover and microwave on High (100%) for 5 minutes, until tender-crisp.

2. Add margarine and stir to combine; microwave, uncovered, on High for 3 minutes. Let stand 1 minute.

3. To serve, transfer to serving platter and garnish with mint sprigs.

APPROXIMATE TOTAL TIME: 20 MINUTES

MAKES 2 SERVINGS

Each serving provides: ½ Fat; 3 Vegetables; ½ Fruit
Per serving: 130 calories; 5 g protein; 2 g fat; 24 g carbohydrate; 82 mg calcium; 67 mg sodium; 0 mg cholesterol; 5 g dietary fiber

Caraway Potatoes

2 teaspoons margarine
2 teaspoons all-purpose flour,
  divided
¼ cup canned ready-to-serve
  low-sodium chicken broth
1 teaspoon chopped fresh parsley
½ teaspoon caraway seed
⅛ teaspoon salt
Dash pepper
9 ounces cooked red potatoes,
  quartered
¼ cup plain low-fat yogurt

In a hurry? Use your microwave oven to cook the potatoes for this recipe in minutes.

1. In 9-inch nonstick skillet melt margarine over medium heat; add 1 teaspoon flour and stir quickly to combine. Continuing to stir, gradually add broth and cook, stirring constantly, until mixture thickens, about 1 minute.

2. Add parsley, caraway seed, salt, and pepper and stir to combine. Reduce heat to low; add potatoes and cook, stirring frequently, until potatoes are heated through, 4 to 5 minutes.

3. In small bowl combine yogurt and remaining flour, stirring to dissolve flour; stir into skillet. Cook, stirring frequently, until mixture thickens, 3 to 4 minutes.

APPROXIMATE TOTAL TIME: 30 MINUTES

MAKES 2 SERVINGS

Each serving provides: ¼ Milk; 1 Fat; 1½ Breads; 20 Optional Calories
Per serving: 170 calories; 5 g protein; 5 g fat; 27 g carbohydrate; 60 mg calcium; 220 mg sodium; 2 mg cholesterol; 2 g dietary fiber (this figure does not include caraway seed; nutrition analysis not available)

Florentine Potatoes ▽C ▽F ▽S

9 ounces pared all-purpose
   potatoes, thinly sliced
½ cup chopped onion
1 tablespoon plus 1 teaspoon
   reduced-calorie margarine (tub)
1 small garlic clove, minced
½ cup thoroughly drained cooked
   spinach
¼ cup plain low-fat yogurt
¼ teaspoon ground nutmeg

1. In 1-quart microwavable casserole combine 2 *cups water* and the potatoes. Cover and microwave on High (100%) for 10 minutes, stirring once halfway through cooking, until potatoes are soft.

2. Drain potatoes; transfer to medium mixing bowl. Using a fork, mash potatoes; set aside.

3. In same casserole combine onion, margarine, and garlic; microwave on High, uncovered, for 1 minute, stirring once halfway through cooking. Add potatoes, spinach, yogurt, and nutmeg and stir to combine. Microwave on High for 1 minute, until heated through.

APPROXIMATE TOTAL TIME: 30 MINUTES

MAKES 2 SERVINGS

Each serving provides: ¼ Milk; 1 Fat; 1 Vegetable; 1½ Breads
Per serving: 179 calories; 6 g protein; 5 g fat; 30 g carbohydrate; 134 mg calcium; 140 mg sodium; 2 mg cholesterol; 4 g dietary fiber

Garlic 'n' Onion-Mashed Potatoes ⦣ᴄ ⦣ꜰ ⦣ꜱ

9 ounces pared all-purpose
    potatoes, cubed
¼ cup diced onion
1½ garlic cloves, chopped
¼ cup evaporated skimmed milk
2 teaspoons margarine
Dash white pepper

1. In 2-quart saucepan bring 1½ quarts water to a boil; add potatoes, onion, and garlic and cook until potatoes are fork-tender, 10 to 15 minutes.

2. While potatoes are cooking prepare milk mixture. In small nonstick saucepan combine milk, margarine, and pepper and cook over low heat until margarine is melted. Keep warm over low heat.

3. Pour potato-onion mixture through colander, discarding cooking liquid. Transfer potato-onion mixture to large mixing bowl. Using mixer on low speed, mash potato-onion mixture. Gradually increase speed to high; add milk mixture and continue beating until potatoes are light and fluffy.

APPROXIMATE TOTAL TIME: 25 MINUTES

MAKES 2 SERVINGS

Each serving provides: ¼ Milk; 1 Fat; ¼ Vegetable; 1½ Breads
Per serving: 170 calories; 5 g protein; 4 g fat; 29 g carbohydrate; 112 mg calcium; 90 mg sodium; 1 mg cholesterol; 2 g dietary fiber

Potato Crêpes

6 ounces pared baking potato, shredded

½ cup grated onion

3 egg whites

1 tablespoon all-purpose flour

Dash *each* white pepper and ground nutmeg

2 teaspoons vegetable oil, divided

12 asparagus spears, cooked

¾ ounce reduced-fat Swiss cheese, shredded

¼ cup plain low-fat yogurt

1. In medium mixing bowl combine potato, onion, egg whites, flour, pepper, and nutmeg; mix well.

2. Spray 9-inch nonstick skillet with nonstick cooking spray and heat; brush with ½ teaspoon oil. Pour ¼ of potato mixture into skillet and, using the back of a spoon, spread mixture over bottom of pan; cook over medium-high heat until bottom is browned, about 1 minute. Using a pancake turner, carefully turn crêpe over and cook over medium heat until other side is browned, about 1 minute longer.

3. Repeat procedure 3 more times, using remaining oil and potato mixture and making 3 more crêpes.

4. Preheat oven to 400°F. Onto center of each crêpe arrange 3 asparagus spears; fold sides of crêpes over to enclose asparagus.

5. In 8 x 8 x 2-inch baking dish arrange crêpes, seam-side down; sprinkle with cheese. Bake until asparagus are heated through, about 10 minutes.

6. Top each crêpe with 1 tablespoon yogurt.

APPROXIMATE TOTAL TIME: 40 MINUTES (includes baking time)

MAKES 2 SERVINGS, 2 CRÊPES EACH

Each serving provides: ¼ Milk; 1 Fat; 1 Protein; 1½ Vegetables; 1 Bread; 15 Optional Calories
Per serving: 233 calories; 16 g protein; 7 g fat; 27 g carbohydrate; 223 mg calcium; 127 mg sodium; 9 mg cholesterol; 3 g dietary fiber

Scalloped Potatoes and Leeks ⟨C⟩ ⟨F⟩ ⟨S⟩

9 ounces pared all-purpose
   potatoes, thinly sliced
½ cup thoroughly washed sliced
   leeks (white portion and
   some green)
1½ ounces reduced-fat Swiss
   cheese, shredded
⅛ teaspoon *each* salt and white
   pepper
½ cup canned ready-to-serve
   low-sodium chicken broth

1. Preheat oven to 400°F. Spray 9-inch pie plate with nonstick cooking spray and arrange half of the potato slices in plate. Top with half of the leeks, half of the cheese, the remaining potato slices, and the remaining leeks. Sprinkle with salt and pepper and then top with remaining cheese.

2. Pour broth evenly over cheese and bake until potatoes are fork-tender, 15 to 20 minutes.

APPROXIMATE TOTAL TIME: 30 MINUTES (includes baking time)

MAKES 2 SERVINGS

Each serving provides: 1 Protein; ½ Vegetable; 1½ Breads; 10 Optional Calories
Per serving: 193 calories; 12 g protein; 5 g fat; 28 g carbohydrate; 288 mg calcium; 199 mg sodium; 15 mg cholesterol; 2 g dietary fiber

Spicy Oven-"Fried" Potato Wedges ⱽC ⱽF ⱽS

¾ pound baking potatoes, cut
   into thin wedges
2 teaspoons vegetable oil
¼ teaspoon *each* onion powder,
   garlic powder, ground red
   pepper, and black pepper

1. Preheat oven to 450°F. Spray nonstick baking sheet with nonstick cooking spray; arrange potatoes on sheet and drizzle with oil. Turn potatoes, coating well with oil.

2. Bake for 10 minutes; turn potatoes over and bake until edges are lightly browned, about 10 minutes longer.

3. Transfer potatoes to mixing bowl; sprinkle with spices and mix well.

APPROXIMATE TOTAL TIME: 25 MINUTES (includes baking time)

MAKES 4 SERVINGS

Each serving provides: ½ Fat; 1 Bread
Per serving: 85 calories; 2 g protein; 2 g fat; 14 g carbohydrate; 12 mg calcium; 6 mg sodium; 0 mg cholesterol; 2 g dietary fiber

Waldorf Potato Salad ▽C ▽F

1 small apple (about ¼ pound),
  cored and cubed
1 tablespoon lemon juice
9 ounces pared cooked all-
  purpose potatoes, cubed
¼ cup diced celery
2 tablespoons *each* diced onion
  and low-fat buttermilk
  (1% milk fat)
1 tablespoon *each* reduced-calorie
  mayonnaise and apple cider
  vinegar
¼ teaspoon granulated sugar
⅛ teaspoon salt
Dash white pepper
¼ ounce shelled walnuts, lightly
  toasted and chopped

1. In medium mixing bowl combine apple and lemon juice; stir to coat. Add potatoes, celery, and onion and stir to combine; set aside.

2. In small mixing bowl combine remaining ingredients except walnuts, stirring until thoroughly combined. Pour over apple-potato mixture and stir to coat. Cover and refrigerate until flavors blend, at least 30 minutes.

3. To serve, sprinkle salad with walnuts.

APPROXIMATE TOTAL TIME: 20 MINUTES (does not include chilling time)

MAKES 2 SERVINGS

Each serving provides: 1 Fat; ¼ Protein; ¼ Vegetable; 1½ Breads; ½ Fruit; 10 Optional Calories
Per serving: 200 calories; 4 g protein; 5 g fat; 38 g carbohydrate; 45 mg calcium; 232 mg sodium; 3 mg cholesterol; 4 g dietary fiber

Fruit-Spiced Rice ▽C ▽F ▽S

2 tablespoons whipped butter
⅛ teaspoon salt
4 ounces uncooked regular long-
  grain rice
3 large dried figs, diced
6 dried apricot halves, diced
¼ teaspoon ground cinnamon
⅛ teaspoon *each* ground
  cardamom and grated lemon
  peel

1. In 1-quart saucepan combine 1½ *cups water*, the butter, and salt and cook over high heat until mixture comes to a boil. Add rice and stir to combine. Reduce heat to low, cover, and let simmer until rice is tender and liquid is almost absorbed, about 15 minutes.

2. Add remaining ingredients and stir to combine. Cover and cook until liquid is fully absorbed and fruits are plumped, 2 to 3 minutes.

APPROXIMATE TOTAL TIME: 25 MINUTES

MAKES 4 SERVINGS

Each serving provides: 1 Bread; 1 Fruit; 25 Optional Calories
Per serving: 157 calories; 2 g protein; 3 g fat; 30 g carbohydrate; 21 mg calcium; 101 mg sodium; 8 mg cholesterol; 1 g dietary fiber

Green Onion Rice ⩔ ⩔ ⩔

1 cup thoroughly washed
 chopped leeks (white portion
 and some green)
2 teaspoons olive *or* vegetable oil
2 ounces uncooked regular long-
 grain rice
1½ cups canned ready-to-serve
 low-sodium chicken broth
½ cup diagonally sliced scallions
 (green onions)
2 tablespoons minced fresh
 chives *or* 1 tablespoon chopped
 chives

1. In 1-quart microwavable casserole combine leeks and oil and stir to coat; microwave on High (100%) for 4 minutes, stirring once halfway through cooking.

2. Stir in rice and broth; cover and microwave on High for 10 minutes, stirring every 4 minutes.

3. Add scallions and stir to combine; cover and microwave on High for 6 minutes until rice is tender.

4. Sprinkle with chives.

APPROXIMATE TOTAL TIME: 30 MINUTES

MAKES 2 SERVINGS

Each serving provides: 1 Fat; 1½ Vegetables; 1 Bread; 30 Optional Calories
Per serving: 204 calories; 5 g protein; 6 g fat; 33 g carbohydrate; 54 mg calcium; 53 mg sodium; 0 mg cholesterol; 2 g dietary fiber

Mushroom Risotto

¼ cup chopped onion
1 teaspoon olive oil
1 garlic clove, minced
3 ounces uncooked short-grain
  rice (arborio rice)
½ cup quartered mushrooms
2 sun-dried tomato halves (not
  packed in oil), chopped
1 packet instant vegetable broth
  and seasoning mix
1 tablespoon *each* grated
  Parmesan cheese and whipped
  butter
Garnish: rosemary sprig

*Arborio rice is a short-grained rice
from Northern Italy that is tradition-
ally used to prepare risotto.*

1. In 1-quart microwavable casserole combine first 3 ingredients and stir to coat; microwave on High (100%) for 1 minute, until onion is softened. Stir in rice and microwave on High for 30 seconds.

2. Stir in 1¾ *cups water*, the mushrooms, tomato, and broth mix. Cover and microwave on High for 15 minutes, stirring every 2 minutes, until rice is tender and liquid is absorbed.

3. Add cheese and butter and stir to combine. Transfer to serving bowl and garnish with rosemary.

APPROXIMATE TOTAL TIME: 25 MINUTES

MAKES 2 SERVINGS

Each serving provides: ½ Fat; 1¼ Vegetables; 1½ Breads; 45 Optional Calories
Per serving: 239 calories; 6 g protein; 6 g fat; 39 g carbohydrate; 59 mg calcium; 465 mg sodium; 10 mg cholesterol; 2 g dietary fiber

Rice-Vermicelli Pilaf ▽C ▽F

1 teaspoon margarine
¾ ounce uncooked vermicelli (thin spaghetti), broken into ½-inch pieces
2 ounces uncooked regular long-grain rice
1 packet instant onion broth and seasoning mix
1 teaspoon chopped fresh mint
⅛ teaspoon white pepper

1. In 2-quart nonstick saucepan melt margarine; add vermicelli and cook over medium heat, stirring frequently, until vermicelli is lightly browned, 1 to 2 minutes. Add *1 cup water* and the remaining ingredients and stir to combine; cover and bring mixture to a boil.

2. Reduce heat to low, cover, and let simmer until rice is tender and liquid is absorbed, 10 to 15 minutes.

APPROXIMATE TOTAL TIME: 20 MINUTES

MAKES 2 SERVINGS

Each serving provides: ½ Fat; 1½ Breads; 5 Optional Calories
Per serving: 165 calories; 4 g protein; 2 g fat; 32 g carbohydrate; 11 mg calcium; 406 mg sodium; 0 mg cholesterol; 1 g dietary fiber

Rice with Sun-Dried Tomatoes (C) (F) (S)

½ cup chopped onion
1 teaspoon vegetable oil
2 small garlic cloves, minced
4 sun-dried tomato halves (not packed in oil), diced
2 ounces uncooked regular long-grain rice
1 tablespoon chopped fresh parsley

1. In 1-quart microwavable casserole combine onion, oil, and garlic and stir to coat. Cover and microwave on High (100%) for 1 minute, until onion is softened.

2. Add tomatoes, rice, and *1¼ cups water*. Cover and microwave on High for 20 minutes.

3. Let stand, covered, for 2 to 3 minutes, until liquid is absorbed. Stir in parsley.

APPROXIMATE TOTAL TIME: 30 MINUTES

MAKES 2 SERVINGS

Each serving provides: ½ Fat; 1½ Vegetables; 1 Bread
Per serving: 157 calories; 3 g protein; 3 g fat; 30 g carbohydrate; 30 mg calcium; 10 mg sodium; 0 mg cholesterol; 2 g dietary fiber

Variation: Rice with Tomatoes—Substitute ½ cup drained canned Italian tomatoes, seeded and chopped, for the sun-dried tomatoes. In Serving Information decrease Vegetables to 1.
Per serving: 153 calories; 3 g protein; 3 g fat; 29 g carbohydrate; 40 mg calcium; 101 mg sodium; 0 mg cholesterol; 1 g dietary fiber

Spinach and Cheddar Rice

C F S

2 tablespoons chopped scallion (green onion)
3 ounces uncooked regular long-grain rice
2 teaspoons *each* reduced-calorie margarine (tub) and all-purpose flour
½ cup low-fat milk (1% milk fat)
¾ ounce sharp reduced-fat Cheddar cheese, shredded
¼ cup thawed frozen chopped spinach

1. In 1-quart saucepan combine *1 ¼ cups water* and the scallion; cover and cook over high heat until mixture comes to a boil. Stir in rice.

2. Reduce heat to low, re-cover, and let simmer until rice is tender and liquid is absorbed, about 15 minutes.

3. While rice is cooking prepare sauce. In small nonstick saucepan melt margarine over high heat. Sprinkle flour over margarine and stir quickly to combine; cook, stirring constantly, for 1 minute.

4. Stir in milk. Reduce heat to medium and cook, stirring frequently, until mixture thickens, about 5 minutes. Stir in cheese and cook until cheese melts.

5. Add spinach to rice mixture and stir to combine. Pour cheese mixture over spinach-rice mixture and stir to combine.

APPROXIMATE TOTAL TIME: 25 MINUTES

MAKES 2 SERVINGS

Each serving provides: ¼ Milk; ½ Fat; ½ Protein; ¼ Vegetable; 1 ½ Breads; 15 Optional Calories
Per serving: 248 calories; 9 g protein; 5 g fat; 41 g carbohydrate; 213 mg calcium; 168 mg sodium; 10 mg cholesterol; 1 g dietary fiber

Vegetable Risotto

2 cups *each* sliced mushrooms and thoroughly washed chopped leeks (white portion only) *or* onions
1 cup chopped red bell peppers
1 tablespoon plus 1 teaspoon olive *or* vegetable oil
4 ounces uncooked short-grain rice (arborio rice)
2 packets instant chicken broth and seasoning mix, dissolved in 2 cups water
1 package (9 ounces) frozen artichoke hearts (halves *or* quarters)
2 tablespoons dry white table wine *or* dry vermouth
1 tablespoon chopped fresh Italian (flat-leaf) parsley
1 teaspoon oregano leaves

1. In 2-quart microwavable casserole combine mushrooms, leeks, peppers, and oil and stir to coat; microwave on High (100%) for 2 minutes, stirring once halfway through cooking, until peppers are tender.

2. Add rice and stir to combine; microwave on High for 1 minute. Stir in dissolved broth mix and microwave on High for 8 minutes, stirring every 2 minutes.

3. Add remaining ingredients; microwave on Medium (50%) for 4 minutes, stirring once halfway through cooking, until artichokes are heated through.

APPROXIMATE TOTAL TIME: 25 MINUTES

MAKES 4 SERVINGS

Each serving provides: 1 Fat; 3½ Vegetables; 1 Bread; 10 Optional Calories
Per serving with wine: 224 calories; 6 g protein; 5 g fat; 39 g carbohydrate; 61 mg calcium; 540 mg sodium; 0 mg cholesterol; 4 g dietary fiber
With vermouth: 227 calories; 6 g protein; 5 g fat; 39 g carbohydrate; 61 mg calcium; 540 mg sodium; 0 mg cholesterol; 4 g dietary fiber

Rum-Baked Plantain $\triangledown_C$ $\triangledown_F$ $\triangledown_S$

6 ounces peeled plantain
2 tablespoons dark rum
1 tablespoon lemon juice
2 teaspoons margarine, melted
1 teaspoon firmly packed light
   brown sugar
¼ teaspoon ground cinnamon

1. Preheat oven to 425°F. Cut plantain in half crosswise, then slice each half lengthwise into thin slices. Spray 10-inch flameproof pie pan or shallow 1-quart casserole with nonstick cooking spray; arrange plantain slices in a single layer in pan. Set aside.

2. In small bowl combine ¼ cup water and the remaining ingredients, stirring to combine; pour evenly over plantain slices. Cover and bake until plantain slices are fork-tender, about 15 minutes.

3. Turn oven control to broil. Remove cover and broil until plantain slices are lightly browned, 1 to 2 minutes.

APPROXIMATE TOTAL TIME: 25 MINUTES (includes baking time)

MAKES 2 SERVINGS

Each serving provides: 1 Fat; 1 Bread; 50 Optional Calories
Per serving: 181 calories; 1 g protein; 4 g fat; 30 g carbohydrate; 10 mg calcium; 51 mg sodium; 0 mg cholesterol; dietary fiber data not available

Tropical Squash Rings

1 acorn squash (about 1 pound)*
½ cup canned crushed pineapple (no sugar added)
⅓ cup pineapple juice (no sugar added)
2 tablespoons dark rum
2 teaspoons margarine, melted
1 teaspoon *each* all-purpose flour and firmly packed light brown sugar
⅛ teaspoon ground nutmeg

1. Preheat oven to 375°F. Cut squash in half crosswise; remove and discard seeds. Cut each squash half crosswise into 2 slices.

2. Spray 9-inch pie plate with nonstick cooking spray and arrange squash slices in plate. Fill center of each squash slice with an equal amount of pineapple.

3. In 1-cup liquid measure combine remaining ingredients, stirring to dissolve flour. Pour mixture evenly over squash slices. Bake until squash slices are fork-tender, 20 to 25 minutes.

* A 1-pound squash yields about 6 ounces cooked squash.

APPROXIMATE TOTAL TIME: 30 MINUTES (includes baking time)

MAKES 4 SERVINGS

Each serving provides: ½ Fat; ½ Bread; ½ Fruit; 25 Optional Calories
Per serving: 102 calories; 1 g protein; 2 g fat; 18 g carbohydrate; 37 mg calcium; 26 mg sodium; 0 mg cholesterol; 3 g dietary fiber

Bibb and Grapefruit Salad $\triangledown_C$ $\triangledown_S$

1½ cups torn Bibb lettuce leaves
1 medium pink grapefruit (about 1 pound), peeled and sectioned (reserve juice)
2 tablespoons sliced scallion (green onion)
1 teaspoon *each* finely chopped cilantro (Chinese parsley) *or* Italian (flat-leaf) parsley, peanut oil, white wine vinegar, and Dijon-style mustard
Dash crushed red pepper

1. Line serving platter with lettuce; decoratively arrange grapefruit over lettuce and sprinkle with scallion.

2. Using a wire whisk, in small mixing bowl beat together reserved grapefruit juice, cilantro, oil, vinegar, mustard, and pepper. Pour over salad.

APPROXIMATE TOTAL TIME: 10 MINUTES

MAKES 2 SERVINGS

Each serving provides: ½ Fat; 1½ Vegetables; 1 Fruit
Per serving: 69 calories; 1 g protein; 3 g fat; 11 g carbohydrate; 46 mg calcium; 79 mg sodium; 0 mg cholesterol; 1 g dietary fiber

Carrot-Radish Salad ⛉ ⛉

2 cups shredded carrots
½ cup sliced radishes
1 tablespoon plus 1½ teaspoons lime juice (no sugar added)
1 tablespoon *each* finely chopped cilantro *or* Italian (flat-leaf) parsley and reduced-sodium soy sauce
1½ teaspoons *each* seeded and finely chopped jalapeño *or* chili pepper and finely chopped pared gingerroot
1 teaspoon Chinese sesame oil
½ teaspoon honey

1. In medium glass or stainless-steel bowl combine all ingredients; stir to combine. Cover and refrigerate until flavors blend, 30 minutes or overnight.

2. Stir salad just before serving.

APPROXIMATE TOTAL TIME: 15 MINUTES (does not include chilling time)

MAKES 2 SERVINGS

Each serving provides: ½ Fat; 2½ Vegetables; 5 Optional Calories
Per serving: 87 calories; 2 g protein; 3 g fat; 16 g carbohydrate; 40 mg calcium; 348 mg sodium; 0 mg cholesterol; 4 g dietary fiber

Confetti Sweet and Sour Slaw ▽C ▽F ▽S

3 cups finely shredded red
    cabbage
1 cup shredded carrots
¼ cup julienne-cut (matchstick
    pieces) red *or* yellow bell
    pepper
2 tablespoons *each* thinly sliced
    onion and celery
2 tablespoons golden raisins,
    plumped
2 teaspoons vegetable oil
¾ teaspoon *each* granulated
    sugar, apple cider vinegar,
    and honey
¼ teaspoon lemon juice
Dash pepper

*A food processor shreds the cabbage
and carrots for this recipe with ease.*

1. In large glass or stainless-steel bowl combine all ingredients; stir to combine. Cover and refrigerate until flavors blend, 30 minutes or overnight.

2. Stir salad just before serving.

APPROXIMATE TOTAL TIME: 20 MINUTES (does not include chilling time)

MAKES 2 SERVINGS

Each serving provides: 1 Fat; 4½ Vegetables; ½ Fruit; 15 Optional Calories
Per serving: 143 calories; 3 g protein; 5 g fat; 25 g carbohydrate; 80 mg calcium; 39 mg sodium; 0 mg cholesterol; 5 g dietary fiber

Cucumber-Corn Salad (C) (F) (S)

¼ cup plain low-fat yogurt
1 tablespoon plus 1 teaspoon reduced-calorie mayonnaise
1 tablespoon lemon juice
1 teaspoon chopped fresh dill
¼ teaspoon granulated sugar
Dash pepper
2 cups thinly sliced cucumbers
½ cup thawed frozen whole-kernel corn
¼ cup *each* sliced scallions (green onions) and diced red bell pepper

1. In medium mixing bowl combine first 6 ingredients, stirring until combined. Add remaining ingredients, stirring to coat.

APPROXIMATE TOTAL TIME: 10 MINUTES

MAKES 2 SERVINGS

Each serving provides: ¼ Milk; 1 Fat; 2½ Vegetables; ½ Bread; 3 Optional Calories
Per serving: 105 calories; 4 g protein; 4 g fat; 17 g carbohydrate; 80 mg calcium; 101 mg sodium; 5 mg cholesterol; 3 g dietary fiber

Cucumber, Orange, and Fennel Salad ▽c ▽s

1 tablespoon raspberry *or* rice
 vinegar
2 teaspoons olive oil
⅛ teaspoon oregano leaves
Dash pepper
3 cups chicory leaves
1 small navel orange (about 6
 ounces), peeled and sectioned
1 cup thinly sliced cucumbers
½ cup thinly sliced fennel
2 tablespoons *each* sliced radishes
 and chopped scallion (green
 onion)

*The fennel you use for this salad
should be the tender inner stalks of
the fennel bulb, rather than the
tougher outer stalks.*

1. In small bowl combine *2 tablespoons water*, the vinegar, oil, oregano, and pepper; mix well and set aside.

2. Line serving platter with chicory leaves; decoratively arrange orange sections, cucumbers, fennel, radishes, and scallion over chicory. Top with vinegar mixture.

APPROXIMATE TOTAL TIME: 10 MINUTES

MAKES 2 SERVINGS

Each serving provides: 1 Fat; 4¾ Vegetables; ½ Fruit
Per serving: 144 calories; 6 g protein; 5 g fat; 23 g carbohydrate; 321 mg calcium; 153 mg sodium; 0 mg cholesterol; 7 g dietary fiber

Fennel-Olive Salad

2 cups chopped fennel
3 large pimiento-stuffed green
   olives, sliced
1 tablespoon *each* finely chopped
   Italian (flat-leaf) parsley and
   balsamic *or* red wine vinegar
1½ teaspoons olive oil
1 teaspoon oregano leaves
1 small garlic clove, mashed
Dash pepper

The licorice flavor of fennel stands out in this attractive salad.

1. In medium glass or stainless-steel bowl combine all ingredients; stir to combine. Cover and refrigerate until flavors blend, 30 minutes or overnight.

2. Stir salad just before serving.

APPROXIMATE TOTAL TIME: 10 MINUTES (does not include chilling time)

MAKES 2 SERVINGS

Each serving provides: 1 Fat; 2 Vegetables
Per serving: 60 calories; 2 g protein; 4 g fat; 4 g carbohydrate; 73 mg calcium; 249 mg sodium; 0 mg cholesterol; 1 g dietary fiber

Greek Eggplant Salad ⬡C ⬡S

1 small eggplant (about
    ¾ pound)
1 medium red bell pepper
1 medium tomato, seeded and
    diced
½ cup diced green bell pepper
¼ cup sliced scallions (green
    onions)
6 large pitted black olives, sliced
1 small garlic clove, minced
2 tablespoons red wine vinegar
1 tablespoon *each* lemon juice
    and olive oil
¼ teaspoon pepper
1½ ounces feta cheese, crumbled

1. Preheat broiler. On baking sheet lined with heavy-duty foil broil eggplant and red bell pepper 4 inches from heat source, turning frequently, until charred on all sides; let stand until cool enough to handle.

2. Over small bowl to catch juice, peel eggplant and red bell pepper; reserve juice. Remove and discard stem end and seeds from red bell pepper. Cut eggplant into ½-inch cubes and dice red bell pepper.

3. In medium mixing bowl combine eggplant, red bell pepper, tomato, green bell pepper, scallions, olives, and garlic; stir well to combine and set aside.

4. In small bowl combine *2 tablespoons water*, the vinegar, lemon juice, oil, and pepper; pour over eggplant mixture and stir to coat. Cover and refrigerate until flavors blend, at least 1 hour or overnight.

5. Onto each of 4 salad plates arrange eggplant mixture and top each portion with an equal amount of cheese.

APPROXIMATE TOTAL TIME: 20 MINUTES (does not include chilling time)

MAKES 4 SERVINGS

Each serving provides: 1 Fat; ½ Protein; 2¼ Vegetables
Per serving: 104 calories; 3 g protein; 7 g fat; 9 g carbohydrate; 93 mg calcium; 172 mg sodium; 9 mg cholesterol; 2 g dietary fiber

Green Bean and Pasta Salad (C) (F) (S)

½ cup *each* thinly sliced onion and red bell pepper strips
2 teaspoons olive oil
1 small garlic clove, minced
2 cups sliced green beans (2-inch pieces), cooked (hot)
1 cup cooked small shell macaroni (hot)
1 tablespoon balsamic *or* red wine vinegar
1 tablespoon chopped fresh basil *or* ½ teaspoon basil leaves
1½ teaspoons chopped fresh Italian (flat-leaf) parsley
Dash pepper

While you prepare this recipe in your microwave oven, cook the macaroni on top of the range.

1. In 1-quart microwavable casserole combine onion, bell pepper, oil, and garlic and stir to coat; microwave on High (100%) for 3 minutes, until bell pepper is tender-crisp, stirring once halfway through cooking.

2. Add remaining ingredients and stir to combine. Serve immediately.

APPROXIMATE TOTAL TIME: 30 MINUTES

MAKES 2 SERVINGS

Each serving provides: 1 Fat; 3 Vegetables; 1 Bread
Per serving: 175 calories; 5 g protein; 5 g fat; 29 g carbohydrate; 69 mg calcium; 10 mg sodium; 0 mg cholesterol; 4 g dietary fiber

Spicy Southwestern Salad ▽C ▽F ▽S

1 cup julienne-cut (matchstick pieces) yellow straightneck squash

½ cup julienne-cut (matchstick pieces) pared jicama

1 small apple (about ¼ pound), cored and cut into matchstick pieces

2 tablespoons sliced scallion (green onion)

8 lettuce leaves

¼ cup spicy mixed vegetable juice

1 tablespoon balsamic *or* red wine vinegar

1½ teaspoons *each* chopped fresh cilantro (Chinese parsley) and fresh parsley

1 teaspoon olive oil

1 garlic clove

1. In medium bowl combine first 4 ingredients; mix well. Line serving platter with lettuce leaves; top with squash mixture.

2. In blender combine remaining ingredients and process until smooth. Pour over salad.

APPROXIMATE TOTAL TIME: 20 MINUTES

MAKES 2 SERVINGS

Each serving provides: ½ Fat; 2¾ Vegetables; ½ Fruit
Per serving: 94 calories; 2 g protein; 3 g fat; 17 g carbohydrate; 60 mg calcium; 108 mg sodium; 0 mg cholesterol; 3 g dietary fiber

Desserts, Snacks, and Beverages

Cinderella's fairy godmother turned a pumpkin into a coach. Our culinary wand does even better, turning nutritious items into sweet-tooth delights. These treats avoid the hazards of empty calories, while providing the satisfied feeling that wards off a "poor me" detour into wrong foods. Sample the magical way oats become Tropical Oatmeal Cookies and low-fat yogurt turns into a luscious treat like Fruit and Nut Pinwheels. Our beverages help you keep your eye on the nutrition goal too. Toast your efforts with a Lite Sea Breeze, using low-calorie cranberry juice as a mixer. Like many of our recipes, it's a breeze to whip up—in a whirlwind five minutes!

Chocolate-Iced Sponge Cake (F) (S)

- ¾ cup cake flour
- 1 teaspoon double-acting baking powder
- 4 eggs (at room temperature)
- ⅓ cup granulated sugar
- 1 cup plain low-fat yogurt
- 1 envelope (four ½-cup servings) reduced-calorie chocolate instant pudding and pie filling mix

1. Preheat oven to 400°F. Spray a 15 x 10½ x 1-inch jelly-roll pan with nonstick cooking spray and line with sheet of parchment paper or wax paper; spray again with nonstick cooking spray and set aside.

2. On sheet of wax paper sift together flour and baking powder; set aside.

3. Using mixer on high speed, in large mixing bowl beat eggs, gradually adding sugar 1 tablespoon at a time, until double in volume; fold in flour mixture.

4. Spread batter evenly in paper-lined pan and bake in middle of center oven rack until golden, 5 to 8 minutes (top should spring back when touched lightly with finger). Remove to wire rack and let cool.

5. While cake cools, prepare icing. In blender combine yogurt and pudding mix and process until smooth.

6. Invert cake onto work surface; remove and discard paper. Cut cake crosswise into 4 equal pieces. Spread ¼ of the yogurt mixture over each portion of cake.

7. On serving platter arrange 1 cake layer, yogurt-mixture side up; repeat with remaining 3 layers.

APPROXIMATE TOTAL TIME: 25 MINUTES (includes baking time)

MAKES 8 SERVINGS

Each serving provides: ½ Milk; ½ Protein; ½ Bread; 40 Optional Calories
Per serving: 150 calories; 6 g protein; 3 g fat; 25 g carbohydrate; 94 mg calcium; 105 mg sodium; 108 mg cholesterol; 0.2 g dietary fiber

Orange-Poppy Cupcakes ⬇️Ⓢ

1 cup plus 2 tablespoons cake
   flour
1½ teaspoons double-acting
   baking powder
2 tablespoons *each* poppy seed
   and grated orange peel
3 eggs
⅓ cup plus 2 teaspoons
   granulated sugar
¼ cup sweet margarine, melted,
   cooled
1 teaspoon confectioners' sugar

Cupcakes aren't just for children. These sophisticated cupcakes bake up fast and can be stored in the freezer for when you want a special treat.

1. Preheat oven to 350°F. Line twelve 2½-inch muffin-pan cups with paper baking cups; set aside.

2. In small mixing bowl sift together flour and baking powder; stir in poppy seed and orange peel and set aside.

3. Using mixer, in large mixing bowl beat together eggs and granulated sugar on medium speed until light and fluffy; add margarine and beat until combined. Stir in flour mixture until moistened.

4. Spoon an equal amount of batter into each lined cup (each will be about ¾ full).

5. Bake in middle of center oven rack for 15 to 20 minutes (until cupcakes are golden and a toothpick, inserted in center, comes out dry). Remove cupcakes to wire rack and let cool at least 10 minutes.

6. Sift confectioners' sugar evenly over cupcakes.

APPROXIMATE TOTAL TIME: 30 MINUTES (includes baking time; does not include cooling time)

MAKES 12 SERVINGS, 1 CUPCAKE EACH

Each serving provides: 1 Fat; ¼ Protein; ½ Bread; 40 Optional Calories
Per serving: 127 calories; 3 g protein; 6 g fat; 16 g carbohydrate; 58 mg calcium; 70 mg sodium; 53 mg cholesterol; 0.2 g dietary fiber (this figure does not include poppy seed; nutrition analysis not available)

Orange Sunshine Cakes ▽F ▽S

2¼ cups cake flour
1 teaspoon baking soda
¼ cup reduced-calorie margarine (tub)
2 tablespoons margarine
⅓ cup less 1 teaspoon granulated sugar
1 cup plain low-fat yogurt
2 eggs
1 tablespoon vanilla extract
¼ cup confectioners' sugar
½ teaspoon grated orange peel

1. Preheat oven to 375°F. On sheet of wax paper sift together flour and baking soda; set aside.

2. Using electric mixer on medium speed, in large mixing bowl beat margarines until combined; gradually add granulated sugar and continue beating until mixture is light and fluffy.

3. Add yogurt, eggs, and vanilla and beat 1 minute longer; add flour mixture and beat on low speed until thoroughly combined.

4. Spray twelve 2½-inch nonstick muffin-pan cups with nonstick cooking spray and fill each cup with an equal amount of batter (about 2 tablespoons). Bake in middle of center oven rack for 15 to 20 minutes (until cakes are golden, and a cake tester, inserted in center, comes out dry). Invert cakes onto wire rack and let cool.

5. In small mixing bowl combine confectioners' sugar, *1½ teaspoons water*, and the orange peel and stir until smooth. Drizzle an equal amount of icing over each cake.

APPROXIMATE TOTAL TIME: 30 MINUTES (includes baking time)

MAKES 12 SERVINGS

Each serving provides: 1 Fat; 1 Bread; 70 Optional Calories
Per serving: 172 calories; 4 g protein; 5 g fat; 27 g carbohydrate; 43 mg calcium; 155 mg sodium; 37 mg cholesterol; 0.4 g dietary fiber

Fruit and Nut Pinwheels ⏦C ⏦S

1½ cups plus 3 tablespoons all-purpose flour, divided
¼ teaspoon salt
⅓ cup reduced-calorie margarine (tub)
½ cup plain low-fat yogurt
Water
½ cup dark raisins, chopped
2 ounces sliced almonds
¼ cup reduced-calorie orange marmalade (16 calories per 2 teaspoons)
1 tablespoon plus 1 teaspoon honey

1. In medium mixing bowl combine 1½ cups flour and the salt; using pastry blender, cut in margarine until mixture resembles coarse meal. Add yogurt and mix thoroughly, adding water by teaspoonfuls, if necessary, to form a dough. Form dough into a ball; cover with plastic wrap and refrigerate for at least 1 hour.

2. In small mixing bowl combine raisins, almonds, and marmalade; stir to combine.

3. Preheat oven to 425°F. Using remaining flour to prevent dough from sticking to work surface, roll dough into a 12 x 9-inch rectangle about ⅛ inch thick. Spread raisin mixture over rectangle. Starting from one of the wide sides, roll dough jelly-roll fashion to enclose filling and press seam to seal.

4. Using a serrated knife, cut roll crosswise into 16 equal slices. Spray nonstick baking sheet with nonstick cooking spray and place slices cut-side down on sheet. Bake in middle of center oven rack until golden, about 18 minutes.

5. Immediately drizzle ¼ teaspoon honey over each pinwheel. Remove to wire rack and let cool.

APPROXIMATE TOTAL TIME: 30 MINUTES (includes baking time; does not include chilling time)

MAKES 8 SERVINGS, 2 PINWHEELS EACH

Each serving provides: 1½ Fats; ½ Protein; 1 Bread; ½ Fruit; 45 Optional Calories
Per serving: 230 calories; 5 g protein; 8 g fat; 36 g carbohydrate; 54 mg calcium; 159 mg sodium; 1 mg cholesterol; 2 g dietary fiber

Iced Apple Turnovers 🔽C 🔽S

1 pound Granny Smith apples, cored, pared, and finely chopped

1 tablespoon lemon juice

½ teaspoon *each* granulated sugar and ground cinnamon

1 refrigerated ready-to-bake 9-inch pie crust

2 tablespoons confectioners' sugar

1 teaspoon grated orange peel

1. Preheat oven to 425°F. In 1-quart saucepan combine apples, lemon juice, granulated sugar, and cinnamon and cook over medium heat, stirring occasionally, until apples are very soft, about 5 minutes. Remove from heat; set aside.

2. On work surface roll pie crust into a 16 x 8-inch rectangle; cut rectangle into eight 4 x 4-inch squares. Spoon an equal amount of apple mixture onto center of each square. Fold square in half, forming a triangle. Using tines of fork, press edges to seal.

3. Arrange turnovers on nonstick baking sheet and bake in middle of center oven rack until golden brown, 8 to 10 minutes. Remove to wire rack and let cool.

4. While turnovers cool, prepare icing. In small bowl combine confectioners' sugar, orange peel, and *1 teaspoon water*, mixing to form icing; decoratively drizzle icing over turnovers.

APPROXIMATE TOTAL TIME: 30 MINUTES (includes baking time)

MAKES 8 SERVINGS, 1 TURNOVER EACH

Each serving provides: ½ Bread; ½ Fruit; 65 Optional Calories
Per serving: 157 calories; 1 g protein; 8 g fat; 22 g carbohydrate; 4 mg calcium; 155 mg sodium; 0 mg cholesterol; 1 g dietary fiber (this figure does not include pie crust; nutrition analysis not available)

Quick Rugalach (Raisin Crescents) Ⓒ Ⓢ

½ cup dark raisins
2 ounces shelled walnuts *or*
blanched almonds
1 tablespoon granulated sugar
1 teaspoon ground cinnamon
1 refrigerated ready-to-bake
9-inch pie crust
1 teaspoon confectioners' sugar

1. Preheat oven to 425°F. In food processor combine first 4 ingredients and, using on-off motion, process until nuts are finely chopped; set aside.

2. On work surface cut pie crust into 16 equal wedges. Spoon an equal amount of raisin-nut mixture evenly over each wedge; roll each wedge from curved end toward point. Place crescents on nonstick cookie sheet, point-side down, and shape each into a half moon.

3. Bake in middle of center oven rack until cookies are golden, 8 to 10 minutes. Transfer to wire rack and let cool.

4. Sift confectioners' sugar evenly over crescents.

APPROXIMATE TOTAL TIME: 30 MINUTES (includes baking time)

MAKES 8 SERVINGS, 2 RUGALACH EACH

Each serving provides: ½ Fat; ½ Protein; ½ Bread; ½ Fruit; 60 Optional Calories
Per serving with walnuts: 200 calories; 2 g protein; 12 g fat; 23 g carbohydrate; 15 mg calcium; 157 mg sodium; 0 mg cholesterol; 1 g dietary fiber (this figure does not include pie crust; nutrition analysis not available)
With almonds: 197 calories; 3 g protein; 11 g fat; 23 g carbohydrate; 25 mg calcium; 157 mg sodium; 0 mg cholesterol; 0.5 g dietary fiber (this figure does not include almonds and pie crust; nutrition analyses not available)

Orange-Poppy Seed Cookies ▽c ▽s

¼ cup reduced-calorie sweet margarine (tub)

3 tablespoons granulated sugar

1 tablespoon plus 1½ teaspoons poppy seed

1 teaspoon *each* grated orange peel and orange juice (no sugar added)

½ cup plus 1 tablespoon all-purpose flour

½ teaspoon double-acting baking powder

Prepare the dough for these cookies in advance and it can be refrigerated overnight.

1. Using mixer, in medium mixing bowl beat together margarine and sugar on medium speed until light and fluffy; add poppy seed, orange peel, and orange juice and stir to combine (mixture may appear curdled).

2. In small mixing bowl combine flour and baking powder and stir well to combine; add margarine mixture, 2 tablespoonfuls at a time, mixing well after each addition, until mixture forms smooth dough but is not sticky. Cover dough with plastic wrap and refrigerate at least 30 minutes.

3. Preheat oven to 375°F. Divide dough into 6 equal portions and, using hands, shape each portion into a ball; arrange balls on nonstick cookie sheet, leaving a space of about 1 inch between each. Using the tines of a fork, slightly press each cookie to flatten, then press down in opposite direction to create a checkerboard pattern.

4. Bake in middle of center oven rack until cookies are golden, 10 to 15 minutes. Transfer to wire rack and let cool.

APPROXIMATE TOTAL TIME: 25 MINUTES (includes baking time; does not include chilling time)

MAKES 6 SERVINGS, 1 COOKIE EACH

Each serving provides: 1 Fat; ½ Bread; 45 Optional Calories
Per serving: 113 calories; 2 g protein; 5 g fat; 16 g carbohydrate; 52 mg calcium; 36 mg sodium; 0 mg cholesterol; 0.3 g dietary fiber (this figure does not include poppy seed; nutrition analysis not available)

Tropical Oatmeal Cookies ⱽ⟨C⟩ ⱽ⟨S⟩

6 ounces uncooked quick oats
¾ cup all-purpose flour
⅓ cup plus 2 teaspoons dark raisins
¼ cup granulated sugar
2 tablespoons shredded coconut
1 ounce chopped walnuts
½ teaspoon baking soda
⅓ cup plus 1 tablespoon plus 1 teaspoon reduced-calorie sweet margarine (tub), melted, cooled
¼ cup thawed frozen egg substitute
1 teaspoon vanilla extract

1. Preheat oven to 375°F. In large mixing bowl combine first 7 ingredients; set aside.

2. In small mixing bowl combine remaining ingredients; add to oat mixture and stir to combine.

3. Using half of dough, drop dough by tablespoonfuls onto nonstick cookie sheet, forming 12 equal cookies and leaving a space of about 1 inch between each. Bake in middle of center oven rack until cookies are golden, 10 to 12 minutes. Transfer cookies to wire rack and let cool (cookies will harden as they cool).

4. Using a cooled cookie sheet, repeat procedure 1 more time, making 12 more cookies.

APPROXIMATE TOTAL TIME: 20 MINUTES (includes baking time)

MAKES 12 SERVINGS, 2 COOKIES EACH

Each serving provides: 1 Fat; ¼ Protein; 1 Bread; ¼ Fruit; 25 Optional Calories
Per serving: 163 calories; 4 g protein; 6 g fat; 24 g carbohydrate; 15 mg calcium; 44 mg sodium; 0 mg cholesterol; 2 g dietary fiber

Canadian Maple-Walnut Chiffon ⬡S⬡

1½ teaspoons unflavored gelatin
½ cup evaporated skimmed milk
2 eggs, separated
2 tablespoons maple syrup
1 teaspoon imitation maple
  extract
⅛ teaspoon cream of tartar
½ cup thawed frozen dairy
  whipped topping
1 ounce chopped walnuts
  (reserve 1 tablespoon plus
  1 teaspoon for garnish)

1. In 1-quart saucepan sprinkle gelatin over milk and let stand 1 minute to soften; cook over low heat, stirring frequently, until gelatin is completely dissolved.

2. Using a wire whisk, in small mixing bowl lightly beat egg yolks; gradually beat in ¼ cup of the gelatin-milk mixture. Gradually stir egg yolk–milk mixture back into saucepan and cook, stirring constantly, until mixture thickens slightly, about 1 minute (do not boil).

3. Remove from heat; stir in maple syrup and extract. Pour egg yolk–milk mixture into large mixing bowl and set aside.

4. Using electric mixer on high speed, in medium mixing bowl beat egg whites until foamy; add cream of tartar and continue beating until whites are stiff but not dry.

5. Gently fold beaten whites into egg yolk–milk mixture; fold in whipped topping and walnuts.

6. Into each of four 6-ounce custard cups or dessert dishes spoon ¼ of chiffon. Top each portion with 1 teaspoon of the reserved walnuts. Cover and refrigerate until set, about 2 hours.

APPROXIMATE TOTAL TIME: 20 MINUTES (does not include chilling time)

MAKES 4 SERVINGS

Each serving provides: ¼ Milk; ½ Fat; 1 Protein; 55 Optional Calories
Per serving: 161 calories; 7 g protein; 9 g fat; 14 g carbohydrate; 122 mg calcium; 81 mg sodium; 108 mg cholesterol; 0.3 g dietary fiber

Lemon-Raspberry Cloud ⬇C ⬇F ⬇S

¼ cup freshly squeezed lemon
  juice
2 tablespoons thawed frozen
  concentrated orange juice (no
  sugar added)
1 tablespoon granulated sugar
½ teaspoon grated lemon peel
1 teaspoon unflavored gelatin
½ cup thawed frozen dairy
  whipped topping
3 egg whites
¼ teaspoon cream of tartar
½ cup raspberries
Garnish: lemon zest*

1. In small nonstick saucepan combine lemon juice, *¼ cup water*, the orange juice, sugar, and lemon peel; sprinkle gelatin over juice mixture and let stand 1 minute to soften. Stir mixture to combine; cook over low heat, stirring frequently, until gelatin is dissolved, 1 to 2 minutes.

2. Transfer mixture to large mixing bowl; stir in whipped topping and set aside.

3. Using mixer on high speed, in large mixing bowl beat egg whites until frothy; add cream of tartar and continue beating until whites are stiff but not dry. Gently fold egg whites into gelatin mixture until mixture is thoroughly combined.

4. Into each of four 6-ounce dessert dishes pour ¼ of gelatin mixture. Cover and refrigerate until firm, at least 1 hour (when gelatin mixture is chilled it will form 2 layers). Garnish each portion with 2 tablespoons raspberries and lemon zest.

* The zest of the lemon is the peel without any of the pith (white membrane). To remove zest from lemon, use a zester or vegetable peeler; wrap lemon in plastic wrap and refrigerate for use at another time.

APPROXIMATE TOTAL TIME: 15 MINUTES (does not include chilling time)

MAKES 4 SERVINGS

Each serving provides: ¼ Protein; ½ Fruit; 40 Optional Calories
Per serving: 76 calories; 4 g protein; 2 g fat; 12 g carbohydrate; 9 mg calcium; 52 mg sodium; 0 mg cholesterol; 1 g dietary fiber

Rum-Raisin Custard ▽c ▽f ▽s

2 cups skim *or* nonfat milk
1 cup thawed frozen egg
  substitute
⅓ cup plus 2 teaspoons all-
  purpose flour
¼ cup granulated sugar
2 tablespoons dark rum
1 teaspoon vanilla extract
1 cup golden raisins
2 ounces sliced almonds

*Custard can be refrigerated over-
night to chill.*

1. Preheat oven to 375°F. In blender combine first 6 ingredients and process until smooth. Spray 9-inch pie plate with nonstick cooking spray and pour milk mixture into plate. Add raisins and stir to combine; sprinkle with almonds.

2. Bake for 25 minutes (until a knife, inserted in center, comes out dry). Transfer to wire rack and let cool. Refrigerate until ready to serve.

APPROXIMATE TOTAL TIME: 30 MINUTES (in-cludes baking time)

MAKES 8 SERVINGS

Each serving provides: ¼ Milk; ½ Fat; 1 Protein; ¼ Bread; 1 Fruit; 40 Optional Calories
Per serving: 186 calories; 7 g protein; 4 g fat; 30 g carbohydrate; 115 mg calcium; 75 mg sodium; 1 mg cholesterol; 1 g dietery fiber

Apple-Wheat Bread Pudding �CᐁᐧFᐁ

1 cup low-fat milk (1% milk fat)
½ cup *each* **thawed frozen egg substitute and applesauce (no sugar added)**
⅓ cup instant nonfat dry milk powder
2 tablespoons granulated sugar
1 teaspoon vanilla extract
½ teaspoon ground cinnamon
4 slices reduced-calorie wheat bread (40 calories per slice), cut into cubes
1 small apple (about ¼ pound), cored, pared, and diced
¼ cup thawed frozen dairy whipped topping

Old-fashioned bread pudding with the nutrition of wheat bread.

1. In medium mixing bowl beat together milk, egg substitute, applesauce, milk powder, sugar, vanilla, and cinnamon until thoroughly combined. Set aside.

2. Into each of four 10-ounce microwavable custard cups arrange ¼ of the bread cubes and apple. Pour ¼ of milk mixture into each custard cup, being sure to moisten bread cubes.

3. Cover cups; fill 4 x 10-inch microwavable baking dish with water to a depth of about 1 inch and set cups in dish. Microwave on Medium (50%) for 20 minutes, rotating dish ½ turn halfway through cooking (until a knife, inserted in center, comes out dry).

4. Remove cups from water bath; set cups on wire rack and let cool at least 5 minutes. Serve each pudding topped with 1 tablespoon whipped topping.

APPROXIMATE TOTAL TIME: 30 MINUTES (does not include cooling time)

MAKES 4 SERVINGS

Each serving provides: ½ Milk; ½ Protein; ½ Bread; ½ Fruit; 50 Optional Calories
Per serving: 169 calories; 9 g protein; 2 g fat; 30 g carbohydrate; 183 mg calcium; 215 mg sodium; 3 mg cholesterol; 1 g dietary fiber

Chunky Chocolate Pudding ⌄C

2 cups skim *or* nonfat milk
1 envelope (four ½-cup servings)
    reduced-calorie instant
    chocolate pudding mix
1¼ ounces mini chocolate chips
1 ounce shelled walnuts, toasted
    and chopped
¼ cup thawed frozen dairy
    whipped topping
1 teaspoon chocolate syrup

1. Using milk, prepare pudding according to package directions. Cover and refrigerate until soft set, about 30 minutes.

2. Stir in chocolate chips and walnuts. Into each of four 6-ounce dessert dishes spoon ¼ of the pudding; top each with 1 tablespoon whipped topping and then drizzle ¼ teaspoon chocolate syrup over whipped topping. Refrigerate until ready to serve.

APPROXIMATE TOTAL TIME: 10 MINUTES (does not include chilling time)

MAKES 4 SERVINGS

Each serving provides: 1 Milk; ½ Fat; ½ Protein; 65 Optional Calories
Per serving: 183 calories; 6 g protein; 9 g fat; 22 g carbohydrate; 164 mg calcium; 321 mg sodium; 2 mg cholesterol; 0.3 g dietary fiber (this figure does not include pudding mix, chocolate, and syrup; nutrition analyses not available)

Double Chocolate-Nut Treat ▽ⓒ

2 cups skim *or* nonfat milk
1 envelope (four ½-cup servings)
  reduced-calorie instant
  chocolate pudding mix
½ cup thawed frozen dairy
  whipped topping
1 tablespoon chocolate syrup
1 ounce shelled almonds, toasted
  and chopped
2 maraschino cherries, cut into
  halves

1. Using milk, prepare pudding according to package directions. Into each of four 6-ounce dessert dishes spoon ¼ of the pudding; set aside.

2. In small mixing bowl combine whipped topping and syrup; stir to combine. Spread ¼ of whipped topping mixture over each portion of pudding.

3. Sprinkle each dessert with ¼ of the almonds and then top each with a cherry half. Cover and refrigerate at least 30 minutes.

APPROXIMATE TOTAL TIME: 15 MINUTES (does not include chilling time)

MAKES 4 SERVINGS

Each serving provides: 1 Milk; ½ Fat; ½ Protein; 45 Optional Calories
Per serving: 155 calories; 6 g protein; 6 g fat; 21 g carbohydrate; 174 mg calcium; 329 mg sodium; 2 mg cholesterol; 0.3 g dietary fiber (this figure does not include pudding mix and chocolate syrup; nutrition analyses not available)

Variation: Double Chocolate Treat—Omit almonds from recipe. In Serving Information omit ½ Protein and ½ Fat.
Per serving: 113 calories; 5 g protein; 3 g fat; 19 g carbohydrate; 156 mg calcium; 328 mg sodium; 2 mg cholesterol; dietary fiber data not available

Mocha Pudding Pie ⌄C

12 graham crackers (2½-inch squares), made into crumbs
1 ounce ground walnuts
2 tablespoons margarine, softened
½ cup plain low-fat yogurt, divided
1 cup skim *or* nonfat milk, divided
2 teaspoons instant espresso coffee powder
1 envelope (four ½-cup servings) reduced-calorie chocolate instant pudding mix
½ cup thawed frozen dairy whipped topping
½ ounce semisweet chocolate, shaved
½ cup raspberries

1. In medium mixing bowl combine graham cracker crumbs and walnuts; with pastry blender, cut in margarine until mixture resembles coarse crumbs. Remove ¼ cup crumb mixture and set aside. Using a fork, add 2 tablespoons yogurt to crumb mixture in mixing bowl and mix thoroughly.

2. Using the back of a spoon, press crumb-yogurt mixture over bottom and up sides of 9-inch microwavable pie plate. Microwave on High (100%) for 4 minutes, rotating plate ½ turn halfway through cooking. Cover pie plate with foil and freeze until ready to fill.

3. In medium microwavable mixing bowl microwave 2 tablespoons milk on High for 15 seconds; add espresso and, using a wire whisk, stir to dissolve. Stir in remaining yogurt, then stir in remaining milk. Add pudding mix, stirring to dissolve.

4. Pour pudding mixture into cooled crust. Sprinkle reserved crumb mixture around edge of pudding mixture. Refrigerate for at least 1 hour.

5. To serve, cut pie into 8 equal wedges and set each wedge on a dessert plate. Top each portion with 1 tablespoon whipped topping and ⅛ of the chocolate shavings. Garnish each portion with 1 tablespoon raspberries.

APPROXIMATE TOTAL TIME: 25 MINUTES (does not include chilling time)

MAKES 8 SERVINGS

Each serving provides: ½ Milk; 1 Fat; ¼ Protein; ½ Bread; 30 Optional Calories
Per serving: 151 calories; 4 g protein; 8 g fat; 18 g carbohydrate; 77 mg calcium; 261 mg sodium; 1 mg cholesterol; 1 g dietary fiber (this figure does not include pudding mix and chocolate; nutrition analyses not available)

Mint Julep Sorbet ▽C ▽F ▽S

1½ cups packed fresh mint,
    divided (reserve 8 mint sprigs
    for garnish)
⅓ cup granulated sugar
2 tablespoons bourbon
1 teaspoon lemon juice

Celebrate the Kentucky Derby with
Mint Julep Sorbet.

1. In 1-quart saucepan combine *2 cups water*, 1 cup mint, and the sugar. Cook over high heat, stirring occasionally, until mixture comes to a boil. Reduce heat to medium and continue to boil until mixture has a syrupy consistency, about 5 minutes.

2. Set sieve over 8 x 8 x 2-inch freezer-safe pan and pour mint mixture through sieve into pan, discarding solids. Set aside and let cool for 15 minutes.

3. Finely chop remaining mint and add to mint mixture; add bourbon and lemon juice and stir to combine. Cover and freeze until frozen, about 3 hours.

4. Into 8 dessert dishes scoop an equal amount of sorbet; garnish each portion with a mint sprig.

APPROXIMATE TOTAL TIME: 25 MINUTES (does not include freezing time)

MAKES 8 SERVINGS

Each serving provides: 50 Optional Calories
Per serving: 43 calories; 0.1 g protein; 0.1 g fat; 9 g carbohydrate; 7 mg calcium; 0.2 mg sodium; 0 mg cholesterol; dietary fiber data not available

Piña Colada Ice

12 ounces pineapple, pared and sliced, *or* 1 cup canned pineapple chunks (no sugar added)

1 medium banana (about 6 ounces), peeled

1½ cups low-fat buttermilk (1% milk fat)

2 tablespoons light rum

1 tablespoon plus 1 teaspoon *each* granulated sugar and shredded coconut, toasted

1. In blender combine all ingredients except coconut and process until smooth. Transfer to 1-quart freezer-safe bowl; stir in coconut. Cover and freeze until solid, about 3 hours.

APPROXIMATE TOTAL TIME: 15 MINUTES (does not include freezing time)

MAKES 4 SERVINGS

Each serving provides: ¼ Milk; 1 Fruit; 70 Optional Calories
Per serving: 120 calories; 4 g protein; 2 g fat; 21 g carbohydrate; 111 mg calcium; 101 mg sodium; 4 mg cholesterol; 1 g dietary fiber

Calypso Plantain Dessert ⊽c⊽ ⊽F⊽ ⊽s⊽

6 ounces peeled plantain, sliced crosswise
¼ cup *each* canned crushed pineapple (no sugar added) and orange juice (no sugar added)
1 teaspoon margarine, melted
½ teaspoon cornstarch
½ ounce finely chopped almonds
2 tablespoons shredded coconut
1 teaspoon firmly packed light brown sugar
½ cup plain low-fat yogurt

1. Preheat oven to 375°F. Spray 10-inch pie pan with nonstick cooking spray; arrange plantain slices in an even layer in bottom of pan. Spread pineapple evenly over plantain slices.

2. In 1-cup liquid measure combine orange juice, margarine, and cornstarch, stirring to dissolve cornstarch; pour evenly over pineapple.

3. In small mixing bowl combine almonds, coconut, and sugar and sprinkle evenly over pineapple. Bake until plantain is soft and coconut mixture is lightly browned, 15 to 20 minutes.

4. To serve, into each of two 6-ounce dessert dishes spoon half of the plantain mixture, then top each with ¼ cup yogurt. Drizzle pan juices over yogurt.

APPROXIMATE TOTAL TIME: 30 MINUTES (includes baking time)

MAKES 2 SERVINGS

Each serving provides: ½ Milk; 1 Fat; ½ Protein; 1 Bread; ½ Fruit; 45 Optional Calories
Per serving: 264 calories; 6 g protein; 8 g fat; 46 g carbohydrate; 136 mg calcium; 79 mg sodium; 3 mg cholesterol; 1 g dietary fiber (this figure does not include plantain; nutrition analysis not available)

Fig and Melon Compote ▽C ▽F ▽S

¼ cup freshly squeezed orange
  juice
2 tablespoons freshly squeezed
  lime juice
1 tablespoon chopped fresh mint
1 teaspoon honey
1 cup seeded and diced melon
  (cantaloupe *or* crenshaw)
1 large fresh fig (2 ounces), cut
  in half and sliced
Garnish: 2 mint sprigs

1. In medium mixing bowl combine first 4 ingredients, stirring to dissolve honey; add melon and fig and stir to coat. Cover and refrigerate until flavors blend, at least 30 minutes.

2. To serve, into each of two 6-ounce dessert dishes spoon half of the fruit mixture and garnish each portion with a mint sprig.

APPROXIMATE TOTAL TIME: 10 MINUTES (does not include chilling time)

MAKES 2 SERVINGS

Each serving provides: 1¼ Fruits; 10 Optional Calories
Per serving: 78 calories; 1 g protein; 0.4 g fat; 20 g carbohydrate; 25 mg calcium; 8 mg sodium; 0 mg cholesterol; 1 g dietary fiber (this figure does not include melon and fig; nutrition analyses not available)

Peaches and Kiwi in Champagne ▽ᶜ ▽ᶠ ▽ˢ

¾ pound peaches, pitted and
   thinly sliced
I medium kiwi fruit (about ¼
   pound), pared and sliced
¼ cup dry champagne
Garnish:
   2 mint sprigs
   I tablespoon *each* julienne-cut
      (matchstick pieces) lime and
      orange zests*

*This elegant dessert is completed in
a mere 15 minutes and can be refrigerated overnight to chill.*

1. In bowl combine all ingredients except garnish.
Cover and refrigerate until chilled, at least 30 minutes.

2. Garnish with mint sprigs and zests before serving.

* The zest is the peel without any of the pith (white membrane).
To remove zest from lime and orange, use a zester or vegetable
peeler; wrap lime and orange in plastic wrap and refrigerate for
use at another time.

**APPROXIMATE TOTAL TIME: 15 MINUTES (does
not include chilling time)**

MAKES 2 SERVINGS

Each serving provides: 1½ Fruits; 25 Optional Calories
Per serving: 99 calories; 1 g protein; 0.3 g fat; 20 g carbohydrate; 19 mg calcium; 3 mg sodium; 0 mg cholesterol;
3 g dietary fiber

Cinnamon Crisp Tortillas ⬇C⬇S

2 flour tortillas (6-inch diameter each)
2 teaspoons reduced-calorie margarine (tub), melted, divided
½ teaspoon *each* ground cinnamon, divided, and granulated sugar

Serve with fresh fruit for a satisfying snack.

1. Preheat broiler. Arrange tortillas on nonstick baking sheet and brush each tortilla with ¼ of the margarine and sprinkle with ¼ of the cinnamon. Broil 6 inches from heat source until margarine is bubbly, 1 to 2 minutes.

2. Combine remaining cinnamon with the sugar. Turn tortillas over; brush each with half of the remaining margarine and then sprinkle each with half of the cinnamon-sugar mixture. Broil until cinnamon-sugar mixture caramelizes, about 1 minute.

APPROXIMATE TOTAL TIME: 10 MINUTES

MAKES 2 SERVINGS, 1 TORTILLA EACH

Each serving provides: ½ Fat; 1 Bread; 5 Optional Calories
Per serving: 92 calories; 2 g protein; 4 g fat; 13 g carbohydrate; 47 mg calcium; 180 mg sodium; 0 mg cholesterol; 1 g dietary fiber

Garlic Bagel Chips

4 small bagels (1 ounce each)
1 tablespoon plus 1 teaspoon
   olive oil, divided
¼ teaspoon *each* garlic powder
   and onion powder

1. Preheat oven to 275°F. Cut bagels horizontally into very thin slices and arrange in a single layer on a nonstick baking sheet. Using a pastry brush, lightly brush 2 teaspoons oil over tops of bagel slices.

2. In small mixing bowl combine garlic and onion powders and sprinkle half of the mixture evenly over bagel slices. Bake for 20 minutes.

3. Increase oven temperature to 425°F. Turn bagel slices over and repeat procedure using remaining oil and garlic-onion powder mixture. Bake until bagel slices are lightly browned, 5 to 10 minutes longer.

APPROXIMATE TOTAL TIME: 40 MINUTES (includes baking time)

MAKES 4 SERVINGS

Each serving provides: 1 Fat; 1 Bread
Per serving: 115 calories; 3 g protein; 5 g fat; 15 g carbohydrate; 11 mg calcium; 175 mg sodium; 0 mg cholesterol; 1 g dietary fiber

Cranberry Cooler

¾ cup seltzer
½ cup dry white *or* rosé table
   wine
⅓ cup cranberry juice
1 teaspoon lemon juice
6 ice cubes
2 lemon slices

1. In 2-cup pitcher or small mixing bowl combine all ingredients except ice and lemon slices; stir well.

2. Into each of two 8-ounce cocktail glasses place 3 ice cubes; add half of the juice mixture to each glass. Garnish each portion with a lemon slice.

APPROXIMATE TOTAL TIME: 5 MINUTES

MAKES 2 SERVINGS, ABOUT ¾ CUP EACH

Each serving provides: ½ Fruit; 50 Optional Calories
Per serving with white wine: 67 calories; 0.2 g protein; 0.1 g fat; 8 g carbohydrate; 15 mg calcium; 5 mg sodium; 0 mg cholesterol; dietary fiber data not available
With rosé wine: 69 calories; 0.3 g protein; 0.1 g fat; 8 g carbohydrate; 14 mg calcium; 5 mg sodium; 0 mg cholesterol; dietary fiber data not available

Lite Sea Breeze ▽C ▽F ▽S

2 cups low-calorie cranberry juice
2 tablespoons plus 2 teaspoons
   vodka *or* gin
12 ice cubes
Garnish:
   1 lemon slice, cut in half
   2 mint sprigs

1. In 3-cup pitcher or small mixing bowl combine juice and vodka.

2. Into each of two 12-ounce glasses place half of the ice cubes; add half of the juice mixture to each glass. Garnish each portion with ½ lemon slice and a mint sprig.

APPROXIMATE TOTAL TIME: 5 MINUTES

MAKES 2 SERVINGS, ABOUT 1 CUP EACH

Each serving provides: 1 Fruit; 50 Optional Calories
Per serving: 91 calories 0.2 g protein; trace fat; 13 g carbohydrate; 30 mg calcium; 8 mg sodium; 0 mg cholesterol; dietary fiber data not available

Cherry-Vanilla "Ice Cream" Soda $\triangledown$ C $\triangledown$ F $\triangledown$ S

1 packet reduced-calorie vanilla-
  flavored dairy drink mix
6 ice cubes
1 cup reduced-calorie black
  cherry soda (2 calories per
  6 fluid ounces)
½ cup vanilla ice milk
2 maraschino cherries

1. In blender combine ½ cup cold water and the drink mix and process on low speed until combined. Add ice cubes, 1 at a time, and process on high speed after each addition until mixture is thick and frothy.

2. Turn blender off; add soda. Process on low speed until thoroughly combined.

3. Into each of two 12-ounce glasses pour half of the drink mix–soda mixture; add ¼ cup ice milk to each glass. Top each with a cherry and serve immediately.

APPROXIMATE TOTAL TIME: 5 MINUTES

MAKES 2 SERVINGS

Each serving provides: ½ Milk; 70 Optional Calories
Per serving: 84 calories; 4 g protein; 1 g fat; 14 g carbo-hydrate; 119 mg calcium; 60 mg sodium; 0 mg cholesterol; dietary fiber data not available

MENU PLANNERS

—On a treasure hunt for new and exciting menu ideas?
—Too busy to plan menus?
—Looking for ways to combine some of our recipes into delicious meals?

If you answered yes to any or all of the above, you've turned to the right section! In the following pages, you'll discover 14 days of menu planners for Levels 1 and 2 and Level 3 of the Weight Watchers food plan. All of them include recipes from this book. As a plus, each of these meals can be prepared in *less than one hour*. So when you're trying to add the spice of variety to your meals, brighten your breakfast, lunch, and dinner by selecting one of our menus.

A few points to keep in mind:

- **Bold type** indicates that the item is a recipe from this book.
- Menus are based on *one* serving of each recipe.
- Weights indicated for poultry, meat, and fish are net cooked or drained weights without skin or bones.
- Canned fish on menus is packed in water.
- The menus were designed for women. Since the daily food requirements differ slightly for men and youths, the menus should be adjusted as follows:

Levels 1 and 2:

Men and Youths: Add 1 Fat, 2 Proteins, 2 Breads, and 1 Fruit.

Youths only: Add 1 Milk.

Level 3:

Men and Youths: Add 1 Fat, 2 Proteins, 2 Breads, and 2 Fruits.

Youths only: Add 2 Milks.

Keep in mind that these menus are a bonus to ward off monotony. However, they are not meant to be combined into a full week's menu, since they weren't designed to fit weekly Program requirements.

MENU 1—LEVELS 1 AND 2

BREAKFAST
½ cup Orange Sections
1 serving **Egg in a Nest** (page 49)
¾ cup Skim Milk
Coffee or Tea

LUNCH
Crunchy Tuna Pocket (1½ ounces tuna with 2 tablespoons chopped celery, 2 teaspoons reduced-calorie mayonnaise, 3 tomato slices, and ¼ cup alfalfa sprouts in 1 small whole wheat pita)
6 *each* Red Bell Pepper Strips and Cucumber Spears
Coffee, Tea, or Mineral Water

DINNER
1 serving **Creamy Chicken Fettuccine** (page 129)
6 Cooked Broccoli Spears
Carrot and Mushroom Salad (½ cup *each* sliced carrot and mushrooms with red wine vinegar and herbs on 4 lettuce leaves)
½ cup Reduced-Calorie Chocolate Pudding topped with 1 tablespoon Whipped Topping
Coffee or Tea

SNACK
1 small Apple; 1 cup Plain Popcorn

Floater: 1 Bread
Optional Calories: 63

MENU 1—LEVEL 3

BREAKFAST
½ cup Orange Sections
1 serving **Egg in a Nest** (page 49)
¾ cup Skim Milk
Coffee or Tea

LUNCH
Crunchy Tuna-Cheese Pocket (1½ ounces tuna with ¾-ounce slice American cheese, 2 tablespoons
    chopped celery, 2 teaspoons reduced-calorie mayonnaise, 3 tomato slices, and ¼ cup alfalfa
    sprouts in 1 small whole wheat pita)
6 *each* Red Bell Pepper Strips and Cucumber Spears
20 small Grapes
Coffee, Tea, or Mineral Water

DINNER
1 serving **Creamy Chicken Fettuccine** (page 129)
¾ ounce Breadsticks
6 Cooked Broccoli Spears
Carrot and Mushroom Salad (½ cup *each* sliced carrot and mushrooms with 1 teaspoon olive oil plus
    red wine vinegar and herbs on 4 lettuce leaves)
½ cup Reduced-Calorie Chocolate Pudding topped with 1 tablespoon Whipped Topping
Coffee or Tea

SNACK
1 small Apple; 1 cup Plain Popcorn

Floater: 1 Bread
Optional Calories: 63

MENU 2—LEVELS 1 AND 2

BREAKFAST
1 cup Strawberries
¾ ounce Cold Cereal
1 cup Skim Milk
Coffee or Tea

LUNCH
1 serving **Tuna-Rice Salad** (page 112)
½ cup *each* Sliced Yellow Squash and Cauliflower Florets
1 medium Peach
Coffee, Tea, or Mineral Water

DINNER
3 ounces Sliced Grilled Steak with ½ cup Cooked Sliced Onion
1 serving **Corn with Chive "Cream"** (page 222)
½ cup Cooked French-Style Green Beans
1½ cups Tossed Salad with 1 tablespoon Reduced-Calorie French Dressing
Iced Tea with Lemon Slice

SNACK
2 × 3-inch wedge Watermelon; 1 serving Reduced-Calorie Vanilla-Flavored Milk Beverage

Floater: 1 Fruit
Optional Calories: 40

MENU 2—LEVEL 3

BREAKFAST
1 cup Strawberries
¾ ounce Cold Cereal
1 cup Skim Milk
Coffee or Tea

LUNCH
1 serving **Tuna-Rice Salad** (page 112)
½ cup *each* Sliced Yellow Squash and Cauliflower Florets
1 medium Peach
Coffee, Tea, or Mineral Water

DINNER
4 ounces Sliced Grilled Steak with ½ cup Cooked Sliced Onion
1 serving **Corn with Chive "Cream"** (page 222)
½ cup Cooked French-Style Green Beans
1½ cups Tossed Salad with 1½ teaspoons French Dressing mixed with 2 teaspoons Lemon Juice and
  ¼ teaspoon Mustard
½ cup Fresh Fruit Salad with Mint Sprig
Iced Tea with Lemon Slice

SNACK
2 × 3-inch wedge Watermelon; 3 Graham Crackers; 1 serving Reduced-Calorie Vanilla-Flavored Milk
  Beverage

Floater: 1 Fruit
Optional Calories: 30

MENU 3—LEVELS 1 AND 2

BREAKFAST
1 serving **Cranberry-Wheat Muffins** (page 41)
2 teaspoons Reduced-Calorie Apricot Spread
1 serving Reduced-Calorie Hot Cocoa

LUNCH
Turkey-Tomato Sandwich (2 ounces sliced turkey with 3 tomato slices, ½ cup shredded lettuce, and
   1 teaspoon Dijon-style mustard on 2 slices reduced-calorie wheat bread)
6 Yellow Squash Sticks and ½ cup Broccoli Florets
1 small Orange
Coffee, Tea, or Mineral Water

DINNER
1 serving **Sesame Flounder Fillets** (page 100)
Maple Carrots (½ cup cooked carrot sticks with ½ teaspoon maple syrup)
Tomato–Red Onion Salad (6 tomato wedges with ½ cup sliced red onion, red wine vinegar, and
   2 teaspoons chopped fresh basil on 2 lettuce leaves)
Coffee or Tea

SNACK
Cherry-Vanilla Yogurt (6 large cherries, pitted and sliced, mixed with ½ cup plain low-fat yogurt and
   ¼ teaspoon vanilla extract)

Floater: 1 Protein
Optional Calories: 106

MENU 3—LEVEL 3

BREAKFAST
⅓ cup Pineapple Juice
1 serving **Cranberry-Wheat Muffins** (page 41)
2 teaspoons Reduced-Calorie Apricot Spread
1 serving Reduced-Calorie Hot Cocoa

LUNCH
Turkey-Tomato Sandwich (3 ounces sliced turkey with 3 tomato slices, ½ cup shredded lettuce, and
   1 teaspoon Dijon-style mustard on 2 slices reduced-calorie wheat bread)
6 Yellow Squash Sticks and ½ cup Broccoli Florets
1 small Orange
Coffee, Tea, or Mineral Water

DINNER
1 serving **Sesame Flounder Fillets** (page 100)
Mushroom Rice (½ cup cooked rice with ¼ cup cooked sliced mushrooms)
Maple Carrots (½ cup cooked carrot sticks with ½ teaspoon maple syrup)
Tomato–Red Onion Salad (6 tomato wedges with ½ cup sliced red onion and 1 teaspoon olive oil
   plus red wine vinegar and 2 teaspoons chopped fresh basil on 2 lettuce leaves)
2-inch wedge Honeydew Melon
Coffee or Tea

SNACK
Cherry-Vanilla Yogurt (6 large cherries, pitted and sliced, mixed with ½ cup plain low-fat yogurt and
   ¼ teaspoon vanilla extract)

Floaters: 1 Protein; 1 Fruit
Optional Calories: 106

BREAKFAST
½ medium Banana, sliced
¾ ounce Cold Cereal
½ cup Skim Milk
Coffee or Tea

LUNCH
Shrimp-Pasta Salad (1½ ounces cooked tiny shrimp with 1 cup cooked elbow macaroni, 2 tablespoons chopped celery, and 2 teaspoons reduced-calorie mayonnaise)
6 *each* Carrot Sticks and Red Bell Pepper Strips
1 cup Strawberries
Coffee, Tea, or Mineral Water

DINNER
Tomato Juice Cocktail (1 cup tomato juice with 4 ice cubes, dash hot sauce, and celery stick stirrer)
1 serving **California Burgers** (page 157)
1 cup Cooked Green Beans
1½ cups Tossed Salad with 1 tablespoon Reduced-Calorie Italian Dressing
½ cup Reduced-Calorie Vanilla Pudding
Coffee or Tea

SNACK
1 serving **Cherry-Vanilla "Ice Cream" Soda** (page 297)

Floater: 1 Bread
Optional Calories: 91

MENU 4—LEVEL 3

BREAKFAST
½ medium Banana, sliced
¾ ounce Cold Cereal
½ cup Skim Milk
Coffee or Tea

LUNCH
Shrimp-Pasta Salad (2½ ounces cooked tiny shrimp with 1 cup cooked elbow macaroni, 2 tablespoons chopped celery, and 2 teaspoons reduced-calorie mayonnaise)
6 *each* Carrot Sticks and Red Bell Pepper Strips
1 cup Strawberries
Coffee, Tea, or Mineral Water

DINNER
Tomato Juice Cocktail (1 cup tomato juice with 4 ice cubes, dash hot sauce, and celery stick stirrer)
1 serving **California Burgers** (page 157)
1 cup Cooked Green Beans
1½ cups Tossed Salad with 1½ teaspoons Italian Dressing mixed with 2 teaspoons Red Wine Vinegar
Peach Pudding (½ cup reduced-calorie vanilla pudding mixed with ½ cup diced peach)
Coffee or Tea

SNACK
3 Graham Crackers; 1 serving **Cherry-Vanilla "Ice Cream" Soda** (page 297)

Floater: 1 Bread
Optional Calories: 85

BREAKFAST
1 cup Honeydew Melon Balls
1 serving **German Egg Cakes** (page 56)
1 cup Skim Milk
Coffee or Tea

LUNCH
Ham 'n' Swiss on Rye (1½ ounces sliced baked Virginia ham with ¾ ounce sliced reduced-fat Swiss cheese, 2 lettuce leaves, 2 green bell pepper rings, and 2 teaspoons country Dijon-style mustard on 2 slices reduced-calorie rye bread)
6 *each* Carrot and Celery Sticks
Coffee, Tea, or Mineral Water

DINNER
1 serving **Tuscan White Bean Soup** (page 181)
Garlic Toast (1½-ounce slice Italian bread with 1 teaspoon reduced-calorie margarine and dash garlic powder, toasted)
Spinach-Mushroom Salad (1 cup torn spinach leaves with ½ cup sliced mushrooms, 3 cherry tomatoes, cut into halves, and 1 teaspoon olive oil plus balsamic vinegar and herbs)
"Jelly"-Topped Pear (1 canned pear half topped with 1 teaspoon reduced-calorie grape spread)
Coffee or Tea

SNACK
Apple-Yogurt Crunch (½ cup plain low-fat yogurt mixed with ¼ cup applesauce, 1 teaspoon wheat germ, and dash cinnamon)

Floaters: 1 Protein; ¼ Bread
Optional Calories: 73

MENU 5—LEVEL 3

BREAKFAST
1 cup Honeydew Melon Balls
1 serving **German Egg Cakes** (page 56)
1 cup Skim Milk
Coffee or Tea

LUNCH
Ham 'n' Swiss on Rye (2½ ounces sliced baked Virginia ham with ¾ ounce sliced reduced-fat Swiss cheese, 2 lettuce leaves, 2 green bell pepper rings, and 2 teaspoons country Dijon-style mustard on 2 slices reduced-calorie rye bread)
6 *each* Carrot and Celery Sticks
Coffee, Tea, or Mineral Water

DINNER
1 serving **Tuscan White Bean Soup** (page 181)
Garlic Toast (1½-ounce slice Italian bread with 1 teaspoon reduced-calorie margarine and dash garlic powder, toasted)
Spinach-Mushroom Salad (1 cup torn spinach leaves with ½ cup sliced mushrooms, 3 cherry tomatoes, cut into halves, and 2 teaspoons olive oil plus balsamic vinegar and herbs)
"Jelly"-Topped Pear (2 canned pear halves topped with 2 teaspoons reduced-calorie grape spread)
Coffee or Tea

SNACK
Apple-Yogurt Crunch (½ cup plain low-fat yogurt mixed with ½ cup applesauce, 1 teaspoon wheat germ, and dash cinnamon); 2 cups Plain Popcorn

Floaters: 1 Protein; ¼ Bread
Optional Calories: 81

BREAKFAST
½ cup Grapefruit Sections
1 Scrambled Egg
1 slice Reduced-Calorie Wheat Bread, toasted
2 teaspoons Reduced-Calorie Raspberry Spread
1 cup Skim Milk
Coffee or Tea

LUNCH
Tuna Salad Pita (1 ounce tuna with 1 tablespoon chopped celery, 1 teaspoon reduced-calorie mayonnaise, 3 tomato slices, and 2 red onion slices in 1 small pita)
½ cup Cauliflower Florets and 6 Zucchini Sticks
1 small Nectarine
Coffee, Tea, or Mineral Water

DINNER
1 serving **Braised Cornish Hen** (page 136)
1 serving **Rice-Vermicelli Pilaf** (page 255)
6 Cooked Asparagus Spears topped with Grated Lemon Peel
1½ cups Tossed Salad with 1 tablespoon Reduced-Calorie French Dressing
Rosé Wine Spritzer (¼ cup *each* rosé wine and club soda)

SNACK
1 serving Reduced-Calorie Chocolate-Flavored Milk Beverage

Floater: 1 Protein
Optional Calories: 126

MENU 6—LEVEL 3

BREAKFAST
½ cup Grapefruit Sections
1 Scrambled Egg
1 slice Reduced-Calorie Wheat Bread, toasted
2 teaspoons Reduced-Calorie Raspberry Spread
1 cup Skim Milk
Coffee or Tea

LUNCH
Tuna Salad Pita (2 ounces tuna with 1 tablespoon chopped celery, 1 teaspoon reduced-calorie mayonnaise, 3 tomato slices, and 2 red onion slices in 1 large pita)
½ cup Cauliflower Florets and 6 Zucchini Sticks
1 small Nectarine
Coffee, Tea, or Mineral Water

DINNER
1 serving **Braised Cornish Hen** (page 136)
1 serving **Rice-Vermicelli Pilaf** (page 255)
6 Cooked Asparagus Spears topped with Grated Lemon Peel
1½ cups Tossed Salad with 1½ teaspoons French Dressing mixed with 2 teaspoons Lemon Juice and ¼ teaspoon Mustard
Rosé Wine Spritzer (¼ cup *each* rosé wine and club soda)

SNACK
½ medium Banana; 1 serving Reduced-Calorie Chocolate-Flavored Milk Beverage

Floater: 1 Protein
Optional Calories: 116

MENU 7—LEVELS 1 AND 2

BREAKFAST
1 cup Cantaloupe Chunks
½ cup Cooked Oatmeal sprinkled with dash Cinnamon
1 cup Skim Milk
Coffee or Tea

LUNCH
Turkey Sandwich (2 ounces sliced turkey with 2 lettuce leaves, ¼ cup alfalfa sprouts, and 1½ teaspoons reduced-calorie Thousand Island dressing on 2 slices reduced-calorie rye bread)
½ cup Broccoli Florets and 6 Red Bell Pepper Strips
Coffee, Tea, or Mineral Water

DINNER
1 serving **Pork Chops in Wine Sauce** (page 168)
½ cup Cooked Sliced Yellow Squash
Spinach Salad (1 cup torn spinach leaves with 4 tomato wedges, 2 tablespoons shredded carrot, and
1 tablespoon reduced-calorie Italian dressing)
Coffee or Tea

SNACK
Tropical Yogurt Treat (½ cup plain low-fat yogurt mixed with ½ cup canned crushed pineapple and
topped with 1 teaspoon shredded coconut); 1 serving **Garlic Bagel Chips** (page 294)

Floater: 1 Protein
Optional Calories: 56

MENU 7—LEVEL 3

BREAKFAST
1 cup Cantaloupe Chunks
1 cup Cooked Oatmeal sprinkled with dash Cinnamon
1 cup Skim Milk
Coffee or Tea

LUNCH
Turkey Sandwich (3 ounces sliced turkey with 2 lettuce leaves, ¼ cup alfalfa sprouts, and 1½ teaspoons Thousand Island dressing on 2 slices reduced-calorie rye bread)
½ cup Broccoli Florets and 6 Red Bell Pepper Strips
1 small Pear
Coffee, Tea, or Mineral Water

DINNER
1 serving **Pork Chops in Wine Sauce** (page 168)
½ cup Cooked Sliced Yellow Squash
Spinach Salad (1 cup torn spinach leaves with 4 tomato wedges, 2 tablespoons shredded carrot, and
1 tablespoon reduced-calorie Italian dressing)
Coffee or Tea

SNACK
Tropical Yogurt Treat (½ cup plain low-fat yogurt mixed with ½ cup canned crushed pineapple and
topped with 1 teaspoon shredded coconut); 1 serving **Garlic Bagel Chips** (page 294)

Floater: 1 Protein
Optional Calories: 41

MENU 8—LEVELS 1 AND 2

BREAKFAST
½ medium Grapefruit sprinkled with ½ teaspoon Sugar
¾ ounce Reduced-Fat Swiss Cheese
½ English Muffin, toasted
1 teaspoon Reduced-Calorie Margarine
¾ cup Skim Milk
Coffee or Tea

LUNCH
Russian Roast Beef Sandwich (1 ounce sliced roast beef with ½ cup shredded lettuce and 1½ teaspoons Russian dressing on 2 slices reduced-calorie wheat bread)
6 Cucumber Spears and 3 Cherry Tomatoes
Coffee, Tea, or Mineral Water

DINNER
1 serving **Salmon with Creamy Horseradish Sauce** (page 104)
Yogurt-Chive Potato (3-ounce baked potato, split and topped with ½ cup plain low-fat yogurt mixed
   with 2 teaspoons chopped chives)
½ cup Cooked Sliced Carrots
Mushroom—Red Cabbage Salad (½ cup sliced mushrooms with ¼ cup shredded red cabbage and
   ½ teaspoon olive oil plus red wine vinegar and herbs)
Coffee or Tea

SNACK
1 serving **Piña Colada Ice** (page 289)

Floater: 1 Protein
Optional Calories: 145

MENU 8—LEVEL 3

BREAKFAST
½ medium Grapefruit sprinkled with ½ teaspoon Sugar
¾ ounce Reduced-Fat Swiss Cheese
1 English Muffin, split in half and toasted
2 teaspoons Reduced-Calorie Margarine
¾ cup Skim Milk
Coffee or Tea

LUNCH
Russian Roast Beef Sandwich (2 ounces sliced roast beef with ½ cup shredded lettuce and 1½ teaspoons Russian dressing on 2 slices reduced-calorie wheat bread)
6 Cucumber Spears and 3 Cherry Tomatoes
1 small Apple
Coffee, Tea, or Mineral Water

DINNER
1 serving **Salmon with Creamy Horseradish Sauce** (page 104)
Yogurt-Chive Potato (3-ounce baked potato, split and topped with ½ cup plain low-fat yogurt mixed
   with 2 teaspoons chopped chives)
½ cup Cooked Sliced Carrots
Mushroom–Red Cabbage Salad (½ cup sliced mushrooms with ¼ cup shredded red cabbage and
   1 teaspoon olive oil plus red wine vinegar and herbs)
Coffee or Tea

SNACK
1 serving **Piña Colada Ice** (page 289)

Floater: 1 Protein
Optional Calories: 145

BREAKFAST
½ cup Orange Juice
1 Poached Egg on 1 slice Rye Bread, toasted
½ cup Skim Milk
Coffee or Tea

LUNCH
Ham Sandwich (1 ounce sliced boiled ham with 2 lettuce leaves, 3 tomato slices, and 2 teaspoons
  country Dijon-style mustard on 2 slices reduced-calorie wheat bread)
6 *each* Carrot and Celery Sticks
2 small Plums
Coffee, Tea, or Mineral Water

DINNER
1 serving **Puree of Green Bean Soup** (page 30)
1 serving **Chicken Burgers** (page 120)
Tomato-Cauliflower Salad (6 tomato slices with ½ cup cauliflower florets, 1 radish rose, and ½ teaspoon olive oil plus red wine vinegar and herbs on 1 cup torn lettuce leaves)
Coffee or Tea

SNACK
3 medium Apricots; 1 cup Skim Milk

Floaters: 1 Bread; 1 Fruit
Optional Calories: 35

MENU 9—LEVEL 3

BREAKFAST
½ cup Orange Juice
1 Poached Egg on 1 slice Rye Bread, toasted
½ cup Skim Milk
Coffee or Tea

LUNCH
Ham Sandwich (1 ounce sliced boiled ham with 2 lettuce leaves, 3 tomato slices, and 2 teaspoons
   country Dijon-style mustard on 2 slices reduced-calorie wheat bread)
6 *each* Carrot and Celery Sticks
2 small Plums
Coffee, Tea, or Mineral Water

DINNER
1 serving **Puree of Green Bean Soup** (page 30)
1 serving **Chicken Burgers** (page 120)
Tomato-Cauliflower Salad (6 tomato slices with 2 ounces rinsed drained canned chick-peas, ½ cup
   cauliflower florets, 1 radish rose, and 1½ teaspoons olive oil plus red wine vinegar and herbs on 1
   cup torn lettuce leaves)
½ cup Warm Applesauce with dash Cinnamon
Coffee or Tea

SNACK
3 medium Apricots; 3 Graham Crackers; 1 cup Skim Milk

Floaters: 1 Bread; 1 Fruit
Optional Calories: 35

MENU 10—LEVELS 1 AND 2

BRUNCH
Mock Mimosa (½ cup orange juice with ¼ cup club soda and a mint sprig)
1 serving **Basil-Vegetable Quiche** (page 53)
3 ounces Cooked Small Red Potatoes
1 teaspoon Reduced-Calorie Margarine
Artichoke Salad Vinaigrette (½ cup chilled cooked artichoke hearts with 3 cherry tomatoes, cut into halves, ¼ cup sliced mushrooms, ½ teaspoon olive oil plus balsamic vinegar and herbs on 4 lettuce leaves)
Cappuccino (½ cup *each* hot espresso and hot skim milk with 1 tablespoon whipped topping and dash cinnamon)

DINNER
1 serving **Italian Chick-Pea Soup** (page 182)
1-ounce slice Italian Bread
1 teaspoon Reduced-Calorie Margarine
1½ cups Tossed Salad with 1 tablespoon Reduced-Calorie Italian Dressing
1 cup Strawberries, sliced and topped with ½ cup Plain Low-Fat Yogurt
Coffee or Tea

SNACK
1 medium Peach; 3 Graham Crackers; ½ cup Skim Milk

Floater: 1 Fruit
Optional Calories: 54

MENU 10—LEVEL 3

BRUNCH

Mock Mimosa (½ cup orange juice with ¼ cup club soda and a mint sprig)
1 serving **Basil-Vegetable Quiche** (page 53)
3 ounces Cooked Small Red Potatoes
1 teaspoon Reduced-Calorie Margarine
Artichoke Salad Vinaigrette (½ cup chilled cooked artichoke hearts with 3 cherry tomatoes, cut into halves, ¼ cup sliced mushrooms, ½ teaspoon olive oil plus balsamic vinegar and herbs on 4 lettuce leaves)
2-inch wedge Honeydew
Cappuccino (½ cup *each* hot espresso and hot skim milk with 1 tablespoon whipped topping and dash cinnamon)

DINNER

1 serving **Italian Chick-Pea Soup** (page 182)
2-ounce slice Italian Bread
1 teaspoon Reduced-Calorie Margarine
1½ cups Tossed Salad with ¾ ounce Diced Mozzarella Cheese and 1½ teaspoons Italian Dressing mixed with 2 teaspoons Red Wine Vinegar
1 cup Strawberries, sliced and topped with ½ cup Plain Low-Fat Yogurt
Coffee or Tea

SNACK

1 medium Peach; 3 Graham Crackers; ½ cup Skim Milk

Floater: 1 Fruit
Optional Calories: 48

MENU 11—LEVELS 1 AND 2

BREAKFAST
Cinnamon-Raisin Oatmeal (½ cup cooked oatmeal with 1 tablespoon dark raisins and dash cinnamon)
1 cup Skim Milk
Coffee or Tea

LUNCH
1 cup Tomato Juice
Tuna Salad Sandwich (2 ounces tuna with 1 tablespoon chopped celery, 1 teaspoon reduced-calorie mayonnaise, 3 tomato slices, and 2 lettuce leaves on 2 slices reduced-calorie rye bread)
6 Red Bell Pepper Strips and ½ cup Broccoli Florets
Coffee, Tea, or Mineral Water

DINNER
1 serving **Orange Veal Marsala** (page 171)
½ cup Cooked Fettuccine Noodles sprinkled with 1 teaspoon Grated Parmesan Cheese
1 serving **Spring Peas and Carrots** (page 244)
Cucumber-Sprout Salad (½ cup cucumber slices with ¼ cup alfalfa sprouts and red wine vinegar and herbs on 1 cup shredded lettuce)
Coffee or Tea

SNACK
½ cup Reduced-Calorie Chocolate Pudding

Floater: 1 Protein
Optional Calories: 55

MENU 11—LEVEL 3

BREAKFAST
Cinnamon-Raisin Oatmeal (½ cup cooked oatmeal with 1 tablespoon dark raisins and dash cinnamon)
1 cup Skim Milk
Coffee or Tea

LUNCH
1 cup Tomato Juice
Tuna Salad Sandwich (3 ounces tuna with 1 tablespoon *each* chopped celery and reduced-calorie mayonnaise, 3 tomato slices, and 2 lettuce leaves on 2 slices reduced-calorie rye bread)
6 Red Bell Pepper Strips and ½ cup Broccoli Florets
20 small Grapes
Coffee, Tea, or Mineral Water

DINNER
1 serving **Orange Veal Marsala** (page 171)
1 cup Cooked Fettuccine Noodles sprinkled with 1 teaspoon Grated Parmesan Cheese
1 serving **Spring Peas and Carrots** (page 244)
Cucumber-Sprout Salad (½ cup cucumber slices with ¼ cup alfalfa sprouts and red wine vinegar and herbs on 1 cup shredded lettuce)
Coffee or Tea

SNACK
½ cup Reduced-Calorie Chocolate Pudding

Floater: 1 Protein
Optional Calories: 55

MENU 12—LEVELS 1 AND 2

BREAKFAST
½ cup Blueberries
¾ ounce Cold Cereal
¾ cup Skim Milk
Coffee or Tea

LUNCH
Egg Salad in a Pita (1 hard-cooked egg, chopped, with 2 tablespoons chopped celery, 2 teaspoons
   reduced-calorie mayonnaise, ½ teaspoon Dijon-style mustard, 3 tomato slices, and ½ cup shredded
   lettuce in 1 small whole wheat pita)
6 Carrot Sticks and ½ cup Cauliflower Florets
Coffee, Tea, or Mineral Water

DINNER
1 serving **Chicken-in-the-Rye** (page 123)
Mushroom Rice (½ cup cooked rice with ¼ cup cooked sliced mushrooms)
6 Cooked Broccoli Spears
Chick-Pea and Tomato Toss (1 cup torn lettuce with 1 ounce rinsed drained canned chick-peas,
   4 tomato wedges, ¼ cup shredded carrot, and 1 tablespoon reduced-calorie Thousand Island
   dressing)
1 serving **Peaches and Kiwi in Champagne** (page 292)
Coffee or Tea

SNACK
1 cup Cantaloupe Chunks; 1 serving Reduced-Calorie Vanilla-Flavored Milk Beverage

Floaters: 1½ Fruits
Optional Calories: 100

MENU 12—LEVEL 3

BREAKFAST
½ cup Blueberries
¾ ounce Cold Cereal
½ cup Skim Milk
Coffee or Tea

LUNCH
Egg Salad in a Pita (1 hard-cooked egg, chopped, with 2 tablespoons chopped celery, 2 teaspoons
   reduced-calorie mayonnaise, ½ teaspoon Dijon-style mustard, 3 tomato slices, and ½ cup shredded
   lettuce in 1 small whole wheat pita)
6 Carrot Sticks and ½ cup Cauliflower Florets
12 large Cherries
Coffee, Tea, or Mineral Water

DINNER
1 serving **Chicken-in-the-Rye** (page 123)
Mushroom Rice (1 cup cooked rice with ¼ cup cooked sliced mushrooms)
Broccoli Melt (6 cooked broccoli spears topped with ¾ ounce reduced-fat Swiss cheese, melted)
Chick-Pea and Tomato Toss (1 cup torn lettuce with 1 ounce rinsed drained canned chick-peas,
   4 tomato wedges, ¼ cup shredded carrot, and 1½ teaspoons Thousand Island dressing mixed with
   2 tablespoons plain low-fat yogurt and dash garlic powder)
1 serving **Peaches and Kiwi in Champagne** (page 292)
Coffee or Tea

SNACK
1 cup Cantaloupe Chunks; 1 serving Reduced-Calorie Vanilla-Flavored Milk Beverage

Floaters: 1½ Fruits
Optional Calories: 70

MENU 13—LEVELS 1 AND 2

BREAKFAST
½ medium Banana, sliced
½ cup Cooked Cream of Wheat
1 cup Skim Milk
Coffee or Tea

LUNCH
Turkey and Swiss Cheese Sandwich (1 ounce sliced turkey with ¾ ounce sliced reduced-fat Swiss cheese, 2 lettuce leaves, and 2 teaspoons reduced-calorie mayonnaise on 2 slices pumpernickel bread)
6 *each* Celery Sticks and Cucumber Spears
Coffee, Tea, or Mineral Water

DINNER
1 serving **Fillets with Peppers and Tomatoes** (page 98)
1 serving **Parmesan Braised Citrus Fennel** (page 214)
1½ cups Tossed Salad with 1 tablespoon Reduced-Calorie French Dressing
Coffee or Tea

SNACK
½ cup Orange Sections; 1 serving Reduced-Calorie Hot Cocoa

Floater: 1 Protein
Optional Calories: 85

MENU 13—LEVEL 3

BREAKFAST
½ medium Banana, sliced
½ cup Cooked Cream of Wheat
1 cup Skim Milk
Coffee or Tea

LUNCH
Turkey and Swiss Cheese Sandwich (2 ounces sliced turkey with ¾ ounce sliced reduced-fat Swiss cheese, 2 lettuce leaves, and 2 teaspoons reduced-calorie mayonnaise on 2 slices pumpernickel bread)
6 *each* Celery Sticks and Cucumber Spears
Coffee, Tea, or Mineral Water

DINNER
1 serving **Fillets with Peppers and Tomatoes** (page 98)
3-ounce Baked Potato, split and topped with 1 teaspoon Margarine
1 serving **Parmesan Braised Citrus Fennel** (page 214)
1½ cups Tossed Salad with 1 tablespoon Reduced-Calorie French Dressing
2 slices Canned Pineapple
Coffee or Tea

SNACK
½ cup Orange Sections; 1 serving Reduced-Calorie Hot Cocoa

Floater: 1 Protein
Optional Calories: 85

MENU 14—LEVELS 1 AND 2

BREAKFAST
½ cup Grapefruit Juice
Pepper and "Egg" Scramble (¼ cup egg substitute scrambled with 2 tablespoons chopped green bell pepper)
½ English Muffin, toasted
1 teaspoon Reduced-Calorie Margarine
1 cup Skim Milk
Coffee or Tea

LUNCH
Tuna–Green Bean Salad (2 ounces tuna with 1 cup sliced chilled cooked green beans, 3 cherry tomatoes, cut into halves, and ½ teaspoon olive oil plus red wine vinegar and herbs)
¾ ounce Flatbreads
Coffee, Tea, or Mineral Water

DINNER
1 serving **Two-Bean Chili** (page 188)
2 Taco Shells, heated and broken into pieces
1½ cups Mixed Green Salad with 1 tablespoon Reduced-Calorie Buttermilk Dressing
1 serving **Fig and Melon Compote** (page 291)
Coffee or Tea

SNACK
½ cup Reduced-Calorie Chocolate Pudding

Floaters: 1 Protein; ¼ Fruit
Optional Calories: 60

MENU 14—LEVEL 3

BREAKFAST

½ cup Grapefruit Juice
Pepper and "Egg" Scramble (¼ cup egg substitute scrambled with 2 tablespoons chopped green bell pepper)
½ English Muffin, toasted
1 teaspoon Reduced-Calorie Margarine
1 cup Skim Milk
Coffee or Tea

LUNCH

Tuna—Green Bean Salad (3 ounces tuna with 1 cup sliced chilled cooked green beans, 3 cherry tomatoes, cut into halves, and 1½ teaspoons olive oil plus red wine vinegar and herbs)
¾ ounce Flatbreads
2 cups Plain Popcorn
Coffee, Tea, or Mineral Water

DINNER

1 serving **Two-Bean Chili** (page 188)
2 Taco Shells, heated and broken into pieces
1½ cups Mixed Green Salad with 1 tablespoon Reduced-Calorie Buttermilk Dressing
1 serving **Fig and Melon Compote** (page 291)
Coffee or Tea

SNACK

1 small Pear; ½ cup Reduced-Calorie Chocolate Pudding

Floaters: 1 Protein; ¼ Fruit
Optional Calories: 60

Appendix

Glossary

Bake: To place food in a container and cook in an oven.

Baste: To moisten food while it cooks in order to add flavor and prevent the surface from drying out by coating with a liquid such as melted fat, a sauce, or meat drippings.

Beat: To make a mixture smooth by mixing ingredients vigorously with a spoon or electric mixer.

Blanch: To cook a food for a few minutes in boiling water to preserve the color, texture, or nutritional value or to loosen the skin from the food for easy removal.

Blend: To mix two or more ingredients thoroughly until smooth.

Boil: To cook in water or a liquid consisting mostly of water in which bubbles rise continually and break on the surface. A rolling boil is when the bubbles form rapidly.

Braise: To cook meat or poultry in a small amount of liquid in a covered container in the oven or over low heat on the range.

Broil: To cook by direct dry heat.

Brown: To cook a food usually in a small amount of fat on the range until the surface of the food changes color.

Chill: To refrigerate food or let it stand in ice or iced water until cold.

Chop: To cut into small pieces.

Combine: To mix together two or more ingredients.

Cool: To let a hot food come to room temperature.

Crimp: To press or pinch together.

Cube: To cut food into ½-inch squares.

Cut in: To distribute solid fat in flour or a flour mixture using a pastry blender until flour-coated fat particles resemble a coarse meal.

Dash: Less than ⅛ teaspoon of an ingredient.

Dice: To cut a food into small squares, less than ½ inch in size.

Dredge: To cover a food with flour or a fine crumb mixture.

Fold: To lightly combine ingredients using a rubber scraper and cutting vertically through the mixture and then sliding the spatula across the bottom of the bowl, turning mixtures over.

Fry: To cook uncovered in a small amount of fat.

Grate: To cut food into tiny particles using the small holes of a grater.

Grill: To cook over direct heat.

Julienne: To cut into slivers that resemble matchstick pieces.

Marinate: To let food stand in a mixture that will tenderize it or add flavor.

Mince: To cut or chop into very small pieces.

Mix: To combine ingredients so they are evenly distributed.

Pare: To cut off the outer covering of a food using a knife or vegetable peeler.

Peel: To remove the outer covering of a food using hands rather than a knife or vegetable peeler.

Pierce: A term applied to microwave cooking. To puncture a cover, thick skin, or membrane to allow steam to escape and prevent bursting.

Poach: To cook a food in a hot liquid.

Puree: To press food through a food mill or to process in a blender or food processor into a smooth, thick mixture.

Rearrange: A term applied to microwave cooking. To move food in its dish to another position for even cooking when the food cannot be stirred.

Reduce: To boil a liquid in an uncovered container until it evaporates, resulting in a specific consistency and flavor.

Roast: To cook meats on a rack, uncovered, in an oven.

Rotate: A term applied to microwave cooking. To turn a dish in a microwave oven one-quarter or one-half turn in order for the food to cook more evenly when it cannot be stirred.

Sauté: To brown or cook in a small amount of fat.

Shred: To cut food into long thin pieces using the large holes of a grater.

Simmer: To cook in liquid just below the boiling point.

Slice: To cut a food into thin flat pieces.

Soften: To let cold butter or margarine stand at room temperature until it has a softer consistency.

Standing time: A term applied to microwave cooking. A period of time, after microwaving, which allows foods to complete heating or cooking in the center or in the thicker areas, without overcooking on the thin areas or edges.

Steam: To cook food on a rack or in a colander in a covered pan over steaming hot water.

Stir: To use a utensil in a circular motion to combine portions of a food.

Strain: To separate solid food from liquid by pouring the mixture into a strainer or sieve.

Whip: To beat a mixture rapidly with a wire whisk or electric mixer to incorporate air and increase volume.

Pan Substitutions

It's best to use the pan size that's recommended in a recipe; however, if your kitchen isn't equipped with that particular pan, chances are a substitution will work just as well. The pan size is determined by the volume of food it holds. When substituting, use a pan as close to the recommended size as possible. Food cooked in too small a pan may boil over; food cooked in too large a pan may dry out or burn. To determine the dimensions of a baking pan, measure across the top, between the inside edges. To determine the volume, measure the amount of water the pan holds when completely filled.

When you use a pan that is a different size from the one recommended, it may be necessary to adjust the suggested cooking time. Depending on the size of the pan and the depth of the food in it, you may need to add or subtract 5 to 10 minutes. If you substitute glass or glass-ceramic for metal, the oven temperature should be reduced by 25°F.

The following chart provides some common pan substitutions.

Recommended Size	Approximate Volume	Possible Substitutions
8 × 1½-inch round baking pan	1½ quarts	10 × 6 × 2-inch baking dish 9 × 1½-inch round baking pan 8 × 4 × 2-inch loaf pan 9-inch pie plate
8 × 8 × 2-inch baking pan	2 quarts	11 × 7 × 1½-inch baking pan 12 × 7½ × 2-inch baking pan 9 × 5 × 3-inch loaf pan two 8 × 1½-inch round baking pans
13 × 9 × 2-inch baking pan	3 quarts	14 × 11 × 2-inch baking dish two 9 × 1½-inch round baking pans two 8 × 1½-inch round baking pans

Dry and Liquid Measure Equivalents

Teaspoons	Tablespoons	Cups	Fluid Ounces
3 teaspoons	1 tablespoon		½ fluid ounce
6 teaspoons	2 tablespoons	⅛ cup	1 fluid ounce
8 teaspoons	2 tablespoons plus 2 teaspoons	⅙ cup	
12 teaspoons	4 tablespoons	¼ cup	2 fluid ounces
15 teaspoons	5 tablespoons	⅓ cup less 1 teaspoon	
16 teaspoons	5 tablespoons plus 1 teaspoon	⅓ cup	
18 teaspoons	6 tablespoons	⅓ cup plus 2 teaspoons	3 fluid ounces
24 teaspoons	8 tablespoons	½ cup	4 fluid ounces
30 teaspoons	10 tablespoons	½ cup plus 2 tablespoons	5 fluid ounces
32 teaspoons	10 tablespoons plus 2 teaspoons	⅔ cup	
36 teaspoons	12 tablespoons	¾ cup	6 fluid ounces
42 teaspoons	14 tablespoons	1 cup less 2 tablespoons	7 fluid ounces
45 teaspoons	15 tablespoons	1 cup less 1 tablespoon	
48 teaspoons	16 tablespoons	1 cup	8 fluid ounces

Note: Measurement of less than ⅛ teaspoon is considered a dash or a pinch.

Metric Conversions

If you are converting the recipes in this book to metric measurements, use the following chart as a guide.

Volume

¼ teaspoon	1 milliliter
½ teaspoon	2 milliliters
1 teaspoon	5 milliliters
1 tablespoon	15 milliliters
2 tablespoons	30 milliliters
3 tablespoons	45 milliliters
¼ cup	50 milliliters
⅓ cup	75 milliliters
½ cup	125 milliliters
⅔ cup	150 milliliters
¾ cup	175 milliliters
1 cup	250 milliliters
1 quart	1 liter

Weight

1 ounce	30 grams
¼ pound	120 grams
½ pound	240 grams
¾ pound	360 grams
1 pound	480 grams

Length

1 inch	25 millimeters
1 inch	2.5 centimeters

Oven Temperatures

250°F	120°C
275°F	140°C
300°F	150°C
325°F	160°C
350°F	180°C
375°F	190°C
400°F	200°C
425°F	220°C
450°F	230°C
475°F	250°C
500°F	260°C
525°F	270°C

Index

Cholesterol-Reduced Recipes Index

Index for Recipes with 30% or Less of Their Calories Coming from Fat

Sodium-Reduced Recipes Index